Cram101 Textbook Outlines to accompany:

International Economics

Husted and Melvin, 6th Edition

An Academic Internet Publishers (AIPI) publication (c) 2007.

You have a discounted membership at www.Cram101.com with this book.

Get all of the practice tests for the chapters of this textbook, and access in-depth reference material for writing essays and papers. Here is an example from a Cram101 Biology text:

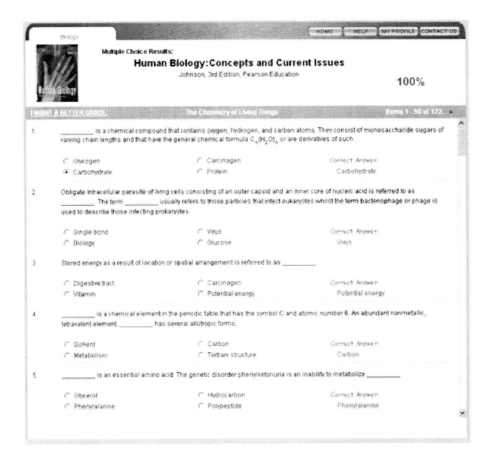

When you need problem solving help with math, stats, and other disciplines, www.Cram101.com will walk through the formulas and solutions step by step.

With Cram101.com online, you also have access to extensive reference material.

You will nail those essays and papers. Here is an example from a Cram101 Biology text:

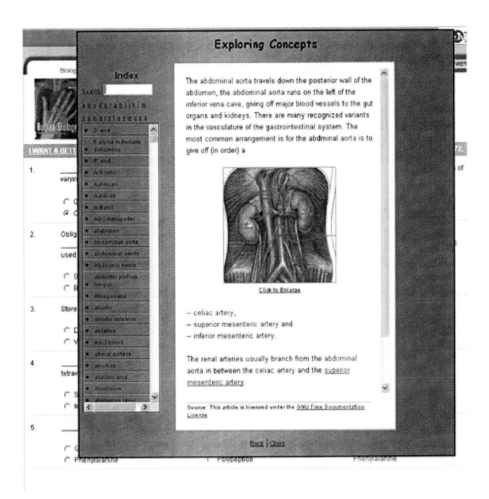

Learning System

Cram101 Textbook Outlines is a learning system. The notes in this book are the highlights of your textbook, you will never have to highlight a book again.

How to use this book. Take this book to class, it is your notebook for the lecture. The notes and highlights on the left hand side of the pages follow the outline and order of the textbook. All you have to do is follow along while your intructor presents the lecture. Circle the items emphasized in class and add other important information on the right side. With Cram101 Textbook Outlines you'll spend less time writing and more time listening. Learning becomes more efficient.

Cram101.com Online

Increase your studying efficiency by using Cram101.com's practice tests and online reference material. It is the perfect complement to Cram101 Textbook Outlines. Use self-teaching matching tests or simulate in-class testing with comprehensive multiple choice tests, or simply use Cram's true and false tests for quick review. Cram101.com even allows you to enter your in-class notes for an integrated studying format combining the textbook notes with your class notes.

Visit **www.Cram101.com**, click Sign Up at the top of the screen, and enter **DK73DW1479** in the promo code box on the registration screen. Access to www.Cram101.com is normally $9.95, but because you have purchased this book, your access fee is only $4.95. Sign up and stop highlighting textbooks forever.

International Economics
Husted and Melvin, 6th

CONTENTS

Microeconomics	The part of economics concerned with such individual units as industries, firms, and households and with individual markets, specific goods and services, and product and resource prices is called microeconomics.
Macroeconomics	Macroeconomics refers to the part of economics concerned with the economy as a whole; with such major aggregates as the household, business, and government sectors; and with measures of the total economy.
Economics	The social science dealing with the use of scarce resources to obtain the maximum satisfaction of society's virtually unlimited economic wants is an economics.
Balance of payments	Balance of payments refers to a list, or accounting, of all of a country's international transactions for a given time period, usually one year.
Interest rate	The rate of return on bonds, loans, or deposits. When one speaks of 'the' interest rate, it is usually in a model where there is only one.
Exchange rate	Exchange rate refers to the price at which one country's currency trades for another, typically on the exchange market.
Exchange	The trade of things of value between buyer and seller so that each is better off after the trade is called the exchange.
Interest	In finance and economics, interest is the price paid by a borrower for the use of a lender's money. In other words, interest is the amount of paid to "rent" money for a period of time.
Balance	In banking and accountancy, the outstanding balance is the amount of money owned, (or due), that remains in a deposit account (or a loan account) at a given date, after all past remittances, payments and withdrawal have been accounted for. It can be positive (then, in the balance sheet of a firm, it is an asset) or negative (a liability).
Policy	Similar to a script in that a policy can be a less than completely rational decision-making method. Involves the use of a pre-existing set of decision steps for any problem that presents itself.
Economy	The income, expenditures, and resources that affect the cost of running a business and household are called an economy.
Large country	Large country refers to a country that is large enough for its international transactions to affect economic variables abroad, usually for its trade to matter for world prices.
Service	Service refers to a "non tangible product" that is not embodied in a physical good and that typically effects some change in another product, person, or institution. Contrasts with good.
Gross domestic product	Gross domestic product refers to the total value of new goods and services produced in a given year within the borders of a country, regardless of by whom.
Gross National Product	Gross National Product is the total value of final goods and services produced in a year by a country's nationals (including profits from capital held abroad).
Domestic	From or in one's own country. A domestic producer is one that produces inside the home country. A domestic price is the price inside the home country. Opposite of 'foreign' or 'world.'.
Final goods	In economics final goods are goods that are ultimately consumed rather than used in the production of another good. When used in measures of national income and output the term final goods only includes new goods.
Final good	Final good refers to a good that requires no further processing or transformation to be ready for use by consumers, investors, or government. Contrasts with intermediate good.
Final goods and services	Goods and services that have been purchased for final use and not for resale or further processing or manufacturing are final goods and services.
Factors of	Economic resources: land, capital, labor, and entrepreneurial ability are called factors of production.

production	
Production	The creation of finished goods and services using the factors of production: land, labor, capital, entrepreneurship, and knowledge.
Capital	Capital generally refers to financial wealth, especially that used to start or maintain a business. In classical economics, capital is one of four factors of production, the others being land and labor and entrepreneurship.
Labor	People's physical and mental talents and efforts that are used to help produce goods and services are called labor.
Standard of living	Standard of living refers to the level of consumption that people enjoy, on the average, and is measured by average income per person.
Gross National Income	Previously known as Gross National Product, Gross National Income comprises the total value of goods and services produced within a country, together with its income received from other countries (notably interest and dividends), less similar payments made to other countries.
National income	National income refers to the income generated by a country's production, and therefore the total income of its factors of production.
Economic agents	Economic agents refers to individuals who engage in production, exchange, specialization, and consumption.
Agent	A person who makes economic decisions for another economic actor. A hired manager operates as an agent for a firm's owner.
International trade	The export of goods and services from a country and the import of goods and services into a country is referred to as the international trade.
Export	In economics, an export is any good or commodity, shipped or otherwise transported out of a country, province, town to another part of the world in a legitimate fashion, typically for use in trade or sale.
Openness	Openness refers to the extent to which an economy is open, often measured by the ratio of its trade to
Per capita	Per capita refers to per person. Usually used to indicate the average per person of any given statistic, commonly income.
Developed country	A developed country is one that enjoys a relatively high standard of living derived through an industrialized, diversified economy. Countries with a very high Human Development Index are generally considered developed countries.
Productivity	Productivity refers to the total output of goods and services in a given period of time divided by work hours.
Value added	The value of output minus the value of all intermediate inputs, representing therefore the contribution of, and payments to, primary factors of production a value added.
World Bank	The World Bank is a group of five international organizations responsible for providing finance and advice to countries for the purposes of economic development and poverty reduction, and for encouraging and safeguarding international investment.
Developing country	Developing country refers to a country whose per capita income is low by world standards. Same as LDC. As usually used, it does not necessarily connote that the country's income is rising.
Per capita income	The per capita income for a group of people may be defined as their total personal income, divided by the total population. Per capita income is usually reported in units of currency per year.
Public utility	A firm that produces an essential good or service, has obtained from a government the right to be the sole supplier of the good or service in the area, and is regulated by that government to prevent the

4

abuse of its monopoly power is a public utility.

Utility	Utility refers to the want-satisfying power of a good or service; the satisfaction or pleasure a consumer obtains from the consumption of a good or service.
Economic infrastructure	Economic infrastructure refers to a country's communications, transportation, financial, and distribution systems.
Commodity	Could refer to any good, but in trade a commodity is usually a raw material or primary product that enters into international trade, such as metals or basic agricultural products.
Technology	The body of knowledge and techniques that can be used to combine economic resources to produce goods and services is called technology.
Endowment	Endowment refers to the amount of something that a person or country simply has, rather than their having somehow to acquire it.
Engine of growth	Term sometimes used to describe the role that exports may have played in economic development, both of some of the regions of recent settlement in the nineteenth century and of today's nics are referred to as engine of growth.
Human capital	Human capital refers to the stock of knowledge and skill, embodied in an individual as a result of education, training, and experience that makes them more productive. The stock of knowledge and skill embodied in the population of an economy.
Accumulation	The acquisition of an increasing quantity of something. The accumulation of factors, especially capital, is a primary mechanism for economic growth.
Physical capital	Physical capital refers to the same as 'capital,' without any adjective, in the sense of plant and equipment. The word 'physical' is used only to distinguish it from human capital.
Investment	Investment refers to spending for the production and accumulation of capital and additions to inventories. In a financial sense, buying an asset with the expectation of making a return.
Acquisition	A company's purchase of the property and obligations of another company is an acquisition.
Premium	Premium refers to the fee charged by an insurance company for an insurance policy. The rate of losses must be relatively predictable: In order to set the premium (prices) insurers must be able to estimate them accurately.
Market	A market is, as defined in economics, a social arrangement that allows buyers and sellers to discover information and carry out a voluntary exchange of goods or services.
Economic growth	Economic growth refers to the increase over time in the capacity of an economy to produce goods and services and to improve the well-being of its citizens.
Financial crisis	A loss of confidence in a country's currency or other financial assets causing international investors to withdraw their funds from the country is referred to as a financial crisis.
Closed economy	Closed economy refers to an economy that does not permit economic transactions with the outside world; a country in autarky.
Open economy	Open economy refers to an economy that permits transactions with the outside world, at least including trade of some goods. Contrasts with closed economy.
Real terms	A wage expressed in real terms is just the real wage.
Tariff	A tax imposed by a nation on an imported good is called a tariff.
Quota	A government-imposed restriction on quantity, or sometimes on total value, used to restrict the import of something to a specific quantity is called a quota.
Manufactured	A manufactured good refers to goods that have been processed in any way.

good	
Free trade	Free trade refers to a situation in which there are no artificial barriers to trade, such as tariffs and quotas. Usually used, often only implicitly, with frictionless trade, so that it implies that there are no barriers to trade of any kind.
Union	A worker association that bargains with employers over wages and working conditions is called a union.
Purchasing	Purchasing refers to the function in a firm that searches for quality material resources, finds the best suppliers, and negotiates the best price for goods and services.
Revenue	Revenue is a U.S. business term for the amount of money that a company receives from its activities, mostly from sales of products and/or services to customers.
Trade deficit	The amount by which imports exceed exports of goods and services is referred to as trade deficit.
Deficit	The deficit is the amount by which expenditure exceed revenue.
Trade surplus	A positive balance of trade is known as a trade surplus and consists of exporting more (in financial capital terms) than one imports.
Holding	The holding is a court's determination of a matter of law based on the issue presented in the particular case. In other words: under this law, with these facts, this result.
Asset	An item of property, such as land, capital, money, a share in ownership, or a claim on others for future payment, such as a bond or a bank deposit is an asset.
Trade balance	Balance of trade in terms of exports versus imports is called trade balance.
Exporter	A firm that sells its product in another country is an exporter.
Remainder	A remainder in property law is a future interest created in a transferee that is capable of becoming possessory upon the natural termination of a prior estate created by the same instrument.
Federal reserve system	The central banking authority responsible for monetary policy in the United States is called federal reserve system or the Fed.
Board of Governors	A board of governors is usually the governing board of a public entity; the Board of Governors of the Federal Reserve System; the Federal Reserve Board.
Federal Reserve	The Federal Reserve System was created via the Federal Reserve Act of December 23rd, 1913. All national banks were required to join the system and other banks could join. The Reserve Banks opened for business on November 16th, 1914. Federal Reserve Notes were created as part of the legislation, to provide an elastic supply of currency.
Trade pattern	What goods a country trades, with whom, and in what direction. Explaining the trade pattern is one of the major purposes of trade theory, especially which goods a country will export and which it will import.
Primary market	The market for the raising of new funds as opposed to the trading of securities already in existence is called primary market.
Accounting	A system that collects and processes financial information about an organization and reports that information to decision makers is referred to as accounting.
Preparation	Preparation refers to usually the first stage in the creative process. It includes education and formal training.
Supply	Supply is the aggregate amount of any material good that can be called into being at a certain price point; it comprises one half of the equation of supply and demand. In classical economic theory, a curve representing supply is one of the factors that produce price.
Closing	The finalization of a real estate sales transaction that passes title to the property from the seller

	to the buyer is referred to as a closing. Closing is a sales term which refers to the process of making a sale. It refers to reaching the final step, which may be an exchange of money or acquiring a signature.
Logo	Logo refers to device or other brand name that cannot be spoken.
Manufacturing	Production of goods primarily by the application of labor and capital to raw materials and other intermediate inputs, in contrast to agriculture, mining, forestry, fishing, and services a manufacturing.
Raw material	Raw material refers to a good that has not been transformed by production; a primary product.
Marketing	Promoting and selling products or services to customers, or prospective customers, is referred to as marketing.
Trade in services	Trade in services refers to the provision of a service to buyers within or from one country by a firm in or from another country.
Commerce	Commerce is the exchange of something of value between two entities. It is the central mechanism from which capitalism is derived.
Industry	A group of firms that produce identical or similar products is an industry. It is also used specifically to refer to an area of economic production focused on manufacturing which involves large amounts of capital investment before any profit can be realized, also called "heavy industry".
Firm	An organization that employs resources to produce a good or service for profit and owns and operates one or more plants is referred to as a firm.
United Nations	An international organization created by multilateral treaty in 1945 to promote social and economic cooperation among nations and to protect human rights is the United Nations.
Economic development	Increase in the economic standard of living of a country's population, normally accomplished by increasing its stocks of physical and human capital and improving its technology is an economic development.

Gains from trade	The net increase in output that countries experience as a result of lowering import tariffs and otherwise liberalizing trade is referred to as gains from trade.
Gain	In finance, gain is a profit or an increase in value of an investment such as a stock or bond. Gain is calculated by fair market value or the proceeds from the sale of the investment minus the sum of the purchase price and all costs associated with it.
International trade	The export of goods and services from a country and the import of goods and services into a country is referred to as the international trade.
Terms of trade	Terms of trade refers to the rate at which units of one product can be exchanged for units of another product; the price of a good or service; the amount of one good or service that must be given up to obtain 1 unit of another good or service.
Economy	The income, expenditures, and resources that affect the cost of running a business and household are called an economy.
Exchange	The trade of things of value between buyer and seller so that each is better off after the trade is called the exchange.
Service	Service refers to a "non tangible product" that is not embodied in a physical good and that typically effects some change in another product, person, or institution. Contrasts with good.
Agent	A person who makes economic decisions for another economic actor. A hired manager operates as an agent for a firm's owner.
Firm	An organization that employs resources to produce a good or service for profit and owns and operates one or more plants is referred to as a firm.
Economic agents	Economic agents refers to individuals who engage in production, exchange, specialization, and consumption.
Economics	The social science dealing with the use of scarce resources to obtain the maximum satisfaction of society's virtually unlimited economic wants is an economics.
Economic model	Economic model refers to a simplified picture of economic reality; an abstract generalization.
Economic theory	Economic theory refers to a statement of a cause-effect relationship; when accepted by all economists, an economic principle.
Abstraction	Abstraction is a model building simplification process that refers to retaining only the essential facts, and the elimination of irrelevant and non-economic facts, to obtain an economic principle.
Milton Friedman	Milton Friedman (born July 31, 1912) is an American economist, known for his work on macroeconomics, microeconomics, economic history, statistics, and for his advocacy of laissez-faire capitalism. In 1976 he won the Nobel Memorial Prize in Economics for his achievements in the fields of consumption analysis, monetary history and theory and for his demonstration of the complexity of stabilization policy.
Variable	A variable is something measured by a number; it is used to analyze what happens to other things when the size of that number changes.
Holding	The holding is a court's determination of a matter of law based on the issue presented in the particular case. In other words: under this law, with these facts, this result.
Economic analysis	The process of deriving economic principles from relevant economic facts are called economic analysis. It is the comparison, with money as the index, of those costs and benefits to the wider economy that can be reasonably quantified, including all social costs and benefits of a

Go to **Cram101.com** for the Practice Tests for this Chapter.

	project.
Value judgment	Value judgment refers to an opinion of what is desirable or undesirable; belief regarding what ought or ought not to be.
Policy	Similar to a script in that a policy can be a less than completely rational decision-making method. Involves the use of a pre-existing set of decision steps for any problem that presents itself.
General equilibrium	Equality of supply and demand in all markets of an economy simultaneously. The number of markets does not have to be large. The simplest Ricardian model has markets only for two goods and one factor, labor, but this is a general equilibrium model.
Consumption	In Keynesian economics consumption refers to personal consumption expenditure, i.e., the purchase of currently produced goods and services out of income, out of savings (net worth), or from borrowed funds. It refers to that part of disposable income that does not go to saving.
Production	The creation of finished goods and services using the factors of production: land, labor, capital, entrepreneurship, and knowledge.
Market	A market is, as defined in economics, a social arrangement that allows buyers and sellers to discover information and carry out a voluntary exchange of goods or services.
Principal	In agency law, one under whose direction an agent acts and for whose benefit that agent acts is a principal.
Drawback	Drawback refers to rebate of import duties when the imported good is re-exported or used as input to the production of an exported good.
Profit	Profit refers to the return to the resource entrepreneurial ability; total revenue minus total cost.
Utility	Utility refers to the want-satisfying power of a good or service; the satisfaction or pleasure a consumer obtains from the consumption of a good or service.
Commodity	Could refer to any good, but in trade a commodity is usually a raw material or primary product that enters into international trade, such as metals or basic agricultural products.
Money illusion	Could cause economic agents to think that a change in the price level is actually a change in real wages or relative prices and so change their production and employment decisions is called money illusion.
Buying power	The dollar amount available to purchase securities on margin is buying power. The amount is calculated by adding the cash held in the brokerage accounts and the amount that could be spent if securities were fully margined to their limit. If an investor uses their buying power, they are purchasing securities on credit.
Real income	Real income refers to the amount of goods and services that can be purchased with nominal income during some period of time; nominal income adjusted for inflation.
Relative price	Relative price refers to the price of one thing in terms of another; i.e., the ratio of two prices.
Price line	A straight line representing the combinations of variables, usually two goods that cost the same at some given prices. The slope of a price line measures relative prices, and changes in prices.
Revenue	Revenue is a U.S. business term for the amount of money that a company receives from its activities, mostly from sales of products and/or services to customers.
Points	Loan origination fees that may be deductible as interest by a buyer of property. A seller of

	property who pays points reduces the selling price by the amount of the points paid for the buyer.
Slope	The slope of a line in the plane containing the x and y axes is generally represented by the letter m, and is defined as the change in the y coordinate divided by the corresponding change in the x coordinate, between two distinct points on the line.
Factor endowments	A country's endowment with resources such as land, labor, and capital are referred to as factor endowments.
Factor endowment	Factor endowment refers to the quantity of a primary factor present in a country.
Technology	The body of knowledge and techniques that can be used to combine economic resources to produce goods and services is called technology.
Endowment	Endowment refers to the amount of something that a person or country simply has, rather than their having somehow to acquire it.
Supply	Supply is the aggregate amount of any material good that can be called into being at a certain price point; it comprises one half of the equation of supply and demand. In classical economic theory, a curve representing supply is one of the factors that produce price.
Value of money	Value of money refers to the quantity of goods and services for which a unit of money can be exchanged; the purchasing power of a unit of money; the reciprocal of the price level.
Barter	Barter is a type of trade where goods or services are exchanged for a certain amount of other goods or services; no money is involved in the transaction.
Insurance	Insurance refers to a system by which individuals can reduce their exposure to risk of large losses by spreading the risks among a large number of persons.
Premium	Premium refers to the fee charged by an insurance company for an insurance policy. The rate of losses must be relatively predictable: In order to set the premium (prices) insurers must be able to estimate them accurately.
Factors of production	Economic resources: land, capital, labor, and entrepreneurial ability are called factors of production.
Industry	A group of firms that produce identical or similar products is an industry. It is also used specifically to refer to an area of economic production focused on manufacturing which involves large amounts of capital investment before any profit can be realized, also called "heavy industry".
Contract	A contract is a "promise" or an "agreement" that is enforced or recognized by the law. In the civil law, a contract is considered to be part of the general law of obligations.
Labor	People's physical and mental talents and efforts that are used to help produce goods and services are called labor.
Opportunity cost	The cost of something in terms of opportunity foregone. The opportunity cost to a country of producing a unit more of a good, such as for export or to replace an import, is the quantity of some other good that could have been produced instead.
Perfect competition	An idealized market structure in which there are large numbers of both buyers and sellers, all of them small, so that they act as price takers. Perfect competition also assumes homogeneous products, free entry and exit, and complete information.
Externality	Externality refers to an effect of one economic agent's actions on another, such that one agent's decisions make another better or worse off by changing their utility or cost.
Social cost	Social cost, in economics, is the total of all the costs associated with an economic activity. It includes both costs borne by the economic agent and also all costs borne by

	society at large. It includes the costs reflected in the organization's production function and the costs external to the firm's private costs.
Market price	Market price is an economic concept with commonplace familiarity; it is the price that a good or service is offered at, or will fetch, in the marketplace; it is of interest mainly in the study of microeconomics.
Competitive firm	Competitive firm refers to a firm without market power, with no ability to alter the market price of the goods it produces.
Microeconomics	The part of economics concerned with such individual units as industries, firms, and households and with individual markets, specific goods and services, and product and resource prices is called microeconomics.
Normal profit	Normal profit refers to the payment made by a firm to obtain and retain entrepreneurial ability; the minimum income entrepreneurial ability must receive to induce it to perform entrepreneurial functions for a firm.
Marginal cost	Marginal cost refers to the increase in cost that accompanies a unit increase in output; the partial derivative of the cost function with respect to output.
Preference	The act of a debtor in paying or securing one or more of his creditors in a manner more favorable to them than to other creditors or to the exclusion of such other creditors is a preference. In the absence of statute, a preference is perfectly good, but to be legal it must be bona fide, and not a mere subterfuge of the debtor to secure a future benefit to himself or to prevent the application of his property to his debts.
Indifference curve	Indifference curve refers to a means of representing the preferences and well being of consumers. Formally, it is a curve representing the combinations of arguments in a utility function that yield a given level of utility.
Property	Assets defined in the broadest legal sense. Property includes the unrealized receivables of a cash basis taxpayer, but not services rendered.
Yield	The interest rate that equates a future value or an annuity to a given present value is a yield.
Autarky	Autarky refers to the situation of not engaging in international trade; self-sufficiency. Not to be confused with 'autarchy,' which in at least some dictionaries is a political term rather than an economic one, and means absolute rule or power.
Community indifference curve	Community indifference curve refers to one of a family of indifference curves intended to represent the preferences, and sometimes the well-being, of a country as a whole. A handy tool for deriving quantities of trade in a two-good model, although its legitimacy depends on the existence of community preferences, which in turn requires very restrictive assumptions.
Consumer demand	Consumer demand or consumption is also known as personal consumption expenditure. It is the largest part of aggregate demand or effective demand at the macroeconomic level.There are two variants of consumption in the aggregate demand model, including induced consumption and autonomous consumption.
Closed economy	Closed economy refers to an economy that does not permit economic transactions with the outside world; a country in autarky.
Innovation	Innovation refers to the first commercially successful introduction of a new product, the use of a new method of production, or the creation of a new form of business organization.
Normative economics	Normative economics refers to the part of economics involving value judgments about what the economy should be like; focused on which economic goals and policies should be implemented; policy economics.

Go to **Cram101.com** for the Practice Tests for this Chapter.

Real gross domestic product	Gross domestic product that has been adjusted to eliminate the impact of changes in the price level is the real gross domestic product.
Gross domestic product	Gross domestic product refers to the total value of new goods and services produced in a given year within the borders of a country, regardless of by whom.
Domestic	From or in one's own country. A domestic producer is one that produces inside the home country. A domestic price is the price inside the home country. Opposite of 'foreign' or 'world.'.
Supply curve	Supply curve refers to the graph of quantity supplied as a function of price, normally upward sloping, straight or curved, and drawn with quantity on the horizontal axis and price on the vertical axis.
Numeraire	The unit in which prices are measured. This may be a currency, but in real models, such as most trade models, the numeraire is usually one of the goods, whose price is then set at one.
Basket	A basket is an economic term for a group of several securities created for the purpose of simultaneous buying or selling. Baskets are frequently used for program trading.
Price index	A measure of the average prices of a group of goods relative to a base year. A typical price index for a vector of quantities q and prices pb, pg in the base and given years respectively would be $I = 100\ Pgq\ /\ Pbq$.
Consumer price index	Consumer price index refers to a price index for the goods purchased by consumers in an economy, usually based on only a representative sample of typical consumer goods and services. Commonly used to measure inflation. Contrasts with the implicit price deflator.
GDP deflator	In economics, the GDP deflator is a measure of the change in prices of all new, domestically produced, final goods and services in an economy.
Base year	The year used as the basis for comparison by a price index such as the CPI. The index for any year is the average of prices for that year compared to the base year; e.g., 110 means that prices are 10% higher than in the base year.
Per capita	Per capita refers to per person. Usually used to indicate the average per person of any given statistic, commonly income.
Excess supply	Supply minus demand. Thus a country's supply of exports of a homogeneous good is its excess supply of that good.
Supply and demand	The partial equilibrium supply and demand economic model originally developed by Alfred Marshall attempts to describe, explain, and predict changes in the price and quantity of goods sold in competitive markets.
Autarky price	Autarky price refers to price in autarky; that is, the price of something within a country when it is not traded by that country. Relative autarky prices turn out to be the most theoretically robust measures of comparative advantage.
Demand curve	Demand curve refers to the graph of quantity demanded as a function of price, normally downward sloping, straight or curved, and drawn with quantity on the horizontal axis and price on the vertical axis.
Equilibrium price	Equilibrium price refers to the price in a competitive market at which the quantity demanded and the quantity supplied are equal, there is neither a shortage nor a surplus, and there is no tendency for price to rise or fall.
Comparative advantage	The ability to produce a good at lower cost, relative to other goods, compared to another country is a comparative advantage.

Division of labor	Division of labor is generally speaking the specialization of cooperative labor in specific, circumscribed tasks and roles, intended to increase efficiency of output.
International division	Division responsible for a firm's international activities is an international division.
Labor theory of value	Labor theory of value refers to the theory that the value of any produced good or service is equal to the amount of labor used, directly and indirectly, to produce it. Sometimes said to underlie the Ricardian Model of international trade.
Absolute advantage	A country has an absolute advantage economically over another when it can produce something more cheaply. This term is often used to differentiate between comparative advantage.
Theory of value	Theory of value is a generic term which encompasses all the theories within economics that explain the worth of goods and services. A key question in economic theory is how the value of goods and services comes about, and how to calculate the correct value of goods and services (if such a value exists).
Classical model	Classical model refers to a model of the economy derived from the ideas of the classical, or pre-Keynesian economists; a model based on the assumptions that wages and prices adjust to clear markets and that monetary policy does not influence real variables. A macroeconomic model that explains how real GDP and other variables are determined at full employment.
Wage	The payment for the service of a unit of labor, per unit time. In trade theory, it is the only payment to labor, usually unskilled labor. In empirical work, wage data may exclude other compenzation, which must be added to get the total cost of employment.

International trade	The export of goods and services from a country and the import of goods and services into a country is referred to as the international trade.
Classical theory	The original theory about organizations that closely resembles military structures is called classical theory.
Contribution	In business organization law, the cash or property contributed to a business by its owners is referred to as contribution.
Trade theory	The body of economic thought that seeks to explain why and how countries engage in international trade and the welfare implication of that trade, encompassing especially the Ricardian Model, the Heckscher-Ohlin Model, and the New Trade Theory.
Law of comparative advantage	The law of comparative advantage is the principle that, given the freedom to respond to market forces, countries will tend to export goods for which they have comparative advantage and import goods for which they have comparative disadvantage.
Comparative advantage	The ability to produce a good at lower cost, relative to other goods, compared to another country is a comparative advantage.
Production	The creation of finished goods and services using the factors of production: land, labor, capital, entrepreneurship, and knowledge.
Absolute advantage	A country has an absolute advantage economically over another when it can produce something more cheaply. This term is often used to differentiate between comparative advantage.
Adam Smith	Adam Smith (baptized June 5, 1723 O.S. (June 16 N.S.) – July 17, 1790) was a Scottish political economist and moral philosopher. His Inquiry into the Nature and Causes of the Wealth of Nations was one of the earliest attempts to study the historical development of industry and commerce in Europe. That work helped to create the modern academic discipline of economics
Operation	A standardized method or technique that is performed repetitively, often on different materials resulting in different finished goods is called an operation.
Industry	A group of firms that produce identical or similar products is an industry. It is also used specifically to refer to an area of economic production focused on manufacturing which involves large amounts of capital investment before any profit can be realized, also called "heavy industry".
Division of labor	Division of labor is generally speaking the specialization of cooperative labor in specific, circumscribed tasks and roles, intended to increase efficiency of output.
Labor	People's physical and mental talents and efforts that are used to help produce goods and services are called labor.
International division	Division responsible for a firm's international activities is an international division.
Autarky	Autarky refers to the situation of not engaging in international trade; self-sufficiency. Not to be confused with 'autarchy,' which in at least some dictionaries is a political term rather than an economic one, and means absolute rule or power.
Expense	In accounting, an expense represents an event in which an asset is used up or a liability is incurred. In terms of the accounting equation, expenses reduce owners' equity.
Standard of living	Standard of living refers to the level of consumption that people enjoy, on the average, and is measured by average income per person.
Mercantilism	Mercantilism refers to an economic philosophy of the 16th and 17th centuries that international commerce should primarily serve to increase a country's financial wealth,

Go to **Cram101.com** for the Practice Tests for this Chapter.

especially of gold and foreign currency.

Domestic	From or in one's own country. A domestic producer is one that produces inside the home country. A domestic price is the price inside the home country. Opposite of 'foreign' or 'world.'.
Export	In economics, an export is any good or commodity, shipped or otherwise transported out of a country, province, town to another part of the world in a legitimate fashion, typically for use in trade or sale.
Policy	Similar to a script in that a policy can be a less than completely rational decision-making method. Involves the use of a pre-existing set of decision steps for any problem that presents itself.
Immigration	Immigration refers to the migration of people into a country.
Corporation	A legal entity chartered by a state or the Federal government that is distinct and separate from the individuals who own it is a corporation. This separation gives the corporation unique powers which other legal entities lack.
Multinational corporations	Firms that own production facilities in two or more countries and produce and sell their products globally are referred to as multinational corporations.
Multinational corporation	An organization that manufactures and markets products in many different countries and has multinational stock ownership and multinational management is referred to as multinational corporation.
Wage	The payment for the service of a unit of labor, per unit time. In trade theory, it is the only payment to labor, usually unskilled labor. In empirical work, wage data may exclude other compenzation, which must be added to get the total cost of employment.
Long run	In economic models, the long run time frame assumes no fixed factors of production. Firms can enter or leave the marketplace, and the cost (and availability) of land, labor, raw materials, and capital goods can be assumed to vary.
Free trade	Free trade refers to a situation in which there are no artificial barriers to trade, such as tariffs and quotas. Usually used, often only implicitly, with frictionless trade, so that it implies that there are no barriers to trade of any kind.
Capital	Capital generally refers to financial wealth, especially that used to start or maintain a business. In classical economics, capital is one of four factors of production, the others being land and labor and entrepreneurship.
Labor theory of value	Labor theory of value refers to the theory that the value of any produced good or service is equal to the amount of labor used, directly and indirectly, to produce it. Sometimes said to underlie the Ricardian Model of international trade.
Theory of value	Theory of value is a generic term which encompasses all the theories within economics that explain the worth of goods and services. A key question in economic theory is how the value of goods and services comes about, and how to calculate the correct value of goods and services (if such a value exists).
Physical capital	Physical capital refers to the same as 'capital,' without any adjective, in the sense of plant and equipment. The word 'physical' is used only to distinguish it from human capital.
Returns to scale	Returns to scale refers to a technical property of production that predicts what happens to output if the quantity of all input factors is increased by some amount of scale.
Inputs	The inputs used by a firm or an economy are the labor, raw materials, electricity and other resources it uses to produce its outputs.

Go to **Cram101.com** for the Practice Tests for this Chapter.
And, **NEVER** highlight a book again!

Constant returns to scale	Constant returns to scale refers to a property of a production function such that scaling all inputs by any positive constant also scales output by the same constant. Such a function is also called homogeneous of degree one or linearly homogeneous.
Factor of production	Factor of production refers to economic resources used in production such as land, labor, and capital.
Classical model	Classical model refers to a model of the economy derived from the ideas of the classical, or pre-Keynesian economists; a model based on the assumptions that wages and prices adjust to clear markets and that monetary policy does not influence real variables. A macroeconomic model that explains how real GDP and other variables are determined at full employment.
Gain	In finance, gain is a profit or an increase in value of an investment such as a stock or bond. Gain is calculated by fair market value or the proceeds from the sale of the investment minus the sum of the purchase price and all costs associated with it.
Market	A market is, as defined in economics, a social arrangement that allows buyers and sellers to discover information and carry out a voluntary exchange of goods or services.
Perfect competition	An idealized market structure in which there are large numbers of both buyers and sellers, all of them small, so that they act as price takers. Perfect competition also assumes homogeneous products, free entry and exit, and complete information.
Layoff	A layoff is the termination of an employee or (more commonly) a group of employees for business reasons, such as the decision that certain positions are no longer necessary.
Closing	The finalization of a real estate sales transaction that passes title to the property from the seller to the buyer is referred to as a closing. Closing is a sales term which refers to the process of making a sale. It refers to reaching the final step, which may be an exchange of money or acquiring a signature.
David Ricardo	David Ricardo (April 18, 1772 – September 11, 1823), a political economist, is often credited with systematizing economics, and was one of the most influential of the classical economists.
Exchange	The trade of things of value between buyer and seller so that each is better off after the trade is called the exchange.
Points	Loan origination fees that may be deductible as interest by a buyer of property. A seller of property who pays points reduces the selling price by the amount of the points paid for the buyer.
Technology	The body of knowledge and techniques that can be used to combine economic resources to produce goods and services is called technology.
Relative price	Relative price refers to the price of one thing in terms of another; i.e., the ratio of two prices.
World price	The price of a good on the 'world market,' meaning the price outside of any country's borders and therefore exclusive of any trade taxes or subsidies is the world price.
Normal profit	Normal profit refers to the payment made by a firm to obtain and retain entrepreneurial ability; the minimum income entrepreneurial ability must receive to induce it to perform entrepreneurial functions for a firm.
Profit	Profit refers to the return to the resource entrepreneurial ability; total revenue minus total cost.
Opportunity cost	The cost of something in terms of opportunity foregone. The opportunity cost to a country of producing a unit more of a good, such as for export or to replace an import, is the quantity of some other good that could have been produced instead.

Terms of trade	Terms of trade refers to the rate at which units of one product can be exchanged for units of another product; the price of a good or service; the amount of one good or service that must be given up to obtain 1 unit of another good or service.
General equilibrium	Equality of supply and demand in all markets of an economy simultaneously. The number of markets does not have to be large. The simplest Ricardian model has markets only for two goods and one factor, labor, but this is a general equilibrium model.
Consumption possibility frontier	Consumption possibility frontier refers to a graph of the maximum quantities of goods that an economy can consume in a specified situation, such as autarky and free trade.
Consumption	In Keynesian economics consumption refers to personal consumption expenditure, i.e., the purchase of currently produced goods and services out of income, out of savings (net worth), or from borrowed funds. It refers to that part of disposable income that does not go to saving.
Community indifference curve	Community indifference curve refers to one of a family of indifference curves intended to represent the preferences, and sometimes the well-being, of a country as a whole. A handy tool for deriving quantities of trade in a two-good model, although its legitimacy depends on the existence of community preferences, which in turn requires very restrictive assumptions.
Indifference curve	Indifference curve refers to a means of representing the preferences and well being of consumers. Formally, it is a curve representing the combinations of arguments in a utility function that yield a given level of utility.
Trade triangle	In the trade-and-transformation-curve diagram, the right triangle formed by the world price line and the production and consumption points, the sides of which represent the quantities exported and imported is referred to as trade triangle.
Slope	The slope of a line in the plane containing the x and y axes is generally represented by the letter m, and is defined as the change in the y coordinate divided by the corresponding change in the x coordinate, between two distinct points on the line.
Economics	The social science dealing with the use of scarce resources to obtain the maximum satisfaction of society's virtually unlimited economic wants is an economics.
Reciprocal demand	Reciprocal demand refers to the concept in international trade, that it is not just supply and demand that interact, but demand and demand. Describes a trading equilibrium in which a reciprocal equilibrium where one country's demand for another country's products matches with the other country's demands for the products of the first.
Supply	Supply is the aggregate amount of any material good that can be called into being at a certain price point; it comprises one half of the equation of supply and demand. In classical economic theory, a curve representing supply is one of the factors that produce price.
Excess supply	Supply minus demand. Thus a country's supply of exports of a homogeneous good is its excess supply of that good.
Supply and demand	The partial equilibrium supply and demand economic model originally developed by Alfred Marshall attempts to describe, explain, and predict changes in the price and quantity of goods sold in competitive markets.
Argument	The discussion by counsel for the respective parties of their contentions on the law and the facts of the case being tried in order to aid the jury in arriving at a correct and just conclusion is called argument.
Enabling	Enabling refers to giving workers the education and tools they need to assume their new decision-making powers.

Go to **Cram101.com** for the Practice Tests for this Chapter.

Gains from trade	The net increase in output that countries experience as a result of lowering import tariffs and otherwise liberalizing trade is referred to as gains from trade.
Economy	The income, expenditures, and resources that affect the cost of running a business and household are called an economy.
Real terms	A wage expressed in real terms is just the real wage.
National income	National income refers to the income generated by a country's production, and therefore the total income of its factors of production.
Trade flow	The quantity or value of a country's bilateral trade with another country is called trade flow.
Supply factor	An increase in the availability of a resource, an improvement in its quality, or an expansion of technological knowledge that makes it possible for an economy to produce a greater output of goods and services is called a supply factor.
Increase in demand	Increase in demand refers to an increase in the quantity demanded of a good or service at every price; a shift of the demand curve to the right.
Labor productivity	In labor economics labor productivity is a measure of the efficiency of the labor force. It is usually measured as output per hour of all people. When comparing labor productivity one mostly looks at the change over time.
Productivity	Productivity refers to the total output of goods and services in a given period of time divided by work hours.
North American Free Trade Agreement	A 1993 agreement establishing, over a 15-year period, a free trade zone composed of Canada, Mexico, and the United States is referred to as the North American Free Trade Agreement.
Manufacturing	Production of goods primarily by the application of labor and capital to raw materials and other intermediate inputs, in contrast to agriculture, mining, forestry, fishing, and services a manufacturing.
Cost advantage	Possession of a lower cost of production or operation than a competing firm or country is cost advantage.
Developing country	Developing country refers to a country whose per capita income is low by world standards. Same as LDC. As usually used, it does not necessarily connote that the country's income is rising.
Direction of trade	Direction of trade is the particular countries and kinds of countries toward which a country's exports are sent, and from which its imports are brought, in contrast to the commodity composition of its exports and imports.
Developed country	A developed country is one that enjoys a relatively high standard of living derived through an industrialized, diversified economy. Countries with a very high Human Development Index are generally considered developed countries.
Welfare	Welfare refers to the economic well being of an individual, group, or economy. For individuals, it is conceptualized by a utility function. For groups, including countries and the world, it is a tricky philosophical concept, since individuals fare differently.
Complete specialization	Complete specialization is the non-production of some of the goods that a country consumes. Also refers to production only of goods that are exported or nontraded, but none that compete with imports; Production of only one good; Being the only country in the world to produce a
Remainder	A remainder in property law is a future interest created in a transferee that is capable of becoming possessory upon the natural termination of a prior estate created by the same

Go to **Cram101.com** for the Practice Tests for this Chapter.

	instrument.
Extension	Extension refers to an out-of-court settlement in which creditors agree to allow the firm more time to meet its financial obligations. A new repayment schedule will be developed, subject to the acceptance of creditors.
Basket	A basket is an economic term for a group of several securities created for the purpose of simultaneous buying or selling. Baskets are frequently used for program trading.
Trade pattern	What goods a country trades, with whom, and in what direction. Explaining the trade pattern is one of the major purposes of trade theory, especially which goods a country will export and which it will import.
Chain of comparative advantage	Chain of comparative advantage refers to a ranking of goods or countries in order of comparative advantage. With two countries and many goods, goods can be ranked by comparative advantage.
Offer curve	Offer curve refers to a curve showing, for a two-good model, the quantity of one good that a country will export for each quantity of the other that it imports.
Option	A contract that gives the purchaser the option to buy or sell the underlying financial instrument at a specified price, called the exercise price or strike price, within a specific period of time.
Factor endowments	A country's endowment with resources such as land, labor, and capital are referred to as factor endowments.
Capital abundant	A country is capital abundant if its endowment of capital is large compared to other countries. Relative capital abundance can be defined by either the quantity definition or the price definition.
Factor endowment	Factor endowment refers to the quantity of a primary factor present in a country.
Labor intensive	Describing an industry or sector of the economy that relies relatively heavily on inputs of labor, usually relative to capital but sometimes to human capital or skilled labor, compared to other industries or sectors is labor intensive.
Economic growth	Economic growth refers to the increase over time in the capacity of an economy to produce goods and services and to improve the well-being of its citizens.
Distribution	Distribution in economics, the manner in which total output and income is distributed among individuals or factors.
Factor price	Factor price refers to the price paid for the services of a unit of a primary factor of production per unit time. Includes the wage or salary of labor and the rental prices of land and capital, and normal profits for the entrepreneur.
Endowment	Endowment refers to the amount of something that a person or country simply has, rather than their having somehow to acquire it.
Factor price equalization	Factor price equalization refers to the tendency for trade to cause factor prices in different countries to become identical.

International trade	The export of goods and services from a country and the import of goods and services into a country is referred to as the international trade.
Classical model	Classical model refers to a model of the economy derived from the ideas of the classical, or pre-Keynesian economists; a model based on the assumptions that wages and prices adjust to clear markets and that monetary policy does not influence real variables. A macroeconomic model that explains how real GDP and other variables are determined at full employment.
Productivity	Productivity refers to the total output of goods and services in a given period of time divided by work hours.
Comparative advantage	The ability to produce a good at lower cost, relative to other goods, compared to another country is a comparative advantage.
Classical theory	The original theory about organizations that closely resembles military structures is called classical theory.
Production	The creation of finished goods and services using the factors of production: land, labor, capital, entrepreneurship, and knowledge.
Factors of production	Economic resources: land, capital, labor, and entrepreneurial ability are called factors of production.
Factor endowments	A country's endowment with resources such as land, labor, and capital are referred to as factor endowments.
Factor endowment	Factor endowment refers to the quantity of a primary factor present in a country.
Endowment	Endowment refers to the amount of something that a person or country simply has, rather than their having somehow to acquire it.
Capital	Capital generally refers to financial wealth, especially that used to start or maintain a business. In classical economics, capital is one of four factors of production, the others being land and labor and entrepreneurship.
Distribution	Distribution in economics, the manner in which total output and income is distributed among individuals or factors.
Appeal	Appeal refers to the act of asking an appellate court to overturn a decision after the trial court's final judgment has been entered.
Economic growth	Economic growth refers to the increase over time in the capacity of an economy to produce goods and services and to improve the well-being of its citizens.
Factor price	Factor price refers to the price paid for the services of a unit of a primary factor of production per unit time. Includes the wage or salary of labor and the rental prices of land and capital, and normal profits for the entrepreneur.
Wage	The payment for the service of a unit of labor, per unit time. In trade theory, it is the only payment to labor, usually unskilled labor. In empirical work, wage data may exclude other compenzation, which must be added to get the total cost of employment.
Economy	The income, expenditures, and resources that affect the cost of running a business and household are called an economy.
Interest	In finance and economics, interest is the price paid by a borrower for the use of a lender's money. In other words, interest is the amount of paid to "rent" money for a period of time.
Service	Service refers to a "non tangible product" that is not embodied in a physical good and that typically effects some change in another product, person, or institution. Contrasts with good.

Labor	People's physical and mental talents and efforts that are used to help produce goods and services are called labor.
Asset	An item of property, such as land, capital, money, a share in ownership, or a claim on others for future payment, such as a bond or a bank deposit is an asset.
Trade pattern	What goods a country trades, with whom, and in what direction. Explaining the trade pattern is one of the major purposes of trade theory, especially which goods a country will export and which it will import.
Technology	The body of knowledge and techniques that can be used to combine economic resources to produce goods and services is called technology.
Returns to scale	Returns to scale refers to a technical property of production that predicts what happens to output if the quantity of all input factors is increased by some amount of scale.
Constant returns to scale	Constant returns to scale refers to a property of a production function such that scaling all inputs by any positive constant also scales output by the same constant. Such a function is also called homogeneous of degree one or linearly homogeneous.
Labor intensive	Describing an industry or sector of the economy that relies relatively heavily on inputs of labor, usually relative to capital but sometimes to human capital or skilled labor, compared to other industries or sectors is labor intensive.
Industry	A group of firms that produce identical or similar products is an industry. It is also used specifically to refer to an area of economic production focused on manufacturing which involves large amounts of capital investment before any profit can be realized, also called "heavy industry".
Factor intensity	Factor intensity refers to the relative importance of one factor versus others in production in an industry, usually compared across industries.
Instrument	Instrument refers to an economic variable that is controlled by policy makers and can be used to influence other variables, called targets. Examples are monetary and fiscal policies used to achieve external and internal balance.
Capital stock	The total amount of physical capital that has been accumulated, usually in a country is capital stock. Also refers to the total issued capital of a firm, including ordinary and preferred shares.
Stock	In financial terminology, stock is the capital raized by a corporation, through the issuance and sale of shares.
Capital abundant	A country is capital abundant if its endowment of capital is large compared to other countries. Relative capital abundance can be defined by either the quantity definition or the price definition.
Labor force	In economics the labor force is the group of people who have a potential for being employed.
Factor abundance	Factor abundance refers to the abundance or scarcity of a primary factor of production. Because, in the short run at least, the supplies of primary factors are more or less fixed, this can be taken as given for determining much about a country's trade and other economic variables. Fundamental to the HO Model.
Demographic	A demographic is a term used in marketing and broadcasting, to describe a demographic grouping or a market segment.
Economic development	Increase in the economic standard of living of a country's population, normally accomplished by increasing its stocks of physical and human capital and improving its technology is an economic development.

Correlation	A correlation is the measure of the extent to which two economic or statistical variables move together, normalized so that its values range from -1 to +1. It is defined as the covariance of the two variables divided by the square root of the product of their variances.
Contract	A contract is a "promise" or an "agreement" that is enforced or recognized by the law. In the civil law, a contract is considered to be part of the general law of obligations.
Export	In economics, an export is any good or commodity, shipped or otherwise transported out of a country, province, town to another part of the world in a legitimate fashion, typically for use in trade or sale.
Demand factor	A demand factor is a factor that determines consumers' willingness and ability to pay for goods and services.
Quantity definition	Quantity definition refers to a method of defining relative factor abundance based on ratios of factor quantities.
Preference	The act of a debtor in paying or securing one or more of his creditors in a manner more favorable to them than to other creditors or to the exclusion of such other creditors is a preference. In the absence of statute, a preference is perfectly good, but to be legal it must be bona fide, and not a mere subterfuge of the debtor to secure a future benefit to himself or to prevent the application of his property to his debts.
Property	Assets defined in the broadest legal sense. Property includes the unrealized receivables of a cash basis taxpayer, but not services rendered.
Autarky	Autarky refers to the situation of not engaging in international trade; self-sufficiency. Not to be confused with 'autarchy,' which in at least some dictionaries is a political term rather than an economic one, and means absolute rule or power.
Relative price	Relative price refers to the price of one thing in terms of another; i.e., the ratio of two prices.
Economic agents	Economic agents refers to individuals who engage in production, exchange, specialization, and consumption.
Trade flow	The quantity or value of a country's bilateral trade with another country is called trade flow.
Profit	Profit refers to the return to the resource entrepreneurial ability; total revenue minus total cost.
Agent	A person who makes economic decisions for another economic actor. A hired manager operates as an agent for a firm's owner.
World price	The price of a good on the 'world market,' meaning the price outside of any country's borders and therefore exclusive of any trade taxes or subsidies is the world price.
Terms of trade	Terms of trade refers to the rate at which units of one product can be exchanged for units of another product; the price of a good or service; the amount of one good or service that must be given up to obtain 1 unit of another good or service.
Price line	A straight line representing the combinations of variables, usually two goods that cost the same at some given prices. The slope of a price line measures relative prices, and changes in prices.
Consumption	In Keynesian economics consumption refers to personal consumption expenditure, i.e., the purchase of currently produced goods and services out of income, out of savings (net worth), or from borrowed funds. It refers to that part of disposable income that does not go to saving.

Go to **Cram101.com** for the Practice Tests for this Chapter.

Exchange	The trade of things of value between buyer and seller so that each is better off after the trade is called the exchange.
Trade triangle	In the trade-and-transformation-curve diagram, the right triangle formed by the world price line and the production and consumption points, the sides of which represent the quantities exported and imported is referred to as trade triangle.
Reciprocal demand	Reciprocal demand refers to the concept in international trade, that it is not just supply and demand that interact, but demand and demand. Describes a trading equilibrium in which a reciprocal equilibrium where one country's demand for another country's products matches with the other country's demands for the products of the first.
Supply	Supply is the aggregate amount of any material good that can be called into being at a certain price point; it comprises one half of the equation of supply and demand. In classical economic theory, a curve representing supply is one of the factors that produce price.
Slope	The slope of a line in the plane containing the x and y axes is generally represented by the letter m, and is defined as the change in the y coordinate divided by the corresponding change in the x coordinate, between two distinct points on the line.
Market	A market is, as defined in economics, a social arrangement that allows buyers and sellers to discover information and carry out a voluntary exchange of goods or services.
Opportunity cost	The cost of something in terms of opportunity foregone. The opportunity cost to a country of producing a unit more of a good, such as for export or to replace an import, is the quantity of some other good that could have been produced instead.
Relative cost	Relative cost refers to the relationship between the price paid for advertising time or space and the size of the audience delivered; it is used to compare the prices of various media vehicles.
Inputs	The inputs used by a firm or an economy are the labor, raw materials, electricity and other resources it uses to produce its outputs.
Complete specialization	Complete specialization is the non-production of some of the goods that a country consumes. Also refers to production only of goods that are exported or nontraded, but none that compete with imports; Production of only one good; Being the only country in the world to produce a
Equilibrium price	Equilibrium price refers to the price in a competitive market at which the quantity demanded and the quantity supplied are equal, there is neither a shortage nor a surplus, and there is no tendency for price to rise or fall.
Supply curve	Supply curve refers to the graph of quantity supplied as a function of price, normally upward sloping, straight or curved, and drawn with quantity on the horizontal axis and price on the vertical axis.
Autarky price	Autarky price refers to price in autarky; that is, the price of something within a country when it is not traded by that country. Relative autarky prices turn out to be the most theoretically robust measures of comparative advantage.
Excess demand	Demand minus supply. Thus a country's demand for imports of a homogeneous good is its excess demand for that good.
Incentive	An incentive is any factor (financial or non-financial) that provides a motive for a particular course of action, or counts as a reason for preferring one choice to the alternatives.
Domestic	From or in one's own country. A domestic producer is one that produces inside the home country. A domestic price is the price inside the home country. Opposite of 'foreign' or 'world.'.

Demand curve	Demand curve refers to the graph of quantity demanded as a function of price, normally downward sloping, straight or curved, and drawn with quantity on the horizontal axis and price on the vertical axis.
Commodity	Could refer to any good, but in trade a commodity is usually a raw material or primary product that enters into international trade, such as metals or basic agricultural products.
Investment	Investment refers to spending for the production and accumulation of capital and additions to inventories. In a financial sense, buying an asset with the expectation of making a return.
Factor price equalization	Factor price equalization refers to the tendency for trade to cause factor prices in different countries to become identical.
Journal	Book of original entry, in which transactions are recorded in a general ledger system, is referred to as a journal.
Free trade	Free trade refers to a situation in which there are no artificial barriers to trade, such as tariffs and quotas. Usually used, often only implicitly, with frictionless trade, so that it implies that there are no barriers to trade of any kind.
Trade barrier	An artificial disincentive to export and/or import, such as a tariff, quota, or other NTB is called a trade barrier.
Trade liberalization	Reduction of tariffs and removal or relaxation of NTBs is referred to as trade liberalization.
Economics	The social science dealing with the use of scarce resources to obtain the maximum satisfaction of society's virtually unlimited economic wants is an economics.
Union	A worker association that bargains with employers over wages and working conditions is called a union.
Factor market	Any place where factors of production, resources, are bought and sold is referred to as factor market.
Scarcity	Scarcity is defined as not having sufficient resources to produce enough to fulfill unlimited subjective wants. Alternatively, scarcity implies that not all of society's goals can be attained at the same time, so that trade-offs one good against others are made.
Competitive bidding	A situation where two or more companies submit bids for a product, service, or project to a potential buyer is competitive bidding.
Labor market	Any arrangement that brings buyers and sellers of labor services together to agree on conditions of work and pay is called a labor market.
Unskilled labor	Unskilled labor refers to labor with a low level of skill or human capital. Identified empirically as labor earning a low wage, with a low level of education, or in an occupational category associated with these.
Manufacturing	Production of goods primarily by the application of labor and capital to raw materials and other intermediate inputs, in contrast to agriculture, mining, forestry, fishing, and services a manufacturing.
Gain	In finance, gain is a profit or an increase in value of an investment such as a stock or bond. Gain is calculated by fair market value or the proceeds from the sale of the investment minus the sum of the purchase price and all costs associated with it.
Policy	Similar to a script in that a policy can be a less than completely rational decision-making method. Involves the use of a pre-existing set of decision steps for any problem that presents itself.
Short run	Short run refers to a period of time that permits an increase or decrease in current

	production volume with existing capacity, but one that is too short to permit enlargement of that capacity itself (eg, the building of new plants, training of additional workers, etc.).
Abundant factor	Abundant factor refers to the factor (resource) in a country's endowment with which it is best endowed, relative to other factors, compared to other countries. May be defined by quantity or by price.
Scarce factor	Scarce factor refers to the factor in a country's endowment with which it is has the least of, relative to other factors, compared to other countries. May be defined by quantity or by price.
General equilibrium	Equality of supply and demand in all markets of an economy simultaneously. The number of markets does not have to be large. The simplest Ricardian model has markets only for two goods and one factor, labor, but this is a general equilibrium model.
Standard of living	Standard of living refers to the level of consumption that people enjoy, on the average, and is measured by average income per person.
Developed country	A developed country is one that enjoys a relatively high standard of living derived through an industrialized, diversified economy. Countries with a very high Human Development Index are generally considered developed countries.
Composition	An out-of-court settlement in which creditors agree to accept a fractional settlement on their original claim is referred to as composition.
Points	Loan origination fees that may be deductible as interest by a buyer of property. A seller of property who pays points reduces the selling price by the amount of the points paid for the buyer.
Principal	In agency law, one under whose direction an agent acts and for whose benefit that agent acts is a principal.
Isoquant	A curve representing the combinations of factor inputs that yield a given level of output in a production function is referred to as isoquant.
Economic theory	Economic theory refers to a statement of a cause-effect relationship; when accepted by all economists, an economic principle.
Perfect substitute	A good that is regarded by its demanders as identical to another good, so that the elasticity of substitution between them is infinite is referred to as perfect substitute.
Production function	Production function refers to a function that specifies the output in an industry for all combinations of inputs.
Marginal cost	Marginal cost refers to the increase in cost that accompanies a unit increase in output; the partial derivative of the cost function with respect to output.
Average cost	Average cost is equal to total cost divided by the number of goods produced (Quantity-Q). It is also equal to the sum of average variable costs (total variable costs divided by Q) plus average fixed costs (total fixed costs divided by Q).
Fixed cost	The cost that a firm bears if it does not produce at all and that is independent of its output. The presence of a fixed cost tends to imply increasing returns to scale. Contrasts with variable cost.
Firm	An organization that employs resources to produce a good or service for profit and owns and operates one or more plants is referred to as a firm.
Other things constant	Other things constant refers to a phrase that signifies that a factor under consideration is changed while all other factors are held constant or unchanged; ceteris paribus.
Holding	The holding is a court's determination of a matter of law based on the issue presented in the

particular case. In other words: under this law, with these facts, this result.

Gains from trade	The net increase in output that countries experience as a result of lowering import tariffs and otherwise liberalizing trade is referred to as gains from trade.
Context	The effect of the background under which a message often takes on more and richer meaning is a context. Context is especially important in cross-cultural interactions because some cultures are said to be high context or low context.
Specific factors model	A model in which some or all factors are specific factors. Most commonly the specific factors model has one specific factor in each industry plus another factor that is mobile between them. But an extreme form of the model can have all factors specific.
Specific factor	Specific factor refers to a factor of production that is unable to move into or out of an industry. The term is used to describe both factors that would not be of any use in other industries and -- more loosely -- factors that could be used elsewhere but are not.
Value marginal product	Value marginal product is defined as the change in total revenue divided by the change in total output. Depending on whether marginal revenue declines as sales increase, this may or may not equal product price.
Marginal product	In a production function, the marginal product of a factor is the increase in output due to a unit increase in the input of the factor; that is, the partial derivative of the production function with respect to the factor.
Marginal product of labor	Marginal product of labor refers to the increase in the amount of output from an additional unit of labor.
Real terms	A wage expressed in real terms is just the real wage.

International trade	The export of goods and services from a country and the import of goods and services into a country is referred to as the international trade.
Production	The creation of finished goods and services using the factors of production: land, labor, capital, entrepreneurship, and knowledge.
Industry	A group of firms that produce identical or similar products is an industry. It is also used specifically to refer to an area of economic production focused on manufacturing which involves large amounts of capital investment before any profit can be realized, also called "heavy industry".
Export	In economics, an export is any good or commodity, shipped or otherwise transported out of a country, province, town to another part of the world in a legitimate fashion, typically for use in trade or sale.
Inputs	The inputs used by a firm or an economy are the labor, raw materials, electricity and other resources it uses to produce its outputs.
Labor	People's physical and mental talents and efforts that are used to help produce goods and services are called labor.
Comparative advantage	The ability to produce a good at lower cost, relative to other goods, compared to another country is a comparative advantage.
Classical model	Classical model refers to a model of the economy derived from the ideas of the classical, or pre-Keynesian economists; a model based on the assumptions that wages and prices adjust to clear markets and that monetary policy does not influence real variables. A macroeconomic model that explains how real GDP and other variables are determined at full employment.
Labor productivity	In labor economics labor productivity is a measure of the efficiency of the labor force. It is usually measured as output per hour of all people. When comparing labor productivity one mostly looks at the change over time.
Productivity	Productivity refers to the total output of goods and services in a given period of time divided by work hours.
Wage	The payment for the service of a unit of labor, per unit time. In trade theory, it is the only payment to labor, usually unskilled labor. In empirical work, wage data may exclude other compenzation, which must be added to get the total cost of employment.
Transport cost	Transport cost refers to the cost of transporting a good, especially in international trade.
Trade barrier	An artificial disincentive to export and/or import, such as a tariff, quota, or other NTB is called a trade barrier.
Product differentiation	A strategy in which one firm's product is distinguished from competing products by means of its design, related services, quality, location, or other attributes is called product differentiation.
Economics	The social science dealing with the use of scarce resources to obtain the maximum satisfaction of society's virtually unlimited economic wants is an economics.
Economy	The income, expenditures, and resources that affect the cost of running a business and household are called an economy.
Intermediate input	Intermediate input refers to an input to production that has itself been produced and that, unlike capital, is used up in production. As an input it is in contrast to a primary input and as an output it is in contrast to a final good.
Raw material	Raw material refers to a good that has not been transformed by production; a primary product.
Service	Service refers to a "non tangible product" that is not embodied in a physical good and that

	typically effects some change in another product, person, or institution. Contrasts with good.
Trade pattern	What goods a country trades, with whom, and in what direction. Explaining the trade pattern is one of the major purposes of trade theory, especially which goods a country will export and which it will import.
Domestic	From or in one's own country. A domestic producer is one that produces inside the home country. A domestic price is the price inside the home country. Opposite of 'foreign' or 'world.'.
Capital	Capital generally refers to financial wealth, especially that used to start or maintain a business. In classical economics, capital is one of four factors of production, the others being land and labor and entrepreneurship.
Ford	Ford is an American company that manufactures and sells automobiles worldwide. Ford introduced methods for large-scale manufacturing of cars, and large-scale management of an industrial workforce, especially elaborately engineered manufacturing sequences typified by the moving assembly lines.
Policy	Similar to a script in that a policy can be a less than completely rational decision-making method. Involves the use of a pre-existing set of decision steps for any problem that presents itself.
Consultant	A professional that provides expert advice in a particular field or area in which customers occassionaly require this type of knowledge is a consultant.
Capital stock	The total amount of physical capital that has been accumulated, usually in a country is capital stock. Also refers to the total issued capital of a firm, including ordinary and preferred shares.
Depression	Depression refers to a prolonged period characterized by high unemployment, low output and investment, depressed business confidence, falling prices, and widespread business failures. A milder form of business downturn is a recession.
Stock	In financial terminology, stock is the capital raized by a corporation, through the issuance and sale of shares.
Leontief paradox	Leontief paradox refers to the empirical finding that, in contrast to the predictions of the Heckscher-Ohlin theory, U.S. exports are less capital intensive than U.S. imports.
Paradox	As used in economics, paradox means something unexpected, rather than the more extreme normal meaning of something seemingly impossible. Some paradoxes are just theoretical results that go against what one thinks of as normal.
Empirical finding	Something that is observed from real-world observation or data, in contrast to something that is deduced from theory is an empirical finding.
Trade flow	The quantity or value of a country's bilateral trade with another country is called trade flow.
Context	The effect of the background under which a message often takes on more and richer meaning is a context. Context is especially important in cross-cultural interactions because some cultures are said to be high context or low context.
Corporation	A legal entity chartered by a state or the Federal government that is distinct and separate from the individuals who own it is a corporation. This separation gives the corporation unique powers which other legal entities lack.
Multinational corporations	Firms that own production facilities in two or more countries and produce and sell their products globally are referred to as multinational corporations.

Multinational corporation	An organization that manufactures and markets products in many different countries and has multinational stock ownership and multinational management is referred to as multinational corporation.
Tariff	A tax imposed by a nation on an imported good is called a tariff.
Consumption	In Keynesian economics consumption refers to personal consumption expenditure, i.e., the purchase of currently produced goods and services out of income, out of savings (net worth), or from borrowed funds. It refers to that part of disposable income that does not go to saving.
Relative price	Relative price refers to the price of one thing in terms of another; i.e., the ratio of two prices.
Factor price	Factor price refers to the price paid for the services of a unit of a primary factor of production per unit time. Includes the wage or salary of labor and the rental prices of land and capital, and normal profits for the entrepreneur.
Labor intensive	Describing an industry or sector of the economy that relies relatively heavily on inputs of labor, usually relative to capital but sometimes to human capital or skilled labor, compared to other industries or sectors is labor intensive.
Union	A worker association that bargains with employers over wages and working conditions is called a union.
Interest	In finance and economics, interest is the price paid by a borrower for the use of a lender's money. In other words, interest is the amount of paid to "rent" money for a period of time.
Factor endowments	A country's endowment with resources such as land, labor, and capital are referred to as factor endowments.
Factor endowment	Factor endowment refers to the quantity of a primary factor present in a country.
Endowment	Endowment refers to the amount of something that a person or country simply has, rather than their having somehow to acquire it.
Capital abundant	A country is capital abundant if its endowment of capital is large compared to other countries. Relative capital abundance can be defined by either the quantity definition or the price definition.
Commodity	Could refer to any good, but in trade a commodity is usually a raw material or primary product that enters into international trade, such as metals or basic agricultural products.
Political economy	Early name for the discipline of economics. A field within economics encompassing several alternatives to neoclassical economics, including Marxist economics. Also called radical political economy.
Journal	Book of original entry, in which transactions are recorded in a general ledger system, is referred to as a journal.
Factor intensity	Factor intensity refers to the relative importance of one factor versus others in production in an industry, usually compared across industries.
Physical capital	Physical capital refers to the same as 'capital,' without any adjective, in the sense of plant and equipment. The word 'physical' is used only to distinguish it from human capital.
Unskilled labor	Unskilled labor refers to labor with a low level of skill or human capital. Identified empirically as labor earning a low wage, with a low level of education, or in an occupational category associated with these.
Technology	The body of knowledge and techniques that can be used to combine economic resources to produce goods and services is called technology.

Daniel Trefler	Daniel Trefler is an economics professor at the University of Toronto specializing in international economics and best known for his empirical research on patterns of trade.
Preference	The act of a debtor in paying or securing one or more of his creditors in a manner more favorable to them than to other creditors or to the exclusion of such other creditors is a preference. In the absence of statute, a preference is perfectly good, but to be legal it must be bona fide, and not a mere subterfuge of the debtor to secure a future benefit to himself or to prevent the application of his property to his debts.
Factor price equalization	Factor price equalization refers to the tendency for trade to cause factor prices in different countries to become identical.
Factors of production	Economic resources: land, capital, labor, and entrepreneurial ability are called factors of production.
Product life cycle	Product life cycle refers to a series of phases in a product's sales and cash flows over time; these phases, in order of occurrence, are introductory, growth, maturity, and decline.
Manufactured good	A manufactured good refers to goods that have been processed in any way.
Cost advantage	Possession of a lower cost of production or operation than a competing firm or country is cost advantage.
Manufacturing	Production of goods primarily by the application of labor and capital to raw materials and other intermediate inputs, in contrast to agriculture, mining, forestry, fishing, and services a manufacturing.
Market share	That fraction of an industry's output accounted for by an individual firm or group of firms is called market share.
Market	A market is, as defined in economics, a social arrangement that allows buyers and sellers to discover information and carry out a voluntary exchange of goods or services.
Gain	In finance, gain is a profit or an increase in value of an investment such as a stock or bond. Gain is calculated by fair market value or the proceeds from the sale of the investment minus the sum of the purchase price and all costs associated with it.
Firm	An organization that employs resources to produce a good or service for profit and owns and operates one or more plants is referred to as a firm.
Manufacturing costs	Costs incurred in a manufacturing process, which consist of direct material, direct labor, and manufacturing overhead are referred to as manufacturing costs.
Fixed capital	Fixed capital is a concept in economics and accounting, first theoretically analysed in some depth by the economist David Ricardo. It refers to any kind of real or physical capital that is not used up in the production of a product. It is contrasted with circulating capital.
Investment	Investment refers to spending for the production and accumulation of capital and additions to inventories. In a financial sense, buying an asset with the expectation of making a return.
Labor force	In economics the labor force is the group of people who have a potential for being employed.
Supply	Supply is the aggregate amount of any material good that can be called into being at a certain price point; it comprises one half of the equation of supply and demand. In classical economic theory, a curve representing supply is one of the factors that produce price.
Direction of trade	Direction of trade is the particular countries and kinds of countries toward which a country's exports are sent, and from which its imports are brought, in contrast to the commodity composition of its exports and imports.
Factor content	The amounts of primary factors used in the production of a good or service, or a vector of

	quantities of goods and services, such as the factor content of trade or the factor content of consumption. Can be either direct or direct-plus-indirect.
Per capita	Per capita refers to per person. Usually used to indicate the average per person of any given statistic, commonly income.
Intraindustry trade	Intraindustry trade refers to trade in which a country exports and imports in the same industry, in contrast to interindustry trade. Ubiquitous in the data, much IIT is due to aggregation.
Airbus	In 2003, for the first time in its 33-year history, Airbus delivered more jet-powered airliners than Boeing. Boeing states that the Boeing 777 has outsold its Airbus counterparts, which include the A340 family as well as the A330-300. The smaller A330-200 competes with the 767, outselling its Boeing counterpart.
Consolidation	The combination of two or more firms, generally of equal size and market power, to form an entirely new entity is a consolidation.
Increasing returns	An increase in a firm's output by a larger percentage than the percentage increase in its inputs is increasing returns.
Returns to scale	Returns to scale refers to a technical property of production that predicts what happens to output if the quantity of all input factors is increased by some amount of scale.
Cost curve	A cost curve is a graph of the costs of production as a function of total quantity produced. In a free market economy, productively efficient firms use these curves to find the optimal point of production, where they make the most profits.
Community indifference curve	Community indifference curve refers to one of a family of indifference curves intended to represent the preferences, and sometimes the well-being, of a country as a whole. A handy tool for deriving quantities of trade in a two-good model, although its legitimacy depends on the existence of community preferences, which in turn requires very restrictive assumptions.
Indifference curve	Indifference curve refers to a means of representing the preferences and well being of consumers. Formally, it is a curve representing the combinations of arguments in a utility function that yield a given level of utility.
Autarky	Autarky refers to the situation of not engaging in international trade; self-sufficiency. Not to be confused with 'autarchy,' which in at least some dictionaries is a political term rather than an economic one, and means absolute rule or power.
Slope	The slope of a line in the plane containing the x and y axes is generally represented by the letter m, and is defined as the change in the y coordinate divided by the corresponding change in the x coordinate, between two distinct points on the line.
Gains from trade	The net increase in output that countries experience as a result of lowering import tariffs and otherwise liberalizing trade is referred to as gains from trade.
Perfect competition	An idealized market structure in which there are large numbers of both buyers and sellers, all of them small, so that they act as price takers. Perfect competition also assumes homogeneous products, free entry and exit, and complete information.
Economies of scale	In economics, returns to scale and economies of scale are related terms that describe what happens as the scale of production increases. They are different terms and not to be used interchangeably.
Market structure	Market structure refers to the way that suppliers and demanders in an industry interact to determine price and quantity. Market structures range from perfect competition to monopoly.
Brand	A name, symbol, or design that identifies the goods or services of one seller or group of sellers and distinguishes them from the goods and services of competitors is a brand.

Perfectly competitive	Perfectly competitive is an economic agent, group of agents, model or analysis that is characterized by perfect competition. Contrasts with imperfectly competitive.
Competitive firm	Competitive firm refers to a firm without market power, with no ability to alter the market price of the goods it produces.
Competitor	Other organizations in the same industry or type of business that provide a good or service to the same set of customers is referred to as a competitor.
Exporting	Selling products to another country is called exporting.
Exchange	The trade of things of value between buyer and seller so that each is better off after the trade is called the exchange.
Imperfect competition	Any departure from perfect competition. However, imperfect competition usually refers to one of the market structures other than perfect competition.
Trade theory	The body of economic thought that seeks to explain why and how countries engage in international trade and the welfare implication of that trade, encompassing especially the Ricardian Model, the Heckscher-Ohlin Model, and the New Trade Theory.

Factors of production	Economic resources: land, capital, labor, and entrepreneurial ability are called factors of production.
Production	The creation of finished goods and services using the factors of production: land, labor, capital, entrepreneurship, and knowledge.
Commercial policy	Commercial policy refers to government policies intended to influence international commerce, including international trade. Includes tariffs and quotas, as well as policies regarding exports.
Composition	An out-of-court settlement in which creditors agree to accept a fractional settlement on their original claim is referred to as composition.
Policy	Similar to a script in that a policy can be a less than completely rational decision-making method. Involves the use of a pre-existing set of decision steps for any problem that presents itself.
Option	A contract that gives the purchaser the option to buy or sell the underlying financial instrument at a specified price, called the exercise price or strike price, within a specific period of time.
Government procurement	Government procurement refers to purchase of goods and services by government and by state-owned enterprises.
Nontariff barrier	Any policy that interferes with exports or imports other than a simple tariff, prominently including quotas and vers is referred to as nontariff barrier.
Procurement	Procurement is the acquisition of goods or services at the best possible total cost of ownership, in the right quantity, at the right time, in the right place for the direct benefit or use of the governments, corporations, or individuals generally via, but not limited to a contract.
Industry	A group of firms that produce identical or similar products is an industry. It is also used specifically to refer to an area of economic production focused on manufacturing which involves large amounts of capital investment before any profit can be realized, also called "heavy industry".
Subsidy	Subsidy refers to government financial assistance to a domestic producer.
Export	In economics, an export is any good or commodity, shipped or otherwise transported out of a country, province, town to another part of the world in a legitimate fashion, typically for use in trade or sale.
Quota	A government-imposed restriction on quantity, or sometimes on total value, used to restrict the import of something to a specific quantity is called a quota.
International trade	The export of goods and services from a country and the import of goods and services into a country is referred to as the international trade.
General equilibrium	Equality of supply and demand in all markets of an economy simultaneously. The number of markets does not have to be large. The simplest Ricardian model has markets only for two goods and one factor, labor, but this is a general equilibrium model.
Free trade	Free trade refers to a situation in which there are no artificial barriers to trade, such as tariffs and quotas. Usually used, often only implicitly, with frictionless trade, so that it implies that there are no barriers to trade of any kind.
Tariff	A tax imposed by a nation on an imported good is called a tariff.
Market	A market is, as defined in economics, a social arrangement that allows buyers and sellers to discover information and carry out a voluntary exchange of goods or services.

Gain	In finance, gain is a profit or an increase in value of an investment such as a stock or bond. Gain is calculated by fair market value or the proceeds from the sale of the investment minus the sum of the purchase price and all costs associated with it.
Consumption	In Keynesian economics consumption refers to personal consumption expenditure, i.e., the purchase of currently produced goods and services out of income, out of savings (net worth), or from borrowed funds. It refers to that part of disposable income that does not go to saving.
Economy	The income, expenditures, and resources that affect the cost of running a business and household are called an economy.
World price	The price of a good on the 'world market,' meaning the price outside of any country's borders and therefore exclusive of any trade taxes or subsidies is the world price.
Price line	A straight line representing the combinations of variables, usually two goods that cost the same at some given prices. The slope of a price line measures relative prices, and changes in prices.
Welfare	Welfare refers to the economic well being of an individual, group, or economy. For individuals, it is conceptualized by a utility function. For groups, including countries and the world, it is a tricky philosophical concept, since individuals fare differently.
Autarky	Autarky refers to the situation of not engaging in international trade; self-sufficiency. Not to be confused with 'autarchy,' which in at least some dictionaries is a political term rather than an economic one, and means absolute rule or power.
Slope	The slope of a line in the plane containing the x and y axes is generally represented by the letter m, and is defined as the change in the y coordinate divided by the corresponding change in the x coordinate, between two distinct points on the line.
Gains from trade	The net increase in output that countries experience as a result of lowering import tariffs and otherwise liberalizing trade is referred to as gains from trade.
Productivity	Productivity refers to the total output of goods and services in a given period of time divided by work hours.
Dynamic gains from trade	Dynamic gains from trade refers to the hoped-for benefits from trade that accrue over time, in addition to the conventional static gains from trade of trade theory.
Economic growth	Economic growth refers to the increase over time in the capacity of an economy to produce goods and services and to improve the well-being of its citizens.
Capital	Capital generally refers to financial wealth, especially that used to start or maintain a business. In classical economics, capital is one of four factors of production, the others being land and labor and entrepreneurship.
Consumer good	Products and services that are ultimately consumed rather than used in the production of another good are a consumer good.
Exchange	The trade of things of value between buyer and seller so that each is better off after the trade is called the exchange.
Capital stock	The total amount of physical capital that has been accumulated, usually in a country is capital stock. Also refers to the total issued capital of a firm, including ordinary and preferred shares.
Stock	In financial terminology, stock is the capital raized by a corporation, through the issuance and sale of shares.
Diffusion	Diffusion is the process by which a new idea or new product is accepted by the market. The

	rate of diffusion is the speed that the new idea spreads from one consumer to the next.
Firm	An organization that employs resources to produce a good or service for profit and owns and operates one or more plants is referred to as a firm.
Technology	The body of knowledge and techniques that can be used to combine economic resources to produce goods and services is called technology.
Marginal cost	Marginal cost refers to the increase in cost that accompanies a unit increase in output; the partial derivative of the cost function with respect to output.
National income	National income refers to the income generated by a country's production, and therefore the total income of its factors of production.
Trade liberalization	Reduction of tariffs and removal or relaxation of NTBs is referred to as trade liberalization.
Dynamic effects	Refers to certain poorly understood effects of trade and trade liberalization, including both multilateral and preferential trade agreements, that extend beyond the static gains from trade: dynamic effects .
Political economy	Early name for the discipline of economics. A field within economics encompassing several alternatives to neoclassical economics, including Marxist economics. Also called radical political economy.
Journal	Book of original entry, in which transactions are recorded in a general ledger system, is referred to as a journal.
Fund	Independent accounting entity with a self-balancing set of accounts segregated for the purposes of carrying on specific activities is referred to as a fund.
Standard of living	Standard of living refers to the level of consumption that people enjoy, on the average, and is measured by average income per person.
Competitor	Other organizations in the same industry or type of business that provide a good or service to the same set of customers is referred to as a competitor.
Domestic	From or in one's own country. A domestic producer is one that produces inside the home country. A domestic price is the price inside the home country. Opposite of 'foreign' or 'world.'.
Trade barrier	An artificial disincentive to export and/or import, such as a tariff, quota, or other NTB is called a trade barrier.
Revenue	Revenue is a U.S. business term for the amount of money that a company receives from its activities, mostly from sales of products and/or services to customers.
Prohibitive tariff	A tariff that reduces imports to zero is referred to as a prohibitive tariff.
Revenue tariff	A tariff designed to produce income for the Federal government is a revenue tariff.
Manufactured good	A manufactured good refers to goods that have been processed in any way.
Most favored nation	Most favored nation refers to the principle, fundamental to the GATT, of treating imports from a country on the same basis as that given to the most favored other nation.
Grant	Grant refers to an intergovernmental transfer of funds . Since the New Deal, state and local governments have become increasingly dependent upon federal grants for an almost infinite variety of programs.
Federal	Federal government refers to the government of the United States, as distinct from the state

government	and local governments.
Compound tariff	A tariff that combines both a specific and an ad valorem component is called a compound tariff.
Developing country	Developing country refers to a country whose per capita income is low by world standards. Same as LDC. As usually used, it does not necessarily connote that the country's income is rising.
Preference	The act of a debtor in paying or securing one or more of his creditors in a manner more favorable to them than to other creditors or to the exclusion of such other creditors is a preference. In the absence of statute, a preference is perfectly good, but to be legal it must be bona fide, and not a mere subterfuge of the debtor to secure a future benefit to himself or to prevent the application of his property to his debts.
Incentive	An incentive is any factor (financial or non-financial) that provides a motive for a particular course of action, or counts as a reason for preferring one choice to the alternatives.
Free market	A free market is a market where price is determined by the unregulated interchange of supply and demand rather than set by artificial means.
Concession	A concession is a business operated under a contract or license associated with a degree of exclusivity in exploiting a business within a certain geographical area. For example, sports arenas or public parks may have concession stands; and public services such as water supply may be operated as concessions.
Economic analysis	The process of deriving economic principles from relevant economic facts are called economic analysis. It is the comparison, with money as the index, of those costs and benefits to the wider economy that can be reasonably quantified, including all social costs and benefits of a project.
Consumer surplus	The difference between the maximum that consumers would be willing to pay for a good and what they actually do pay is consumer surplus. For each unit of the good, this is the vertical distance between the demand curve and price.
Producer surplus	The difference between the revenue of producers and production cost, measured as the area above the supply curve and below price, out to the quantity supplied, and net of fixed cost and losses at low output is producer surplus. If input prices are constant, this is profit.
Demand curve	Demand curve refers to the graph of quantity demanded as a function of price, normally downward sloping, straight or curved, and drawn with quantity on the horizontal axis and price on the vertical axis.
Market price	Market price is an economic concept with commonplace familiarity; it is the price that a good or service is offered at, or will fetch, in the marketplace; it is of interest mainly in the study of microeconomics.
Fixed cost	The cost that a firm bears if it does not produce at all and that is independent of its output. The presence of a fixed cost tends to imply increasing returns to scale. Contrasts with variable cost.
Profit	Profit refers to the return to the resource entrepreneurial ability; total revenue minus total cost.
Variable	A variable is something measured by a number; it is used to analyze what happens to other things when the size of that number changes.
Total variable Cost	The total of all costs that vary with output in the short run is called total variable cost.

Go to **Cram101.com** for the Practice Tests for this Chapter.

Variable cost	The portion of a firm or industry's cost that changes with output, in contrast to fixed cost is referred to as variable cost.
Total revenue	Total revenue refers to the total number of dollars received by a firm from the sale of a product; equal to the total expenditures for the product produced by the firm; equal to the quantity sold multiplied by the price at which it is sold.
Supply curve	Supply curve refers to the graph of quantity supplied as a function of price, normally upward sloping, straight or curved, and drawn with quantity on the horizontal axis and price on the vertical axis.
Supply	Supply is the aggregate amount of any material good that can be called into being at a certain price point; it comprises one half of the equation of supply and demand. In classical economic theory, a curve representing supply is one of the factors that produce price.
Economic policy	Economic policy refers to the actions that governments take in the economic field. It covers the systems for setting interest rates and government deficit as well as the labor market, national ownership, and many other areas of government.
Quantity supplied	The amount of a good or service that producers offer to sell at a particular price during a given time period is called quantity supplied.
Quantity demanded	The amount of a good or service that buyers desire to purchase at a particular price during some period is a quantity demanded.
Interest	In finance and economics, interest is the price paid by a borrower for the use of a lender's money. In other words, interest is the amount of paid to "rent" money for a period of time.
Elasticity	In economics, elasticity is the ratio of the incremental percentage change in one variable with respect to an incremental percentage change in another variable. Elasticity is usually expressed as a positive number (i.e., an absolute value) when the sign is already clear from context.
Perfectly competitive market	Exists when there is a homogeneous product and where no individual buyers or sellers can affect those prices by their own actions are referred to as perfectly competitive market.
Perfectly competitive	Perfectly competitive is an economic agent, group of agents, model or analysis that is characterized by perfect competition. Contrasts with imperfectly competitive.
Competitive market	A market in which no buyer or seller has market power is called a competitive market.
Economic cost	Economic cost refers to payments made or incomes forgone to obtain and retain the services of a resource.
Economics	The social science dealing with the use of scarce resources to obtain the maximum satisfaction of society's virtually unlimited economic wants is an economics.
Boot	Boot is any type of personal property received in a real property transaction that is not like kind, such as cash, mortgage notes, a boat or stock. The exchanger pays taxes on the boot to the extent of recognized capital gain. In an exchange if any funds are not used in purchasing the replacement property, that also will be called boot.
Market power	The ability of a single economic actor to have a substantial influence on market prices is market power.
Exporting	Selling products to another country is called exporting.
Large country	Large country refers to a country that is large enough for its international transactions to affect economic variables abroad, usually for its trade to matter for world prices.

Excess demand	Demand minus supply. Thus a country's demand for imports of a homogeneous good is its excess demand for that good.
Traded good	A good that is exported or imported or -- sometimes -- a good that could be exported or imported if it weren't tariffs, or quotas, is referred to as traded good.
Optimal tariff	The level of a tariff that maximizes a country's welfare. In a non-distorted small open economy, the optimal tariff is zero. In a large country it is positive, due to its effect on the terms of trade.
Expense	In accounting, an expense represents an event in which an asset is used up or a liability is incurred. In terms of the accounting equation, expenses reduce owners' equity.
Trade war	Trade war refers to generally, a period in which each of two countries alternate in further restricting trade from the other. More specifically, the process of tariffs and retaliation.
Tariff escalation	The tendency of tariffs and other import barriers to be higher on finished goods sold to consumers than on intermediate manufactured goods sold to industry is tariff escalation.
Retaliation	The use of an increased trade barrier in response to another country increasing its trade barrier, either as a way of undoing the adverse effects of the latter's action or of punishing it is retaliation.
Escalation	Regarding the structure of tariffs. In the context of a trade war, escalation refers to the increase in tariffs that occurs as countries retaliate again and again.
Authority	Authority in agency law, refers to an agent's ability to affect his principal's legal relations with third parties. Also used to refer to an actor's legal power or ability to do something. In addition, sometimes used to refer to a statute, case, or other legal source that justifies a particular result.
Commerce	Commerce is the exchange of something of value between two entities. It is the central mechanism from which capitalism is derived.
Manufacturing	Production of goods primarily by the application of labor and capital to raw materials and other intermediate inputs, in contrast to agriculture, mining, forestry, fishing, and services a manufacturing.
Testimony	In some contexts, the word bears the same import as the word evidence, but in most connections it has a much narrower meaning. Testimony are the words heard from the witness in court, and evidence is what the jury considers it worth.
Committee	A long-lasting, sometimes permanent team in the organization structure created to deal with tasks that recur regularly is the committee.
Dutiable imports	Dutiable imports refers to imports on which a positive duty, or tariff, is levied. The term seems like it ought to include imports on which the duty is zero but which a government is somehow free, or able, to levy a positive duty.
Great Depression	The period of severe economic contraction and high unemployment that began in 1929 and continued throughout the 1930s is referred to as the Great Depression.
Depression	Depression refers to a prolonged period characterized by high unemployment, low output and investment, depressed business confidence, falling prices, and widespread business failures. A milder form of business downturn is a recession.
Boycott	To protest by refusing to purchase from someone, or otherwise do business with them. In international trade, a boycott most often takes the form of refusal to import a country's goods.
Negotiation	Negotiation is the process whereby interested parties resolve disputes, agree upon courses of

action, bargain for individual or collective advantage, and/or attempt to craft outcomes which serve their mutual interests.

Union	A worker association that bargains with employers over wages and working conditions is called a union.
Inputs	The inputs used by a firm or an economy are the labor, raw materials, electricity and other resources it uses to produce its outputs.
Primary factor	Primary factor refers to an input that exists as a stock, providing services that contribute to production. The stock is not used up in production, although it may deteriorate with use, providing a smaller flow of services later.
Wage	The payment for the service of a unit of labor, per unit time. In trade theory, it is the only payment to labor, usually unskilled labor. In empirical work, wage data may exclude other compenzation, which must be added to get the total cost of employment.
Effective protection	Effective protection refers to the concept that the protection provided to an industry depends on the tariffs and other trade barriers on both its inputs and its outputs, since a tariff on inputs raises cost. Measured by the effective rate of protection.
Perfect substitute	A good that is regarded by its demanders as identical to another good, so that the elasticity of substitution between them is infinite is referred to as perfect substitute.
Labor	People's physical and mental talents and efforts that are used to help produce goods and services are called labor.
Effective rate of protection	Effective rate of protection refers to a measure of the protection provided to an industry by the entire structure of tariffs, taking into account the effects of tariffs on inputs as well as on outputs.
Value added	The value of output minus the value of all intermediate inputs, representing therefore the contribution of, and payments to, primary factors of production a value added.
Final goods	In economics final goods are goods that are ultimately consumed rather than used in the production of another good. When used in measures of national income and output the term final goods only includes new goods.
Final good	Final good refers to a good that requires no further processing or transformation to be ready for use by consumers, investors, or government. Contrasts with intermediate good.
Intermediate good	Same as intermediate input are called intermediate good. In the production process, a intermediate good either become part of the final product, or are changed beyond recognition in the process.
Raw material	Raw material refers to a good that has not been transformed by production; a primary product.
Elastic demand	Elastic demand refers to product or resource demand whose price elasticity is greater than 1. This means the resulting change in quantity demanded is greater than the percentage change in price.
Inelastic demand	Inelastic demand refers to product or resource demand for which the elasticity coefficient for price is less than 1. This means the resulting percentage change in quantity demanded is less than the percentage change in price. In other words, consumers are relatively less sensitive to changes in price.
Inelastic	Inelastic refers to having an elasticity less than one. For a price elasticity of demand, this means that expenditure falls as price falls. For an income elasticity, it means that expenditure share falls with income.
World Bank	The World Bank is a group of five international organizations responsible for providing

Go to **Cram101.com** for the Practice Tests for this Chapter.
And, **NEVER** highlight a book again!

finance and advice to countries for the purposes of economic development and poverty reduction, and for encouraging and safeguarding international investment.

Trade barrier	An artificial disincentive to export and/or import, such as a tariff, quota, or other NTB is called a trade barrier.
Quota	A government-imposed restriction on quantity, or sometimes on total value, used to restrict the import of something to a specific quantity is called a quota.
International trade	The export of goods and services from a country and the import of goods and services into a country is referred to as the international trade.
Nontariff barrier	Any policy that interferes with exports or imports other than a simple tariff, prominently including quotas and vers is referred to as nontariff barrier.
Federal Reserve	The Federal Reserve System was created via the Federal Reserve Act of December 23rd, 1913. All national banks were required to join the system and other banks could join. The Reserve Banks opened for business on November 16th, 1914. Federal Reserve Notes were created as part of the legislation, to provide an elastic supply of currency.
Market share	That fraction of an industry's output accounted for by an individual firm or group of firms is called market share.
Value quota	Value quota refers to a quota specifying value -- price times quantity -- of a good.
Distortion	Distortion refers to any departure from the ideal of perfect competition that interferes with economic agents maximizing social welfare when they maximize their own.
World Bank	The World Bank is a group of five international organizations responsible for providing finance and advice to countries for the purposes of economic development and poverty reduction, and for encouraging and safeguarding international investment.
Shares	Shares refer to an equity security, representing a shareholder's ownership of a corporation. Shares are one of a finite number of equal portions in the capital of a company, entitling the owner to a proportion of distributed, non-reinvested profits known as dividends and to a portion of the value of the company in case of liquidation.
Market	A market is, as defined in economics, a social arrangement that allows buyers and sellers to discover information and carry out a voluntary exchange of goods or services.
Petition	A petition is a request to an authority, most commonly a government official or public entity. In the colloquial sense, a petition is a document addressed to some official and signed by numerous individuals.
Tariff	A tax imposed by a nation on an imported good is called a tariff.
Economic sanction	A economic sanction can vary from imposing import duties on goods from, or blocking the export of certain goods to the target country, to a full naval blockade of its ports in an effort to verify, and curb or block specified imported goods.
Policy	Similar to a script in that a policy can be a less than completely rational decision-making method. Involves the use of a pre-existing set of decision steps for any problem that presents itself.
Uruguay round	The eighth and most recent round of trade negotiations under GATT is referred to as Uruguay round.
World Trade Organization	The World Trade Organization is an international, multilateral organization, which sets the rules for the global trading system and resolves disputes between its member states, all of whom are signatories to its approximately 30 agreements.
International trade law	International trade law includes the appropriate rules and customs for handling trade between countries or between private companies across borders.
Industry	A group of firms that produce identical or similar products is an industry. It is also used

specifically to refer to an area of economic production focused on manufacturing which involves large amounts of capital investment before any profit can be realized, also called "heavy industry".

Balance	In banking and accountancy, the outstanding balance is the amount of money owned, (or due), that remains in a deposit account (or a loan account) at a given date, after all past remittances, payments and withdrawal have been accounted for. It can be positive (then, in the balance sheet of a firm, it is an asset) or negative (a liability).
Aid	Assistance provided by countries and by international institutions such as the World Bank to developing countries in the form of monetary grants, loans at low interest rates, in kind, or a combination of these is called aid. Aid can also refer to assistance of any type rendered to benefit some group or individual.
Exporting	Selling products to another country is called exporting.
Export	In economics, an export is any good or commodity, shipped or otherwise transported out of a country, province, town to another part of the world in a legitimate fashion, typically for use in trade or sale.
Embargo	Embargo refers to the prohibition of some category of trade. May apply to exports and/or imports, of particular products or of all trade, vis a vis the world or a particular country or countries.
Global quota	Global quota refers to an import quota that specifies the permitted quantity of imports from all sources combined.
Customs	Customs is an authority or agency in a country responsible for collecting customs duties and for controlling the flow of people, animals and goods (including personal effects and hazardous items) in and out of the country.
License	A license in the sphere of Intellectual Property Rights (IPR) is a document, contract or agreement giving permission or the 'right' to a legally-definable entity to do something (such as manufacture a product or to use a service), or to apply something (such as a trademark), with the objective of achieving commercial gain.
Bearer	A person in possession of a negotiable instrument that is payable to him, his order, or to whoever is in possession of the instrument is referred to as bearer.
Supply curve	Supply curve refers to the graph of quantity supplied as a function of price, normally upward sloping, straight or curved, and drawn with quantity on the horizontal axis and price on the vertical axis.
Domestic	From or in one's own country. A domestic producer is one that produces inside the home country. A domestic price is the price inside the home country. Opposite of 'foreign' or 'world.'.
Supply	Supply is the aggregate amount of any material good that can be called into being at a certain price point; it comprises one half of the equation of supply and demand. In classical economic theory, a curve representing supply is one of the factors that produce price.
Demand curve	Demand curve refers to the graph of quantity demanded as a function of price, normally downward sloping, straight or curved, and drawn with quantity on the horizontal axis and price on the vertical axis.
World price	The price of a good on the 'world market,' meaning the price outside of any country's borders and therefore exclusive of any trade taxes or subsidies is the world price.
Free trade	Free trade refers to a situation in which there are no artificial barriers to trade, such as tariffs and quotas. Usually used, often only implicitly, with frictionless trade, so that it

Go to **Cram101.com** for the Practice Tests for this Chapter.

	implies that there are no barriers to trade of any kind.
Welfare	Welfare refers to the economic well being of an individual, group, or economy. For individuals, it is conceptualized by a utility function. For groups, including countries and the world, it is a tricky philosophical concept, since individuals fare differently.
Consumer surplus	The difference between the maximum that consumers would be willing to pay for a good and what they actually do pay is consumer surplus. For each unit of the good, this is the vertical distance between the demand curve and price.
Producer surplus	The difference between the revenue of producers and production cost, measured as the area above the supply curve and below price, out to the quantity supplied, and net of fixed cost and losses at low output is producer surplus. If input prices are constant, this is profit.
Profit	Profit refers to the return to the resource entrepreneurial ability; total revenue minus total cost.
Firm	An organization that employs resources to produce a good or service for profit and owns and operates one or more plants is referred to as a firm.
Quota rent	Quota rent refers to the economic rent received by the holder of the right to import under a quota. Equals the domestic price of the imported good, net of any tariff, minus the world price, times the quantity of imports.
Domestic price	The price of a good or service within a country, determined by domestic demand and supply is referred to as domestic price.
Competitive bidding	A situation where two or more companies submit bids for a product, service, or project to a potential buyer is competitive bidding.
Economy	The income, expenditures, and resources that affect the cost of running a business and household are called an economy.
Economic cost	Economic cost refers to payments made or incomes forgone to obtain and retain the services of a resource.
Revenue	Revenue is a U.S. business term for the amount of money that a company receives from its activities, mostly from sales of products and/or services to customers.
Auction	A preexisting business model that operates successfully on the Internet by announcing an item for sale and permitting multiple purchasers to bid on them under specified rules and condition is an auction.
Competitiveness	Competitiveness usually refers to characteristics that permit a firm to compete effectively with other firms due to low cost or superior technology, perhaps internationally.
Markup	Markup is a term used in marketing to indicate how much the price of a product is above the cost of producing and distributing the product.
Voluntary export restraint	Voluntary export restraint refers to a restriction on a country's imports that is achieved by negotiating with the foreign exporting country for it to restrict its exports. The restraint agreement may be concluded at either industry or government level. In the latter case, sometimes referred to as an orderly marketing arrangement.
Normal profit	Normal profit refers to the payment made by a firm to obtain and retain entrepreneurial ability; the minimum income entrepreneurial ability must receive to induce it to perform entrepreneurial functions for a firm.
Exporter	A firm that sells its product in another country is an exporter.
Principal	In agency law, one under whose direction an agent acts and for whose benefit that agent acts is a principal.

Potential competition	Potential competition refers to the new competitors that may be induced to enter an industry if firms now in that industry are receiving large economic profits.
Monopoly power	Monopoly power is an example of market failure which occurs when one or more of the participants has the ability to influence the price or other outcomes in some general or specialized market.
Monopoly	A monopoly is defined as a persistent market situation where there is only one provider of a kind of product or service.
Holding	The holding is a court's determination of a matter of law based on the issue presented in the particular case. In other words: under this law, with these facts, this result.
Corruption	The unauthorized use of public office for private gain. The most common forms of corruption are bribery, extortion, and the misuse of inside information.
Incentive	An incentive is any factor (financial or non-financial) that provides a motive for a particular course of action, or counts as a reason for preferring one choice to the alternatives.
Authority	Authority in agency law, refers to an agent's ability to affect his principal's legal relations with third parties. Also used to refer to an actor's legal power or ability to do something. In addition, sometimes used to refer to a statute, case, or other legal source that justifies a particular result.
Contribution	In business organization law, the cash or property contributed to a business by its owners is referred to as contribution.
Beneficiary	The person for whose benefit an insurance policy, trust, will, or contract is established is a beneficiary. In the case of a contract, the beneficiary is called a third-party beneficiary.
Objection	In the trial of a case the formal remonstrance made by counsel to something that has been said or done, in order to obtain the court's ruling thereon is an objection.
Argument	The discussion by counsel for the respective parties of their contentions on the law and the facts of the case being tried in order to aid the jury in arriving at a correct and just conclusion is called argument.
Rent seeking	Rent seeking is the process by which an individual or firm seeks to gain through manipulation of the economic environment, rather than through trade and the production of added wealth.
Gain	In finance, gain is a profit or an increase in value of an investment such as a stock or bond. Gain is calculated by fair market value or the proceeds from the sale of the investment minus the sum of the purchase price and all costs associated with it.
Export subsidies	Government payments to domestic producers to enable them to reduce the price of a good or service to foreign buyers are referred to as export subsidies.
Subsidy	Subsidy refers to government financial assistance to a domestic producer.
Production	The creation of finished goods and services using the factors of production: land, labor, capital, entrepreneurship, and knowledge.
Countervailing duty	A tariff levied against imports that are subsidized by the exporting country's government, designed to offset the effect of the subsidy, is referred to as countervailing duty.
Government procurement	Government procurement refers to purchase of goods and services by government and by state-owned enterprises.
Procurement	Procurement is the acquisition of goods or services at the best possible total cost of ownership, in the right quantity, at the right time, in the right place for the direct

Go to **Cram101.com** for the Practice Tests for this Chapter.

benefit or use of the governments, corporations, or individuals generally via, but not limited to a contract.

Service	Service refers to a "non tangible product" that is not embodied in a physical good and that typically effects some change in another product, person, or institution. Contrasts with good.
Purchasing	Purchasing refers to the function in a firm that searches for quality material resources, finds the best suppliers, and negotiates the best price for goods and services.
Preference	The act of a debtor in paying or securing one or more of his creditors in a manner more favorable to them than to other creditors or to the exclusion of such other creditors is a preference. In the absence of statute, a preference is perfectly good, but to be legal it must be bona fide, and not a mere subterfuge of the debtor to secure a future benefit to himself or to prevent the application of his property to his debts.
Agent	A person who makes economic decisions for another economic actor. A hired manager operates as an agent for a firm's owner.
Contract	A contract is a "promise" or an "agreement" that is enforced or recognized by the law. In the civil law, a contract is considered to be part of the general law of obligations.
Grant	Grant refers to an intergovernmental transfer of funds . Since the New Deal, state and local governments have become increasingly dependent upon federal grants for an almost infinite variety of programs.
Enterprise	Enterprise refers to another name for a business organization. Other similar terms are business firm, sometimes simply business, sometimes simply firm, as well as company, and entity.
Appropriation	A privacy tort that consists of using a person's name or likeness for commercial gain without the person's permission is an appropriation.
Distribution	Distribution in economics, the manner in which total output and income is distributed among individuals or factors.
Regulation	Regulation refers to restrictions state and federal laws place on business with regard to the conduct of its activities.
Prohibitive tariff	A tariff that reduces imports to zero is referred to as a prohibitive tariff.
Negotiation	Negotiation is the process whereby interested parties resolve disputes, agree upon courses of action, bargain for individual or collective advantage, and/or attempt to craft outcomes which serve their mutual interests.
Trademark	A distinctive word, name, symbol, device, or combination thereof, which enables consumers to identify favored products or services and which may find protection under state or federal law is a trademark.
Intellectual property protection	Intellectual property protection refers to laws that establish and maintain ownership rights to intellectual property. The principal forms of this protection are patents, trademarks, and copyrights.
Intellectual property	In law, intellectual property is an umbrella term for various legal entitlements which attach to certain types of information, ideas, or other intangibles in their expressed form. The holder of this legal entitlement is generally entitled to exercise various exclusive rights in relation to its subject matter.
Property	Assets defined in the broadest legal sense. Property includes the unrealized receivables of a cash basis taxpayer, but not services rendered.

Developing country	Developing country refers to a country whose per capita income is low by world standards. Same as LDC. As usually used, it does not necessarily connote that the country's income is rising.
Patent	The legal right to the proceeds from and control over the use of an invented product or process, granted for a fixed period of time, usually 20 years. Patent is one form of intellectual property that is subject of the TRIPS agreement.
Research and development	The use of resources for the deliberate discovery of new information and ways of doing things, together with the application of that information in inventing new products or processes is referred to as research and development.
Intellectual property rights	Intellectual property rights, such as patents, copyrights, trademarks, trade secrets, trade names, and domain names are very valuable business assets. Federal and state laws protect intellectual property rights from misappropriation and infringement.
Intellectual property right	Intellectual property right refers to the right to control and derive the benefits from something one has invented, discovered, or created.
Property rights	Bundle of legal rights over the use to which a resource is put and over the use made of any income that may be derived from that resource are referred to as property rights.
Copyright	The legal right to the proceeds from and control over the use of a created product, such a written work, audio, video, film, or software is a copyright. This right generally extends over the life of the author plus fifty years.
Price discrimination	Price discrimination refers to the sale by a firm to buyers at two different prices. When this occurs internationally and the lower price is charged for export, it is regarded as dumping.
Consideration	Consideration in contract law, a basic requirement for an enforceable agreement under traditional contract principles, defined in this text as legal value, bargained for and given in exchange for an act or promise. In corporation law, cash or property contributed to a corporation in exchange for shares, or a promise to contribute such cash or property.
Trade flow	The quantity or value of a country's bilateral trade with another country is called trade flow.
Frequency	Frequency refers to the speed of the up and down movements of a fluctuating economic variable; that is, the number of times per unit of time that the variable completes a cycle of up and down movement.
Advance deposit requirement	Advance deposit requirement refers to a requirement that some proportion of the value of imports, or of import duties, be deposited prior to payment, without competitive interest being paid.
Countervailing duties	countervailing duties are tariffs imposed by a country on imported goods in cases where imports have been unfairly subsidized by a foreign government and hurt domestic producers. Antidumping duties are referred to as countervailing duties.
Border tax adjustment	Border tax adjustment refers to the rebate of indirect taxes on exported goods and the levying of them on imported goods. May distort trade when tax rates differ or when adjustment does not match the tax paid.
Variable levy	Variable levy refers to a tax on imports that varies over time so as to stabilize the domestic price of the imported good. Essentially, the tax is set equal to the difference between the target domestic price and the world price.
Variable	A variable is something measured by a number; it is used to analyze what happens to other things when the size of that number changes.

Go to **Cram101.com** for the Practice Tests for this Chapter.

Levy	Levy refers to imposing and collecting a tax or tariff.
Developed country	A developed country is one that enjoys a relatively high standard of living derived through an industrialized, diversified economy. Countries with a very high Human Development Index are generally considered developed countries.
Trend	Trend refers to the long-term movement of an economic variable, such as its average rate of increase or decrease over enough years to encompass several business cycles.
Anticipation	In finance, anticipation is where debts are paid off early, generally in order to pay less interest.
General equilibrium	Equality of supply and demand in all markets of an economy simultaneously. The number of markets does not have to be large. The simplest Ricardian model has markets only for two goods and one factor, labor, but this is a general equilibrium model.
Keynes	English economist Keynes (1883-1946) radical ideas impacted modern economics as well as political theory. He is most noted for his advocation of interventionist government policy in which the government fiscal and monetary measures to handle the effects of economic recessions, depressions, and booms.
Fallacy of composition	Fallacy of composition refers to the false notion that what is true for the individual is necessarily true for the group.
Composition	An out-of-court settlement in which creditors agree to accept a fractional settlement on their original claim is referred to as composition.
Consumption	In Keynesian economics consumption refers to personal consumption expenditure, i.e., the purchase of currently produced goods and services out of income, out of savings (net worth), or from borrowed funds. It refers to that part of disposable income that does not go to saving.
Stockholder	A stockholder is an individual or company (including a corporation) that legally owns one or more shares of stock in a joined stock company. The shareholders are the owners of a corporation. Companies listed at the stock market strive to enhance shareholder value.
Allegation	An allegation is a statement of a fact by a party in a pleading, which the party claims it will prove. Allegations remain assertions without proof, only claims until they are proved.
Level playing field	The objective of those who advocate protection on the grounds the foreign firms have an unfair advantage. A level playing field would remove such advantages, although it is not usually clear what sorts of advantage would be permitted to remain.
Commerce	Commerce is the exchange of something of value between two entities. It is the central mechanism from which capitalism is derived.
Appeal	Appeal refers to the act of asking an appellate court to overturn a decision after the trial court's final judgment has been entered.
Optimal tariff	The level of a tariff that maximizes a country's welfare. In a non-distorted small open economy, the optimal tariff is zero. In a large country it is positive, due to its effect on the terms of trade.
Optimal tariff argument	Optimal tariff argument refers to an argument in favor of levying a tariff in order to improve the terms of trade. The argument is valid only in a large country, and then only if other countries do not retaliate by raising tariffs themselves.
International Monetary Fund	The International Monetary Fund is the international organization entrusted with overseeing the global financial system by monitoring exchange rates and balance of payments, as well as offering technical and financial assistance when asked.

Go to **Cram101.com** for the Practice Tests for this Chapter.

Fund	Independent accounting entity with a self-balancing set of accounts segregated for the purposes of carrying on specific activities is referred to as a fund.
Slope	The slope of a line in the plane containing the x and y axes is generally represented by the letter m, and is defined as the change in the y coordinate divided by the corresponding change in the x coordinate, between two distinct points on the line.
Factor of production	Factor of production refers to economic resources used in production such as land, labor, and capital.
Abundant factor	Abundant factor refers to the factor (resource) in a country's endowment with which it is best endowed, relative to other factors, compared to other countries. May be defined by quantity or by price.
Scarce factor	Scarce factor refers to the factor in a country's endowment with which it is has the least of, relative to other factors, compared to other countries. May be defined by quantity or by price.
Commercial policy	Commercial policy refers to government policies intended to influence international commerce, including international trade. Includes tariffs and quotas, as well as policies regarding exports.
Capital	Capital generally refers to financial wealth, especially that used to start or maintain a business. In classical economics, capital is one of four factors of production, the others being land and labor and entrepreneurship.
Labor	People's physical and mental talents and efforts that are used to help produce goods and services are called labor.
Testimony	In some contexts, the word bears the same import as the word evidence, but in most connections it has a much narrower meaning. Testimony are the words heard from the witness in court, and evidence is what the jury considers it worth.
Economics	The social science dealing with the use of scarce resources to obtain the maximum satisfaction of society's virtually unlimited economic wants is an economics.
Intervention	Intervention refers to an activity in which a government buys or sells its currency in the foreign exchange market in order to affect its currency's exchange rate.
Political economy	Early name for the discipline of economics. A field within economics encompassing several alternatives to neoclassical economics, including Marxist economics. Also called radical political economy.
Journal	Book of original entry, in which transactions are recorded in a general ledger system, is referred to as a journal.
National defense argument for protection	National defense argument for protection refers to the argument that imports should be restricted in order to sustain a domestic industry so that it will be available in case of trade disruption due to war. Aircraft and auto manufacturing usually fall in this category of protected industry.
Argument for protection	Argument for protection refers to a reason given for restricting imports by tariffs and/or quotas.
Comparative advantage	The ability to produce a good at lower cost, relative to other goods, compared to another country is a comparative advantage.
Domestic output	Domestic output refers to gross domestic product; the total output of final goods and services produced in the economy.
Remainder	A remainder in property law is a future interest created in a transferee that is capable of

Go to **Cram101.com** for the Practice Tests for this Chapter.

	becoming possessory upon the natural termination of a prior estate created by the same instrument.
Infant industry	Infant industry refers to a young industry that may need temporary protection from competition from the established industries of other countries to develop an acquired comparative advantage.
Infant industry protection	Infant industry protection refers to protection of a newly established domestic industry that is less productive than foreign producers.
Infant industry argument	The theoretical rationale for infant industry protection is referred to as the infant industry argument.
Expense	In accounting, an expense represents an event in which an asset is used up or a liability is incurred. In terms of the accounting equation, expenses reduce owners' equity.
Marketing	Promoting and selling products or services to customers, or prospective customers, is referred to as marketing.
Perfect competition	An idealized market structure in which there are large numbers of both buyers and sellers, all of them small, so that they act as price takers. Perfect competition also assumes homogeneous products, free entry and exit, and complete information.
Price support	Price support refers to government action to increase the price of a product, usually by buying it. May be associated with a price floor.
Autarky	Autarky refers to the situation of not engaging in international trade; self-sufficiency. Not to be confused with 'autarchy,' which in at least some dictionaries is a political term rather than an economic one, and means absolute rule or power.
Negative externality	Negative externality refers to a harmful externality; that is, a harmful effect of one economic agent's actions on another. Considered a distortion because the first agent has inadequate incentive to curtail their action.
Externality	Externality refers to an effect of one economic agent's actions on another, such that one agent's decisions make another better or worse off by changing their utility or cost.
Market failure	Any departure from the ideal benchmark of perfect competition, especially the complete absence of a market due to incomplete or asymmetric information is called market failure.
Case study	A case study is a particular method of qualitative research. Rather than using large samples and following a rigid protocol to examine a limited number of variables, case study methods involve an in-depth, longitudinal examination of a single instance or event: a case. They provide a systematic way of looking at events, collecting data, analyzing information, and reporting the results.
Leverage	Leverage is using given resources in such a way that the potential positive or negative outcome is magnified. In finance, this generally refers to borrowing.
Points	Loan origination fees that may be deductible as interest by a buyer of property. A seller of property who pays points reduces the selling price by the amount of the points paid for the buyer.
Manufacturing	Production of goods primarily by the application of labor and capital to raw materials and other intermediate inputs, in contrast to agriculture, mining, forestry, fishing, and services a manufacturing.
Value added	The value of output minus the value of all intermediate inputs, representing therefore the contribution of, and payments to, primary factors of production a value added.
Abatement	Abatement in pleading, a legal defence to civil and criminal actions based purely on

95

	procedural and technical issues involving the death of parties and changes in their status. Abatement of debts and legacies is a common law doctrine of wills that holds that when the equitable assets of a deceased person are not sufficient to satisfy fully all the creditors, their debts must abate proportionately, and they must accept a dividend.
Strategic trade policy	Strategic trade policy refers to the use of trade policies, including tariffs, subsidies, and even export subsidies, in a context of imperfect competition and/or increasing returns, to alter the outcome of international competition in a country.
Increasing returns	An increase in a firm's output by a larger percentage than the percentage increase in its inputs is increasing returns.
Returns to scale	Returns to scale refers to a technical property of production that predicts what happens to output if the quantity of all input factors is increased by some amount of scale.
Marginal revenue curve	A graph of the relationship between the change in total revenue and the quantity sold is referred to as the marginal revenue curve.
Marginal revenue	Marginal revenue refers to the change in total revenue obtained by selling one additional unit.
Marginal cost	Marginal cost refers to the increase in cost that accompanies a unit increase in output; the partial derivative of the cost function with respect to output.
Cost curve	A cost curve is a graph of the costs of production as a function of total quantity produced. In a free market economy, productively efficient firms use these curves to find the optimal point of production, where they make the most profits.
Monopoly profit	In economics, a firm is said to reap monopoly profit when a lack of viable market competition allows it to set its prices above the equilibrium price for a good or service without losing profits to competitors.
Airbus	In 2003, for the first time in its 33-year history, Airbus delivered more jet-powered airliners than Boeing. Boeing states that the Boeing 777 has outsold its Airbus counterparts, which include the A340 family as well as the A330-300. The smaller A330-200 competes with the 767, outselling its Boeing counterpart.
Boeing	Boeing is the world's largest aircraft manufacturer by revenue. Headquartered in Chicago, Illinois, Boeing is the second-largest defense contractor in the world. In 2005, the company was the world's largest civil aircraft manufacturer in terms of value.
Economic perspective	A viewpoint that envisions individuals and institutions making rational decisions by comparing the marginal benefits and marginal costs associated with their actions is an economic perspective.
Import quota	Import quota refers to a limit imposed by a nation on the quantity of a good that may be imported during some period of time.
Yield	The interest rate that equates a future value or an annuity to a given present value is a yield.
Committee	A long-lasting, sometimes permanent team in the organization structure created to deal with tasks that recur regularly is the committee.
Statute	A statute is a formal, written law of a country or state, written and enacted by its legislative authority, perhaps to then be ratified by the highest executive in the government, and finally published.
Trade adjustment assistance	Trade adjustment assistance provides special unemployment benefits, loans, retraining programs, and other aid to workers and firms that are harmed by foreign competition.

Adjustment assistance	Adjustment assistance refers to government program to assist those workers and/or firms whose industry has declined, either due to competition from imports or from other causes.
Most favored nation	Most favored nation refers to the principle, fundamental to the GATT, of treating imports from a country on the same basis as that given to the most favored other nation.
Predatory dumping	Predatory dumping refers to dumping for the purpose of driving competitors out of business and then raising price. This is the one motivation for dumping that most economists agree is undesirable, like predatory pricing in other contexts.
Dumping margin	Dumping margin in a case of dumping, the difference between the 'fair price' and the price charged for export. Used as the basis for setting anti-dumping duties.
Escape clause	The portion of a legal text that permits departure from ts provisions in the event of specified adverse circumstances is the escape clause.
Dumping	Dumping refers to a practice of charging a very low price in a foreign market for such economic purposes as putting rival suppliers out of business.
Margin	A deposit by a buyer in stocks with a seller or a stockbroker, as security to cover fluctuations in the market in reference to stocks that the buyer has purchased but for which he has not paid is a margin. Commodities are also traded on margin.

Commercial policy	Commercial policy refers to government policies intended to influence international commerce, including international trade. Includes tariffs and quotas, as well as policies regarding exports.
Policy	Similar to a script in that a policy can be a less than completely rational decision-making method. Involves the use of a pre-existing set of decision steps for any problem that presents itself.
World Trade Organization	The World Trade Organization is an international, multilateral organization, which sets the rules for the global trading system and resolves disputes between its member states, all of whom are signatories to its approximately 30 agreements.
Economy	The income, expenditures, and resources that affect the cost of running a business and household are called an economy.
Trade barrier	An artificial disincentive to export and/or import, such as a tariff, quota, or other NTB is called a trade barrier.
Trend	Trend refers to the long-term movement of an economic variable, such as its average rate of increase or decrease over enough years to encompass several business cycles.
Authority	Authority in agency law, refers to an agent's ability to affect his principal's legal relations with third parties. Also used to refer to an actor's legal power or ability to do something. In addition, sometimes used to refer to a statute, case, or other legal source that justifies a particular result.
Commerce	Commerce is the exchange of something of value between two entities. It is the central mechanism from which capitalism is derived.
Grant	Grant refers to an intergovernmental transfer of funds . Since the New Deal, state and local governments have become increasingly dependent upon federal grants for an almost infinite variety of programs.
Tariff	A tax imposed by a nation on an imported good is called a tariff.
Industry	A group of firms that produce identical or similar products is an industry. It is also used specifically to refer to an area of economic production focused on manufacturing which involves large amounts of capital investment before any profit can be realized, also called "heavy industry".
International trade	The export of goods and services from a country and the import of goods and services into a country is referred to as the international trade.
Exchange	The trade of things of value between buyer and seller so that each is better off after the trade is called the exchange.
Market	A market is, as defined in economics, a social arrangement that allows buyers and sellers to discover information and carry out a voluntary exchange of goods or services.
Federal government	Federal government refers to the government of the United States, as distinct from the state and local governments.
Revenue	Revenue is a U.S. business term for the amount of money that a company receives from its activities, mostly from sales of products and/or services to customers.
Raw material	Raw material refers to a good that has not been transformed by production; a primary product.
Fund	Independent accounting entity with a self-balancing set of accounts segregated for the purposes of carrying on specific activities is referred to as a fund.
Production	The creation of finished goods and services using the factors of production: land, labor, capital, entrepreneurship, and knowledge.

Infant industry	Infant industry refers to a young industry that may need temporary protection from competition from the established industries of other countries to develop an acquired comparative advantage.
Depression	Depression refers to a prolonged period characterized by high unemployment, low output and investment, depressed business confidence, falling prices, and widespread business failures. A milder form of business downturn is a recession.
Export	In economics, an export is any good or commodity, shipped or otherwise transported out of a country, province, town to another part of the world in a legitimate fashion, typically for use in trade or sale.
Writ	Writ refers to a commandment of a court given for the purpose of compelling certain action from the defendant, and usually executed by a sheriff or other judicial officer.
Manufactured good	A manufactured good refers to goods that have been processed in any way.
Compromise	Compromise occurs when the interaction is moderately important to meeting goals and the goals are neither completely compatible nor completely incompatible.
Federal budget	The annual statement of the expenditures and tax revenues of the government of the United States together with the laws and regulations that approve and support those expenditures and taxes is the federal budget.
Budget	Budget refers to an account, usually for a year, of the planned expenditures and the expected receipts of an entity. For a government, the receipts are tax revenues.
Administration	Administration refers to the management and direction of the affairs of governments and institutions; a collective term for all policymaking officials of a government; the execution and implementation of public policy.
Recession	A significant decline in economic activity. In the U.S., recession is approximately defined as two successive quarters of falling GDP, as judged by NBER.
Closing	The finalization of a real estate sales transaction that passes title to the property from the seller to the buyer is referred to as a closing. Closing is a sales term which refers to the process of making a sale. It refers to reaching the final step, which may be an exchange of money or acquiring a signature.
Legislative branch	The part of the government that consists of Congress and has the power to adopt laws is called the legislative branch.
Reciprocal trade agreements act	Reciprocal Trade Agreements Act refers to a 1934 U.S. Federal law that authorized the president to negotiate up to 50 percent lower tariffs with foreign nations that agreed to reduce their tariffs on U.S. goods.
Negotiation	Negotiation is the process whereby interested parties resolve disputes, agree upon courses of action, bargain for individual or collective advantage, and/or attempt to craft outcomes which serve their mutual interests.
Reciprocal trade agreement	Reciprocal trade agreement refers to agreement between two countries to open their markets to each other's exports, usually by each reducing tariffs.
Most favored nation	Most favored nation refers to the principle, fundamental to the GATT, of treating imports from a country on the same basis as that given to the most favored other nation.
General Agreement on Tariffs and Trade	The General Agreement on Tariffs and Trade was originally created by the Bretton Woods Conference as part of a larger plan for economic recovery after World War II. It included a reduction in tariffs and other international trade barriers and is generally considered the precursor to the World Trade Organization.

Concession	A concession is a business operated under a contract or license associated with a degree of exclusivity in exploiting a business within a certain geographical area. For example, sports arenas or public parks may have concession stands; and public services such as water supply may be operated as concessions.
Quota	A government-imposed restriction on quantity, or sometimes on total value, used to restrict the import of something to a specific quantity is called a quota.
Public policy	Decision making by government. Governments are constantly concerned about what they should or should not do. And whatever they do or do not do is public policy. public program All those activities designed to implement a public policy; often this calls for the creation of organizations, public agencies, and bureaus.
Uruguay round	The eighth and most recent round of trade negotiations under GATT is referred to as Uruguay round.
Mfn status	MFN status refers to Most Favored Nation status, the status given by the U.S. to some non-members of the GATT/WTO whereby they are charged MFN tariffs even though they are eligible for higher tariffs.
Interest	In finance and economics, interest is the price paid by a borrower for the use of a lender's money. In other words, interest is the amount of paid to "rent" money for a period of time.
Enabling	Enabling refers to giving workers the education and tools they need to assume their new decision-making powers.
Structural change	Changes in the relative importance of different areas of an economy over time, usually measured in terms of their share of output, employment, or total spending is structural change.
Inflation	An increase in the overall price level of an economy, usually as measured by the CPI or by the implicit price deflator is called inflation.
Trade minister	Trade minister refers to the government official, at the ministerial or cabinet level, primarily responsible for issues of international trade policy; the minister of international trade.
Procedural rule	A rule that governs the internal processes of an administrative agency is referred to as the procedural rule.
Developing country	Developing country refers to a country whose per capita income is low by world standards. Same as LDC. As usually used, it does not necessarily connote that the country's income is rising.
National treatment	The principle of providing foreign producers and sellers the same treatment provided to domestic firms is national treatment.
Regulation	Regulation refers to restrictions state and federal laws place on business with regard to the conduct of its activities.
Domestic	From or in one's own country. A domestic producer is one that produces inside the home country. A domestic price is the price inside the home country. Opposite of 'foreign' or 'world.'.
Customs procedure	Customs procedure refers to the practices used by customs officers to clear goods into a country and levy tariffs. Includes clearance procedures such as documentation and inspection, methods of determining a good's classification, and methods of assignment.
Customs	Customs is an authority or agency in a country responsible for collecting customs duties and for controlling the flow of people, animals and goods (including personal effects and hazardous items) in and out of the country.

Dumping margin	Dumping margin in a case of dumping, the difference between the 'fair price' and the price charged for export. Used as the basis for setting anti-dumping duties.
Dumping	Dumping refers to a practice of charging a very low price in a foreign market for such economic purposes as putting rival suppliers out of business.
Margin	A deposit by a buyer in stocks with a seller or a stockbroker, as security to cover fluctuations in the market in reference to stocks that the buyer has purchased but for which he has not paid is a margin. Commodities are also traded on margin.
Countervailing duty	A tariff levied against imports that are subsidized by the exporting country's government, designed to offset the effect of the subsidy, is referred to as countervailing duty.
Subsidy	Subsidy refers to government financial assistance to a domestic producer.
Quantitative restriction	Quantitative restriction refers to a restriction on trade, usually imports, limiting the quantity of the good or service that is traded; a quota is the most common example.
Balance of payments	Balance of payments refers to a list, or accounting, of all of a country's international transactions for a given time period, usually one year.
Currency control	Currency control is a system whereby a country tries to regulate the value of money (currency) within its borders. From simple to complex policy changes, it can be characterized as a government initiated system to control currency fluctuations through interest rates, bonds, laws, money printing, and many more.
Escape clause	The portion of a legal text that permits departure from ts provisions in the event of specified adverse circumstances is the escape clause.
Balance	In banking and accountancy, the outstanding balance is the amount of money owned, (or due), that remains in a deposit account (or a loan account) at a given date, after all past remittances, payments and withdrawal have been accounted for. It can be positive (then, in the balance sheet of a firm, it is an asset) or negative (a liability).
Export subsidies	Government payments to domestic producers to enable them to reduce the price of a good or service to foreign buyers are referred to as export subsidies.
Primary product	A good that has not been processed and is therefore in its natural state, specifically products of agriculture, forestry, fishing, and mining is referred to as primary product.
Consideration	Consideration in contract law, a basic requirement for an enforceable agreement under traditional contract principles, defined in this text as legal value, bargained for and given in exchange for an act or promise. In corporation law, cash or property contributed to a corporation in exchange for shares, or a promise to contribute such cash or property.
Procurement	Procurement is the acquisition of goods or services at the best possible total cost of ownership, in the right quantity, at the right time, in the right place for the direct benefit or use of the governments, corporations, or individuals generally via, but not limited to a contract.
Enterprise	Enterprise refers to another name for a business organization. Other similar terms are business firm, sometimes simply business, sometimes simply firm, as well as company, and entity.
Buyer	A buyer refers to a role in the buying center with formal authority and responsibility to select the supplier and negotiate the terms of the contract.
Security	Security refers to a claim on the borrower future income that is sold by the borrower to the lender. A security is a type of transferable interest representing financial value.
Accession	Accession refers to the process of adding a country to an international agreement, such as

the GATT, WTO, EU, or NAFTA.

Developed country	A developed country is one that enjoys a relatively high standard of living derived through an industrialized, diversified economy. Countries with a very high Human Development Index are generally considered developed countries.
Reciprocity	An industrial buying practice in which two organizations agree to purchase each other's products and services is called reciprocity.
Labor	People's physical and mental talents and efforts that are used to help produce goods and services are called labor.
Executive branch	The executive branch is the part of government charged with implementing or enforcing the laws. Consists of the President and Vice President.
Credit	Credit refers to a recording as positive in the balance of payments, any transaction that gives rise to a payment into the country, such as an export, the sale of an asset, or borrowing from abroad.
Exporter	A firm that sells its product in another country is an exporter.
Firm	An organization that employs resources to produce a good or service for profit and owns and operates one or more plants is referred to as a firm.
Trade liberalization	Reduction of tariffs and removal or relaxation of NTBs is referred to as trade liberalization.
Specificity	The property that a policy measure applies to one or a group of enterprises or industries, as opposed to all industries, is called specificity.
Extension	Extension refers to an out-of-court settlement in which creditors agree to allow the firm more time to meet its financial obligations. A new repayment schedule will be developed, subject to the acceptance of creditors.
Intellectual property rights	Intellectual property rights, such as patents, copyrights, trademarks, trade secrets, trade names, and domain names are very valuable business assets. Federal and state laws protect intellectual property rights from misappropriation and infringement.
Intellectual property right	Intellectual property right refers to the right to control and derive the benefits from something one has invented, discovered, or created.
Intellectual property	In law, intellectual property is an umbrella term for various legal entitlements which attach to certain types of information, ideas, or other intangibles in their expressed form. The holder of this legal entitlement is generally entitled to exercise various exclusive rights in relation to its subject matter.
Nontariff barrier	Any policy that interferes with exports or imports other than a simple tariff, prominently including quotas and vers is referred to as nontariff barrier.
Trade in services	Trade in services refers to the provision of a service to buyers within or from one country by a firm in or from another country.
Property rights	Bundle of legal rights over the use to which a resource is put and over the use made of any income that may be derived from that resource are referred to as property rights.
Property	Assets defined in the broadest legal sense. Property includes the unrealized receivables of a cash basis taxpayer, but not services rendered.
Service	Service refers to a "non tangible product" that is not embodied in a physical good and that typically effects some change in another product, person, or institution. Contrasts with good.

Go to **Cram101.com** for the Practice Tests for this Chapter.

Political economy	Early name for the discipline of economics. A field within economics encompassing several alternatives to neoclassical economics, including Marxist economics. Also called radical political economy.
Economics	The social science dealing with the use of scarce resources to obtain the maximum satisfaction of society's virtually unlimited economic wants is an economics.
Target price	Target price refers to estimated price for a product or service that potential customers will
Exporting	Selling products to another country is called exporting.
Data processing	Data processing refers to a name for business technology in the 1970s; included technology that supported an existing business and was primarily used to improve the flow of financial information.
Insurance	Insurance refers to a system by which individuals can reduce their exposure to risk of large losses by spreading the risks among a large number of persons.
Licensing	Licensing is a form of strategic alliance which involves the sale of a right to use certain proprietary knowledge (so called intellectual property) in a defined way.
Investment	Investment refers to spending for the production and accumulation of capital and additions to inventories. In a financial sense, buying an asset with the expectation of making a return.
Appeal	Appeal refers to the act of asking an appellate court to overturn a decision after the trial court's final judgment has been entered.
Consumption	In Keynesian economics consumption refers to personal consumption expenditure, i.e., the purchase of currently produced goods and services out of income, out of savings (net worth), or from borrowed funds. It refers to that part of disposable income that does not go to saving.
Market access	The ability of firms from one country to sell in another is market access.
Waiver	Waiver refers to an authorized deviation from the terms of a previously negotiated and legally binding agreement. Many countries have sought and obtained waivers from particular obligations of the GATT and WTO.
Case study	A case study is a particular method of qualitative research. Rather than using large samples and following a rigid protocol to examine a limited number of variables, case study methods involve an in-depth, longitudinal examination of a single instance or event: a case. They provide a systematic way of looking at events, collecting data, analyzing information, and reporting the results.
Embargo	Embargo refers to the prohibition of some category of trade. May apply to exports and/or imports, of particular products or of all trade, vis a vis the world or a particular country or countries.
Specie	Specie refers to coins, normally including only those made of precious metal.
Tariff escalation	The tendency of tariffs and other import barriers to be higher on finished goods sold to consumers than on intermediate manufactured goods sold to industry is tariff escalation.
Escalation	Regarding the structure of tariffs. In the context of a trade war, escalation refers to the increase in tariffs that occurs as countries retaliate again and again.
Peak	Peak refers to the point in the business cycle when an economic expansion reaches its highest point before turning down. Contrasts with trough.
Market value	Market value refers to the price of an asset agreed on between a willing buyer and a willing seller; the price an asset could demand if it is sold on the open market.

Free trade	Free trade refers to a situation in which there are no artificial barriers to trade, such as tariffs and quotas. Usually used, often only implicitly, with frictionless trade, so that it implies that there are no barriers to trade of any kind.
Holding	The holding is a court's determination of a matter of law based on the issue presented in the particular case. In other words: under this law, with these facts, this result.
Welfare	Welfare refers to the economic well being of an individual, group, or economy. For individuals, it is conceptualized by a utility function. For groups, including countries and the world, it is a tricky philosophical concept, since individuals fare differently.
Profit	Profit refers to the return to the resource entrepreneurial ability; total revenue minus total cost.
Competitor	Other organizations in the same industry or type of business that provide a good or service to the same set of customers is referred to as a competitor.
Predatory dumping	Predatory dumping refers to dumping for the purpose of driving competitors out of business and then raising price. This is the one motivation for dumping that most economists agree is undesirable, like predatory pricing in other contexts.
Market power	The ability of a single economic actor to have a substantial influence on market prices is market power.
Demand curve	Demand curve refers to the graph of quantity demanded as a function of price, normally downward sloping, straight or curved, and drawn with quantity on the horizontal axis and price on the vertical axis.
Price discrimination	Price discrimination refers to the sale by a firm to buyers at two different prices. When this occurs internationally and the lower price is charged for export, it is regarded as dumping.
Marginal revenue	Marginal revenue refers to the change in total revenue obtained by selling one additional unit.
Marginal cost	Marginal cost refers to the increase in cost that accompanies a unit increase in output; the partial derivative of the cost function with respect to output.
Fair value	Fair value is a concept used in finance and economics, defined as a rational and unbiased estimate of the potential market price of a good, service, or asset.
Fair market value	Fair market value refers to the amount at which property would change hands between a willing buyer and a willing seller, neither being under any compulsion to buy or to sell, and both having reasonable knowledge of the relevant facts.
Complaint	The pleading in a civil case in which the plaintiff states his claim and requests relief is called complaint. In the common law, it is a formal legal document that sets out the basic facts and legal reasons that the filing party (the plaintiffs) believes are sufficient to support a claim against another person, persons, entity or entities (the defendants) that entitles the plaintiff(s) to a remedy (either money damages or injunctive relief).
Trade union	A Trade Union, as we understand the term, is a continuous association of wage-earners for the purpose of maintaining or improving the conditions of their employment. They may organise strikes or resistance to lockouts in furtherance of particular goals.
Union	A worker association that bargains with employers over wages and working conditions is called a union.
Inventory	Tangible property held for sale in the normal course of business or used in producing goods or services for sale is an inventory.

Go to **Cram101.com** for the Practice Tests for this Chapter.

Capital	Capital generally refers to financial wealth, especially that used to start or maintain a business. In classical economics, capital is one of four factors of production, the others being land and labor and entrepreneurship.
Wage	The payment for the service of a unit of labor, per unit time. In trade theory, it is the only payment to labor, usually unskilled labor. In empirical work, wage data may exclude other compenzation, which must be added to get the total cost of employment.
Assessment	Collecting information and providing feedback to employees about their behavior, communication style, or skills is an assessment.
Statute	A statute is a formal, written law of a country or state, written and enacted by its legislative authority, perhaps to then be ratified by the highest executive in the government, and finally published.
Market price	Market price is an economic concept with commonplace familiarity; it is the price that a good or service is offered at, or will fetch, in the marketplace; it is of interest mainly in the study of microeconomics.
Petition	A petition is a request to an authority, most commonly a government official or public entity. In the colloquial sense, a petition is a document addressed to some official and signed by numerous individuals.
Expense	In accounting, an expense represents an event in which an asset is used up or a liability is incurred. In terms of the accounting equation, expenses reduce owners' equity.
Markup	Markup is a term used in marketing to indicate how much the price of a product is above the cost of producing and distributing the product.
Brand	A name, symbol, or design that identifies the goods or services of one seller or group of sellers and distinguishes them from the goods and services of competitors is a brand.
Hearing	A hearing is a proceeding before a court or other decision-making body or officer. A hearing is generally distinguished from a trial in that it is usually shorter and often less formal.
Option	A contract that gives the purchaser the option to buy or sell the underlying financial instrument at a specified price, called the exercise price or strike price, within a specific period of time.
Fair trade	The Fair Trade movement promotes international labor, environmental and social standards for the production of labelled and unlabelled goods ranging from handcrafts to agricultural commodities. The movement focuses in particular on exports from developing countries to developed countries.
Fraud	Tax fraud falls into two categories: civil and criminal. Under civil fraud, the IRS may impose as a penalty of an amount equal to as much as 75 percent of the underpayment.
Mfn tariff	The tariff level that a member of the GATT/WTO charges on a good to other members is a MFN tariff.
Actionable	Actionable refers to capable of being remedied by a legal action or claim.
Prohibited subsidy	Prohibited subsidy refers to a subsidy that is prohibited under the rules of the WTO. These include subsidies that are specifically designed to distort international trade.
Dispute settlement body	A board comprized of one representative from each WTO member nation that reviews panel reports and deals with disputes between members is referred to as the dispute settlement body.
Actionable subsidy	A subsidy that is not prohibited by the WTO but that member countries are permitted to levy countervailing duties against is an actionable subsidy.

Go to **Cram101.com** for the Practice Tests for this Chapter.

Countervailing duties	countervailing duties are tariffs imposed by a country on imported goods in cases where imports have been unfairly subsidized by a foreign government and hurt domestic producers. Antidumping duties are referred to as countervailing duties.
Market economy	A market economy is an economic system in which the production and distribution of goods and services takes place through the mechanism of free markets guided by a free price system rather than by the state in a planned economy.
Per capita	Per capita refers to per person. Usually used to indicate the average per person of any given statistic, commonly income.
Trade negotiation	A negotiation between pairs of governments, or among groups of governments, exchanging commitments to alter their trade policies, usually involving reductions in tariffs and sometimes nontariff barriers is a trade negotiation.
Cabinet	The heads of the executive departments of a jurisdiction who report to and advise its chief executive; examples would include the president's cabinet, the governor's cabinet, and the mayor's cabinet.
Retaliation	The use of an increased trade barrier in response to another country increasing its trade barrier, either as a way of undoing the adverse effects of the latter's action or of punishing it is retaliation.
Status quo	Status quo is a Latin term meaning the present, current, existing state of affairs.
Leverage	Leverage is using given resources in such a way that the potential positive or negative outcome is magnified. In finance, this generally refers to borrowing.
Gain	In finance, gain is a profit or an increase in value of an investment such as a stock or bond. Gain is calculated by fair market value or the proceeds from the sale of the investment minus the sum of the purchase price and all costs associated with it.
License	A license in the sphere of Intellectual Property Rights (IPR) is a document, contract or agreement giving permission or the 'right' to a legally-definable entity to do something (such as manufacture a product or to use a service), or to apply something (such as a trademark), with the objective of achieving commercial gain.
Market share	That fraction of an industry's output accounted for by an individual firm or group of firms is called market share.
Trade dispute	Trade dispute refers to any disagreement between nations involving their international trade or trade policies.
Arbitration	Arbitration is a form of mediation or conciliation, where the mediating party is given power by the disputant parties to settle the dispute by making a finding. In practice arbitration is generally used as a substitute for judicial systems, particularly when the judicial processes are viewed as too slow, expensive or biased. Arbitration is also used by communities which lack formal law, as a substitute for formal law.
Points	Loan origination fees that may be deductible as interest by a buyer of property. A seller of property who pays points reduces the selling price by the amount of the points paid for the buyer.
Quota rent	Quota rent refers to the economic rent received by the holder of the right to import under a quota. Equals the domestic price of the imported good, net of any tariff, minus the world price, times the quantity of imports.
Import quota	Import quota refers to a limit imposed by a nation on the quantity of a good that may be imported during some period of time.
Wall Street	Dow Jones & Company was founded in 1882 by reporters Charles Dow, Edward Jones and Charles

Go to **Cram101.com** for the Practice Tests for this Chapter.

Journal	Bergstresser. Jones converted the small Customers' Afternoon Letter into The Wall Street Journal, first published in 1889, and began delivery of the Dow Jones News Service via telegraph. The Journal featured the Jones 'Average', the first of several indexes of stock and bond prices on the New York Stock Exchange.
Trade war	Trade war refers to generally, a period in which each of two countries alternate in further restricting trade from the other. More specifically, the process of tariffs and retaliation.
Journal	Book of original entry, in which transactions are recorded in a general ledger system, is referred to as a journal.
Serious injury	The injury requirement of the escape clause, understood to be more stringent than material injury but otherwise apparently not rigorously defined, is referred to as serious injury.
Trade association	An industry trade group or trade association is generally a public relations organization founded and funded by corporations that operate in a specific industry. Its purpose is generally to promote that industry through PR activities such as advertizing, education, political donations, political pressure, publishing, and astroturfing.
Accord	An agreement whereby the parties agree to accept something different in satisfaction of the original contract is an accord.
Import relief	Import relief usually refers to some form of restraint of imports in a particular sector in order to assist domestic producers, and with the connotation that these producers have been suffering from the competition with imports.
Bankruptcy	Bankruptcy is a legally declared inability or impairment of ability of an individual or organization to pay their creditors.
Excess capacity	Excess capacity refers to plant resources that are underused when imperfectly competitive firms produce less output than that associated with purely competitive firms, who by definiation, are achieving minimum average total cost.
Trade adjustment assistance	Trade adjustment assistance provides special unemployment benefits, loans, retraining programs, and other aid to workers and firms that are harmed by foreign competition.
Adjustment assistance	Adjustment assistance refers to government program to assist those workers and/or firms whose industry has declined, either due to competition from imports or from other causes.
Health insurance	Health insurance is a type of insurance whereby the insurer pays the medical costs of the insured if the insured becomes sick due to covered causes, or due to accidents. The insurer may be a private organization or a government agency.
Corporation	A legal entity chartered by a state or the Federal government that is distinct and separate from the individuals who own it is a corporation. This separation gives the corporation unique powers which other legal entities lack.
Tax credit	Allows a firm to reduce the taxes paid to the home government by the amount of taxes paid to the foreign government is referred to as tax credit.
Pension	A pension is a steady income given to a person (usually after retirement). Pensions are typically payments made in the form of a guaranteed annuity to a retired or disabled employee.
Trade sanction	Use of a trade policy as a sanction, most commonly an embargo imposed against a country for violating human rights is referred to as trade sanction.
Product development	In business and engineering, new product development is the complete process of bringing a new product to market. There are two parallel aspects to this process : one involves product engineering ; the other marketing analysis. Marketers see new product development as the

Go to **Cram101.com** for the Practice Tests for this Chapter.

	first stage in product life cycle management, engineers as part of Product Lifecycle Management.
New product development	New product development is the complete process of bringing a new product to market. There are two parallel aspects to this process : one involves product engineering ; the other marketing analysis.
Patent infringement	Patent infringement refers to unauthorized use of another's patent. A patent holder may recover damages and other remedies against a patent infringer.
Patent	The legal right to the proceeds from and control over the use of an invented product or process, granted for a fixed period of time, usually 20 years. Patent is one form of intellectual property that is subject of the TRIPS agreement.
Adoption	In corporation law, a corporation's acceptance of a pre-incorporation contract by action of its board of directors, by which the corporation becomes liable on the contract, is referred to as adoption.
Users	Users refer to people in the organization who actually use the product or service purchased by the buying center.
Sunset clause	A provision within a piece of legislation providing for its demise on a specified date unless it is deliberately renewed is referred to as a sunset clause.
Prohibition	Prohibition refers to denial of the right to import or export, applying to particular products and/or particular countries. Includes embargo.
Orderly marketing arrangement	Orderly marketing arrangement refers to an agreement among a group of exporting and importing countries to restrict the quantities traded of a good or group of goods.
Marketing	Promoting and selling products or services to customers, or prospective customers, is referred to as marketing.
Comprehensive	A comprehensive refers to a layout accurate in size, color, scheme, and other necessary details to show how a final ad will look. For presentation only, never for reproduction.
Administrator	Administrator refers to the personal representative appointed by a probate court to settle the estate of a deceased person who died.
Milton Friedman	Milton Friedman (born July 31, 1912) is an American economist, known for his work on macroeconomics, microeconomics, economic history, statistics, and for his advocacy of laissez-faire capitalism. In 1976 he won the Nobel Memorial Prize in Economics for his achievements in the fields of consumption analysis, monetary history and theory and for his demonstration of the complexity of stabilization policy.
Committee	A long-lasting, sometimes permanent team in the organization structure created to deal with tasks that recur regularly is the committee.
North American Free Trade Agreement	A 1993 agreement establishing, over a 15-year period, a free trade zone composed of Canada, Mexico, and the United States is referred to as the North American Free Trade Agreement.
Multilateralism	Multilateralism is an international relations term that refers to multiple countries working in concert.
Economic analysis	The process of deriving economic principles from relevant economic facts are called economic analysis. It is the comparison, with money as the index, of those costs and benefits to the wider economy that can be reasonably quantified, including all social costs and benefits of a project.

Go to **Cram101.com** for the Practice Tests for this Chapter.

Trade diversion	Trade diversion refers to trade that occurs between members of a preferential trading arrangement that replaces what would have been imports from a country outside the PTA.
Trade creation	Trade creation refers to trade that occurs between members of a preferential trading arrangement that replaces what would have been production in the importing country were it not for the PTA.
Customs union	Customs union refers to a group of countries that adopt free trade on trade among themselves, and that also, on each product, agree to levy the same tariff on imports from outside the group. Equivalent to an FTA plus a common external tariff.
Regionalism	Regionalism refers to the formation or proliferation of preferential trading arrangements within a geographical region.

Trade liberalization	Reduction of tariffs and removal or relaxation of NTBs is referred to as trade liberalization.
Customs union	Customs union refers to a group of countries that adopt free trade on trade among themselves, and that also, on each product, agree to levy the same tariff on imports from outside the group. Equivalent to an FTA plus a common external tariff.
Customs	Customs is an authority or agency in a country responsible for collecting customs duties and for controlling the flow of people, animals and goods (including personal effects and hazardous items) in and out of the country.
Union	A worker association that bargains with employers over wages and working conditions is called a union.
Trade barrier	An artificial disincentive to export and/or import, such as a tariff, quota, or other NTB is called a trade barrier.
Exporter	A firm that sells its product in another country is an exporter.
Commercial policy	Commercial policy refers to government policies intended to influence international commerce, including international trade. Includes tariffs and quotas, as well as policies regarding exports.
Free trade	Free trade refers to a situation in which there are no artificial barriers to trade, such as tariffs and quotas. Usually used, often only implicitly, with frictionless trade, so that it implies that there are no barriers to trade of any kind.
Policy	Similar to a script in that a policy can be a less than completely rational decision-making method. Involves the use of a pre-existing set of decision steps for any problem that presents itself.
Tariff	A tax imposed by a nation on an imported good is called a tariff.
Labor law	Labor law is the body of laws, administrative rulings, and precedents which addresses the legal rights of, and restrictions on, workers and their organizations.
Accord	An agreement whereby the parties agree to accept something different in satisfaction of the original contract is an accord.
Labor	People's physical and mental talents and efforts that are used to help produce goods and services are called labor.
Intellectual property rights	Intellectual property rights, such as patents, copyrights, trademarks, trade secrets, trade names, and domain names are very valuable business assets. Federal and state laws protect intellectual property rights from misappropriation and infringement.
Intellectual property right	Intellectual property right refers to the right to control and derive the benefits from something one has invented, discovered, or created.
Intellectual property	In law, intellectual property is an umbrella term for various legal entitlements which attach to certain types of information, ideas, or other intangibles in their expressed form. The holder of this legal entitlement is generally entitled to exercise various exclusive rights in relation to its subject matter.
Property rights	Bundle of legal rights over the use to which a resource is put and over the use made of any income that may be derived from that resource are referred to as property rights.
Property	Assets defined in the broadest legal sense. Property includes the unrealized receivables of a cash basis taxpayer, but not services rendered.
Economic analysis	The process of deriving economic principles from relevant economic facts are called economic analysis. It is the comparison, with money as the index, of those costs and benefits to the

	wider economy that can be reasonably quantified, including all social costs and benefits of a project.
Trade diversion	Trade diversion refers to trade that occurs between members of a preferential trading arrangement that replaces what would have been imports from a country outside the PTA.
Comparative advantage	The ability to produce a good at lower cost, relative to other goods, compared to another country is a comparative advantage.
Production	The creation of finished goods and services using the factors of production: land, labor, capital, entrepreneurship, and knowledge.
Trade creation	Trade creation refers to trade that occurs between members of a preferential trading arrangement that replaces what would have been production in the importing country were it not for the PTA.
Welfare	Welfare refers to the economic well being of an individual, group, or economy. For individuals, it is conceptualized by a utility function. For groups, including countries and the world, it is a tricky philosophical concept, since individuals fare differently.
Consumer surplus	The difference between the maximum that consumers would be willing to pay for a good and what they actually do pay is consumer surplus. For each unit of the good, this is the vertical distance between the demand curve and price.
Producer surplus	The difference between the revenue of producers and production cost, measured as the area above the supply curve and below price, out to the quantity supplied, and net of fixed cost and losses at low output is producer surplus. If input prices are constant, this is profit.
Revenue	Revenue is a U.S. business term for the amount of money that a company receives from its activities, mostly from sales of products and/or services to customers.
Yield	The interest rate that equates a future value or an annuity to a given present value is a yield.
Domestic	From or in one's own country. A domestic producer is one that produces inside the home country. A domestic price is the price inside the home country. Opposite of 'foreign' or 'world.'.
Remainder	A remainder in property law is a future interest created in a transferee that is capable of becoming possessory upon the natural termination of a prior estate created by the same instrument.
Gain	In finance, gain is a profit or an increase in value of an investment such as a stock or bond. Gain is calculated by fair market value or the proceeds from the sale of the investment minus the sum of the purchase price and all costs associated with it.
Export	In economics, an export is any good or commodity, shipped or otherwise transported out of a country, province, town to another part of the world in a legitimate fashion, typically for use in trade or sale.
Market	A market is, as defined in economics, a social arrangement that allows buyers and sellers to discover information and carry out a voluntary exchange of goods or services.
Trading arrangement	An agreement between two or more countries concerning the rules under which trade among them will be conducted, either in a particular industry or more broadly is called a trading arrangement.
Economy	The income, expenditures, and resources that affect the cost of running a business and household are called an economy.
Economies of	In economics, returns to scale and economies of scale are related terms that describe what

Go to **Cram101.com** for the Practice Tests for this Chapter.

scale	happens as the scale of production increases. They are different terms and not to be used interchangeably.
Developing country	Developing country refers to a country whose per capita income is low by world standards. Same as LDC. As usually used, it does not necessarily connote that the country's income is rising.
Preference	The act of a debtor in paying or securing one or more of his creditors in a manner more favorable to them than to other creditors or to the exclusion of such other creditors is a preference. In the absence of statute, a preference is perfectly good, but to be legal it must be bona fide, and not a mere subterfuge of the debtor to secure a future benefit to himself or to prevent the application of his property to his debts.
North American Free Trade Agreement	A 1993 agreement establishing, over a 15-year period, a free trade zone composed of Canada, Mexico, and the United States is referred to as the North American Free Trade Agreement.
Service	Service refers to a "non tangible product" that is not embodied in a physical good and that typically effects some change in another product, person, or institution. Contrasts with good.
Negotiation	Negotiation is the process whereby interested parties resolve disputes, agree upon courses of action, bargain for individual or collective advantage, and/or attempt to craft outcomes which serve their mutual interests.
Regulation	Regulation refers to restrictions state and federal laws place on business with regard to the conduct of its activities.
Economic growth	Economic growth refers to the increase over time in the capacity of an economy to produce goods and services and to improve the well-being of its citizens.
Enterprise	Enterprise refers to another name for a business organization. Other similar terms are business firm, sometimes simply business, sometimes simply firm, as well as company, and entity.
Inflation	An increase in the overall price level of an economy, usually as measured by the CPI or by the implicit price deflator is called inflation.
Financial assets	Financial assets refer to monetary claims or obligations by one party against another party. Examples are bonds, mortgages, bank loans, and equities.
Balance	In banking and accountancy, the outstanding balance is the amount of money owned, (or due), that remains in a deposit account (or a loan account) at a given date, after all past remittances, payments and withdrawal have been accounted for. It can be positive (then, in the balance sheet of a firm, it is an asset) or negative (a liability).
Asset	An item of property, such as land, capital, money, a share in ownership, or a claim on others for future payment, such as a bond or a bank deposit is an asset.
Import substitution	Import substitution refers to a strategy for economic development that replaces imports with domestic production. It may be motivated by the infant industry argument, or simply by the desire to mimic the industrial structure of advanced countries.
Capital flight	Large financial capital outflows from a country prompted by fear of default or, especially, by fear of devaluation is called capital flight.
Economics	The social science dealing with the use of scarce resources to obtain the maximum satisfaction of society's virtually unlimited economic wants is an economics.
Capital	Capital generally refers to financial wealth, especially that used to start or maintain a business. In classical economics, capital is one of four factors of production, the others

Go to **Cram101.com** for the Practice Tests for this Chapter.

being land and labor and entrepreneurship.

Tight money	A term to indicate time periods in which financing may be difficult to find and interest rates may be quite high by normal standards is called tight money.
Recession	A significant decline in economic activity. In the U.S., recession is approximately defined as two successive quarters of falling GDP, as judged by NBER.
Interest	In finance and economics, interest is the price paid by a borrower for the use of a lender's money. In other words, interest is the amount of paid to "rent" money for a period of time.
Principal	In agency law, one under whose direction an agent acts and for whose benefit that agent acts is a principal.
Leadership	Management merely consists of leadership applied to business situations; or in other words: management forms a sub-set of the broader process of leadership.
Firm	An organization that employs resources to produce a good or service for profit and owns and operates one or more plants is referred to as a firm.
Government spending	Government spending refers to spending by all levels of government on goods and services.
Deficit	The deficit is the amount by which expenditure exceed revenue.
Wage	The payment for the service of a unit of labor, per unit time. In trade theory, it is the only payment to labor, usually unskilled labor. In empirical work, wage data may exclude other compenzation, which must be added to get the total cost of employment.
Pact	Pact refers to a set of principles endorsed by 21 of the largest U.S. ad agencies aimed at improving the research used in preparing and testing ads, providing a better creative product for clients, and controlling the cost of TV commercials.
Money supply	There are several formal definitions, but all include the quantity of currency in circulation plus the amount of demand deposits. The money supply, together with the amount of real economic activity in a country, is an important determinant of price.
Supply	Supply is the aggregate amount of any material good that can be called into being at a certain price point; it comprises one half of the equation of supply and demand. In classical economic theory, a curve representing supply is one of the factors that produce price.
Investment	Investment refers to spending for the production and accumulation of capital and additions to inventories. In a financial sense, buying an asset with the expectation of making a return.
Nontariff barrier	Any policy that interferes with exports or imports other than a simple tariff, prominently including quotas and vers is referred to as nontariff barrier.
Quota	A government-imposed restriction on quantity, or sometimes on total value, used to restrict the import of something to a specific quantity is called a quota.
Comprehensive	A comprehensive refers to a layout accurate in size, color, scheme, and other necessary details to show how a final ad will look. For presentation only, never for reproduction.
Trade in services	Trade in services refers to the provision of a service to buyers within or from one country by a firm in or from another country.
Draft	A signed, written order by which one party instructs another party to pay a specified sum to a third party, at sight or at a specific date is a draft.
Consideration	Consideration in contract law, a basic requirement for an enforceable agreement under traditional contract principles, defined in this text as legal value, bargained for and given in exchange for an act or promise. In corporation law, cash or property contributed to a

	corporation in exchange for shares, or a promise to contribute such cash or property.
Rules of origin	Rules of origin refer to rules included in a FTA specifying when a good will be regarded as produced within the FTA, so as to cross between members without tariff. Typical rules of origin are based on percentage of value added or on changes in tariff heading.
License	A license in the sphere of Intellectual Property Rights (IPR) is a document, contract or agreement giving permission or the 'right' to a legally-definable entity to do something (such as manufacture a product or to use a service), or to apply something (such as a trademark), with the objective of achieving commercial gain.
Exporting	Selling products to another country is called exporting.
Corporation	A legal entity chartered by a state or the Federal government that is distinct and separate from the individuals who own it is a corporation. This separation gives the corporation unique powers which other legal entities lack.
Profit	Profit refers to the return to the resource entrepreneurial ability; total revenue minus total cost.
Foreign ownership	Foreign ownership refers to the complete or majority ownership/control of businesses or resources in a country, by individuals who are not citizens of that country, or by companies whose headquarters are not in that country.
Appeal	Appeal refers to the act of asking an appellate court to overturn a decision after the trial court's final judgment has been entered.
Intellectual property protection	Intellectual property protection refers to laws that establish and maintain ownership rights to intellectual property. The principal forms of this protection are patents, trademarks, and copyrights.
Security	Security refers to a claim on the borrower future income that is sold by the borrower to the lender. A security is a type of transferable interest representing financial value.
Patent	The legal right to the proceeds from and control over the use of an invented product or process, granted for a fixed period of time, usually 20 years. Patent is one form of intellectual property that is subject of the TRIPS agreement.
Trade secret	Trade secret refers to a secret formula, pattern, process, program, device, method, technique, or compilation of information that is used in its owner's business and affords that owner a competitive advantage. Trade secrets are protected by state law.
Service mark	A mark that distinguishes the services rather than the product of the holder from those of its competitors is a service mark.
Trade sanction	Use of a trade policy as a sanction, most commonly an embargo imposed against a country for violating human rights is referred to as trade sanction.
Labor market	Any arrangement that brings buyers and sellers of labor services together to agree on conditions of work and pay is called a labor market.
Child labor	Originally, the employment of children in a manner detrimental to their health and social development. Now that the law contains strong child labor prohibitions, the term refers to the employment of children below the legal age limit.
Collaboration	Collaboration occurs when the interaction between groups is very important to goal attainment and the goals are compatible. Wherein people work together —applying both to the work of individuals as well as larger collectives and societies.
Exchange	The trade of things of value between buyer and seller so that each is better off after the trade is called the exchange.

Arbitration	Arbitration is a form of mediation or conciliation, where the mediating party is given power by the disputant parties to settle the dispute by making a finding. In practice arbitration is generally used as a substitute for judicial systems, particularly when the judicial processes are viewed as too slow, expensive or biased. Arbitration is also used by communities which lack formal law, as a substitute for formal law.
Assessment	Collecting information and providing feedback to employees about their behavior, communication style, or skills is an assessment.
Labor union	A group of workers organized to advance the interests of the group is called a labor union.
Administration	Administration refers to the management and direction of the affairs of governments and institutions; a collective term for all policymaking officials of a government; the execution and implementation of public policy.
Manufacturing	Production of goods primarily by the application of labor and capital to raw materials and other intermediate inputs, in contrast to agriculture, mining, forestry, fishing, and services a manufacturing.
Exchange rate	Exchange rate refers to the price at which one country's currency trades for another, typically on the exchange market.
Objection	In the trial of a case the formal remonstrance made by counsel to something that has been said or done, in order to obtain the court's ruling thereon is an objection.
Labor productivity	In labor economics labor productivity is a measure of the efficiency of the labor force. It is usually measured as output per hour of all people. When comparing labor productivity one mostly looks at the change over time.
Productivity	Productivity refers to the total output of goods and services in a given period of time divided by work hours.
World Bank	The World Bank is a group of five international organizations responsible for providing finance and advice to countries for the purposes of economic development and poverty reduction, and for encouraging and safeguarding international investment.
Operation	A standardized method or technique that is performed repetitively, often on different materials resulting in different finished goods is called an operation.
Mass production	The process of making a large number of a limited variety of products at very low cost is referred to as mass production.
Legal system	Legal system refers to system of rules that regulate behavior and the processes by which the laws of a country are enforced and through which redress of grievances is obtained.
Trade deficit	The amount by which imports exceed exports of goods and services is referred to as trade deficit.
Integration	Economic integration refers to reducing barriers among countries to transactions and to movements of goods, capital, and labor, including harmonization of laws, regulations, and standards. Integrated markets theoretically function as a unified market.
Commodity	Could refer to any good, but in trade a commodity is usually a raw material or primary product that enters into international trade, such as metals or basic agricultural products.
Unskilled labor	Unskilled labor refers to labor with a low level of skill or human capital. Identified empirically as labor earning a low wage, with a low level of education, or in an occupational category associated with these.
Industry	A group of firms that produce identical or similar products is an industry. It is also used specifically to refer to an area of economic production focused on manufacturing which

involves large amounts of capital investment before any profit can be realized, also called "heavy industry".

Euro	The common currency of a subset of the countries of the EU, adopted January 1, 1999 is called euro.
Accession	Accession refers to the process of adding a country to an international agreement, such as the GATT, WTO, EU, or NAFTA.
Statute	A statute is a formal, written law of a country or state, written and enacted by its legislative authority, perhaps to then be ratified by the highest executive in the government, and finally published.
Common currency	A situation where several countries form a monetary union with a single currency and a unified central bank is referred to as common currency.
Administrative agency	Administrative agency refers to a unit of government charged with the administration of particular laws. In the United States, those most important for administering laws related to international trade are the ITC and ITA.
Legislative branch	The part of the government that consists of Congress and has the power to adopt laws is called the legislative branch.
Guardian	A person to whom the law has entrusted the custody and control of the person, or estate, or both, of an incompetent person is a guardian.
International trade	The export of goods and services from a country and the import of goods and services into a country is referred to as the international trade.
Trade negotiation	A negotiation between pairs of governments, or among groups of governments, exchanging commitments to alter their trade policies, usually involving reductions in tariffs and sometimes nontariff barriers is a trade negotiation.
Price support	Price support refers to government action to increase the price of a product, usually by buying it. May be associated with a price floor.
Forming	The first stage of team development, where the team is formed and the objectives for the team are set is referred to as forming.
Treaties	The first source of international law, consisting of agreements or contracts between two or more nations that are formally signed by an authorized representative and ratified by the supreme power of each nation are called treaties.
Judiciary	The branch of government chosen to oversee the legal system through the court system is referred to as judiciary.
Budget	Budget refers to an account, usually for a year, of the planned expenditures and the expected receipts of an entity. For a government, the receipts are tax revenues.
Procurement	Procurement is the acquisition of goods or services at the best possible total cost of ownership, in the right quantity, at the right time, in the right place for the direct benefit or use of the governments, corporations, or individuals generally via, but not limited to a contract.
Subsidy	Subsidy refers to government financial assistance to a domestic producer.
Deregulation	The lessening or complete removal of government regulations on an industry, especially concerning the price that firms are allowed to charge and leaving price to be determined by market forces a deregulation.
Regionalism	Regionalism refers to the formation or proliferation of preferential trading arrangements within a geographical region.

Standardization	Standardization, in the context related to technologies and industries, is the process of establishing a technical standard among competing entities in a market, where this will bring benefits without hurting competition.
Government procurement	Government procurement refers to purchase of goods and services by government and by state-owned enterprises.
Integration process	The way information such as product knowledge, meanings, and beliefs is combined to evaluate two or more alternatives is referred to as an integration process.
Monetary union	An arrangement by which several nations adopt a common currency as a unit of account and medium of exchange. The European Monetary Union is scheduled to adopt the 'Euro' as the common currency in 1999.
Monetary policy	The use of the money supply and/or the interest rate to influence the level of economic activity and other policy objectives including the balance of payments or the exchange rate is called monetary policy.
Central Bank	Central bank refers to the institution in a country that is normally responsible for managing the supply of the country's money and the value of its currency on the foreign exchange market.
Charter	Charter refers to an instrument or authority from the sovereign power bestowing the right or power to do business under the corporate form of organization. Also, the organic law of a city or town, and representing a portion of the statute law of the state.
Common external tariff	When a group of countries form a customs union they must introduce a common external tariff. The same customs duties, quotas, preferences or other non-tariff barriers to trade apply to all goods entering the area, regardless of which country within the area they are entering. It is designed to end re-exportation.
Common market	Common market refers to a group of countries that eliminate all barriers to movement of both goods and factors among themselves, and that also, on each product, agree to levy the same tariff on imports from outside the group.
Association of Southeast Asian Nations	The Association of Southeast Asian Nations is a political, economic, and cultural organization of countries located in Southeast Asia.
Trade association	An industry trade group or trade association is generally a public relations organization founded and funded by corporations that operate in a specific industry. Its purpose is generally to promote that industry through PR activities such as advertizing, education, political donations, political pressure, publishing, and astroturfing.
Andean Pact	A 1969 agreement between Bolivia, Chile, Ecuador, Colombia, and Peru to establish a customs union is called Andean Pact.
Mercosur	Pact between Argentina, Brazil, Paraguay, and Uruguay to establish a free trade area is called mercosur.
Multilateralism	Multilateralism is an international relations term that refers to multiple countries working in concert.
Trend	Trend refers to the long-term movement of an economic variable, such as its average rate of increase or decrease over enough years to encompass several business cycles.
Complement	A good that is used in conjunction with another good is a complement. For example, cameras and film would complement eachother.
Trading bloc	Trading bloc refers to a group of countries that are somehow closely associated in international trade, usually in some sort of PTA.

Go to **Cram101.com** for the Practice Tests for this Chapter.

Federal Reserve	The Federal Reserve System was created via the Federal Reserve Act of December 23rd, 1913. All national banks were required to join the system and other banks could join. The Reserve Banks opened for business on November 16th, 1914. Federal Reserve Notes were created as part of the legislation, to provide an elastic supply of currency.
Free trade zone	A free trade zone is one or more areas of a country where tariffs and quotas are eliminated and bureaucratic requirements are lowered in order to attract companies by raising the incentives for doing business there.
Argument	The discussion by counsel for the respective parties of their contentions on the law and the facts of the case being tried in order to aid the jury in arriving at a correct and just conclusion is called argument.
Mfn status	MFN status refers to Most Favored Nation status, the status given by the U.S. to some non-members of the GATT/WTO whereby they are charged MFN tariffs even though they are eligible for higher tariffs.
World Trade Organization	The World Trade Organization is an international, multilateral organization, which sets the rules for the global trading system and resolves disputes between its member states, all of whom are signatories to its approximately 30 agreements.
Gross domestic product	Gross domestic product refers to the total value of new goods and services produced in a given year within the borders of a country, regardless of by whom.
Value marginal product	Value marginal product is defined as the change in total revenue divided by the change in total output. Depending on whether marginal revenue declines as sales increase, this may or may not equal product price.
Economic development	Increase in the economic standard of living of a country's population, normally accomplished by increasing its stocks of physical and human capital and improving its technology is an economic development.
Diminishing returns	The fall in the marginal product of a factor or factors that eventually occurs as input of that factor rises, holding the input of at least one other factor fixed, according to the Law of Diminishing Returns.
Marginal product	In a production function, the marginal product of a factor is the increase in output due to a unit increase in the input of the factor; that is, the partial derivative of the production function with respect to the factor.
Capital flow	International capital movement is referred to as capital flow.
Guest worker	Guest worker refers to a foreign worker who is permitted to enter a country temporarily in order to take a job for which there is shortage of domestic labor.
Immigration	Immigration refers to the migration of people into a country.
Brain drain	Brain drain refers to the migration of skilled workers out of a country. First applied to the migration of British-trained scientists, physicians, and university teachers in the early 1960's, mostly to the United States.
Multinational corporations	Firms that own production facilities in two or more countries and produce and sell their products globally are referred to as multinational corporations.
Multinational corporation	An organization that manufactures and markets products in many different countries and has multinational stock ownership and multinational management is referred to as multinational corporation.
Marginal product of labor	Marginal product of labor refers to the increase in the amount of output from an additional unit of labor.

141

Go to **Cram101.com** for the Practice Tests for this Chapter.

Economic development	Increase in the economic standard of living of a country's population, normally accomplished by increasing its stocks of physical and human capital and improving its technology is an economic development.
Economic growth	Economic growth refers to the increase over time in the capacity of an economy to produce goods and services and to improve the well-being of its citizens.
Economy	The income, expenditures, and resources that affect the cost of running a business and household are called an economy.
Consumption	In Keynesian economics consumption refers to personal consumption expenditure, i.e., the purchase of currently produced goods and services out of income, out of savings (net worth), or from borrowed funds. It refers to that part of disposable income that does not go to saving.
Unemployment rate	The unemployment rate is the number of unemployed workers divided by the total civilian labor force, which includes both the unemployed and those with jobs (all those willing and able to work for pay).
Production	The creation of finished goods and services using the factors of production: land, labor, capital, entrepreneurship, and knowledge.
Export	In economics, an export is any good or commodity, shipped or otherwise transported out of a country, province, town to another part of the world in a legitimate fashion, typically for use in trade or sale.
Capital	Capital generally refers to financial wealth, especially that used to start or maintain a business. In classical economics, capital is one of four factors of production, the others being land and labor and entrepreneurship.
Developing country	Developing country refers to a country whose per capita income is low by world standards. Same as LDC. As usually used, it does not necessarily connote that the country's income is rising.
Brief	Brief refers to a statement of a party's case or legal arguments, usually prepared by an attorney. Also used to make legal arguments before appellate courts.
Policy	Similar to a script in that a policy can be a less than completely rational decision-making method. Involves the use of a pre-existing set of decision steps for any problem that presents itself.
Comparative advantage	The ability to produce a good at lower cost, relative to other goods, compared to another country is a comparative advantage.
Manufactured good	A manufactured good refers to goods that have been processed in any way.
Exporting	Selling products to another country is called exporting.
Firm	An organization that employs resources to produce a good or service for profit and owns and operates one or more plants is referred to as a firm.
Investment	Investment refers to spending for the production and accumulation of capital and additions to inventories. In a financial sense, buying an asset with the expectation of making a return.
Industry	A group of firms that produce identical or similar products is an industry. It is also used specifically to refer to an area of economic production focused on manufacturing which involves large amounts of capital investment before any profit can be realized, also called "heavy industry".
Economic	Economic infrastructure refers to a country's communications, transportation, financial, and

infrastructure	distribution systems.
Gains from trade	The net increase in output that countries experience as a result of lowering import tariffs and otherwise liberalizing trade is referred to as gains from trade.
Growth strategy	A strategy based on investing in companies and sectors which are growing faster than their peers is a growth strategy. The benefits are usually in the form of capital gains rather than dividends.
Gain	In finance, gain is a profit or an increase in value of an investment such as a stock or bond. Gain is calculated by fair market value or the proceeds from the sale of the investment minus the sum of the purchase price and all costs associated with it.
Dynamic gains from trade	Dynamic gains from trade refers to the hoped-for benefits from trade that accrue over time, in addition to the conventional static gains from trade of trade theory.
Primary product	A good that has not been processed and is therefore in its natural state, specifically products of agriculture, forestry, fishing, and mining is referred to as primary product.
Terms of trade	Terms of trade refers to the rate at which units of one product can be exchanged for units of another product; the price of a good or service; the amount of one good or service that must be given up to obtain 1 unit of another good or service.
Exporter	A firm that sells its product in another country is an exporter.
Trend	Trend refers to the long-term movement of an economic variable, such as its average rate of increase or decrease over enough years to encompass several business cycles.
Welfare	Welfare refers to the economic well being of an individual, group, or economy. For individuals, it is conceptualized by a utility function. For groups, including countries and the world, it is a tricky philosophical concept, since individuals fare differently.
United Nations	An international organization created by multilateral treaty in 1945 to promote social and economic cooperation among nations and to protect human rights is the United Nations.
Distribution	Distribution in economics, the manner in which total output and income is distributed among individuals or factors.
Principal	In agency law, one under whose direction an agent acts and for whose benefit that agent acts is a principal.
Argument	The discussion by counsel for the respective parties of their contentions on the law and the facts of the case being tried in order to aid the jury in arriving at a correct and just conclusion is called argument.
Long run	In economic models, the long run time frame assumes no fixed factors of production. Firms can enter or leave the marketplace, and the cost (and availability) of land, labor, raw materials, and capital goods can be assumed to vary.
Downturn	A decline in a stock market or economic cycle is a downturn.
Infant industry	Infant industry refers to a young industry that may need temporary protection from competition from the established industries of other countries to develop an acquired comparative advantage.
Infant industry argument	The theoretical rationale for infant industry protection is referred to as the infant industry argument.
Argument for protection	Argument for protection refers to a reason given for restricting imports by tariffs and/or quotas.
Profit	Profit refers to the return to the resource entrepreneurial ability; total revenue minus

total cost.

Market	A market is, as defined in economics, a social arrangement that allows buyers and sellers to discover information and carry out a voluntary exchange of goods or services.
Inputs	The inputs used by a firm or an economy are the labor, raw materials, electricity and other resources it uses to produce its outputs.
Tariff	A tax imposed by a nation on an imported good is called a tariff.
Minimum wage	The lowest wage employers may legally pay for an hour of work is the minimum wage.
Labor	People's physical and mental talents and efforts that are used to help produce goods and services are called labor.
Wage	The payment for the service of a unit of labor, per unit time. In trade theory, it is the only payment to labor, usually unskilled labor. In empirical work, wage data may exclude other compenzation, which must be added to get the total cost of employment.
Preference	The act of a debtor in paying or securing one or more of his creditors in a manner more favorable to them than to other creditors or to the exclusion of such other creditors is a preference. In the absence of statute, a preference is perfectly good, but to be legal it must be bona fide, and not a mere subterfuge of the debtor to secure a future benefit to himself or to prevent the application of his property to his debts.
Economic cost	Economic cost refers to payments made or incomes forgone to obtain and retain the services of a resource.
Effective rate of protection	Effective rate of protection refers to a measure of the protection provided to an industry by the entire structure of tariffs, taking into account the effects of tariffs on inputs as well as on outputs.
Manufacturing	Production of goods primarily by the application of labor and capital to raw materials and other intermediate inputs, in contrast to agriculture, mining, forestry, fishing, and services a manufacturing.
Integration	Economic integration refers to reducing barriers among countries to transactions and to movements of goods, capital, and labor, including harmonization of laws, regulations, and standards. Integrated markets theoretically function as a unified market.
Quota	A government-imposed restriction on quantity, or sometimes on total value, used to restrict the import of something to a specific quantity is called a quota.
Licensing	Licensing is a form of strategic alliance which involves the sale of a right to use certain proprietary knowledge (so called intellectual property) in a defined way.
Peak	Peak refers to the point in the business cycle when an economic expansion reaches its highest point before turning down. Contrasts with trough.
Industrial policy	Industrial policy refers to government policy to influence which industries expand and, perhaps implicitly, which contract, via subsidies, tax breaks, and other aids for favored industries.
Distortion	Distortion refers to any departure from the ideal of perfect competition that interferes with economic agents maximizing social welfare when they maximize their own.
Per capita	Per capita refers to per person. Usually used to indicate the average per person of any given statistic, commonly income.
Labor force	In economics the labor force is the group of people who have a potential for being employed.
Capital stock	The total amount of physical capital that has been accumulated, usually in a country is

Go to **Cram101.com** for the Practice Tests for this Chapter.

	capital stock. Also refers to the total issued capital of a firm, including ordinary and preferred shares.
Stock	In financial terminology, stock is the capital raized by a corporation, through the issuance and sale of shares.
Innovation	Innovation refers to the first commercially successful introduction of a new product, the use of a new method of production, or the creation of a new form of business organization.
Continuity	A media scheduling strategy where a continuous pattern of advertising is used over the time span of the advertising campaign is continuity.
International trade	The export of goods and services from a country and the import of goods and services into a country is referred to as the international trade.
Supply	Supply is the aggregate amount of any material good that can be called into being at a certain price point; it comprises one half of the equation of supply and demand. In classical economic theory, a curve representing supply is one of the factors that produce price.
Factors of production	Economic resources: land, capital, labor, and entrepreneurial ability are called factors of production.
Technological change	The introduction of new methods of production or new products intended to increase the productivity of existing inputs or to raise marginal products is a technological change.
Slope	The slope of a line in the plane containing the x and y axes is generally represented by the letter m, and is defined as the change in the y coordinate divided by the corresponding change in the x coordinate, between two distinct points on the line.
Points	Loan origination fees that may be deductible as interest by a buyer of property. A seller of property who pays points reduces the selling price by the amount of the points paid for the buyer.
Trade triangle	In the trade-and-transformation-curve diagram, the right triangle formed by the world price line and the production and consumption points, the sides of which represent the quantities exported and imported is referred to as trade triangle.
World price	The price of a good on the 'world market,' meaning the price outside of any country's borders and therefore exclusive of any trade taxes or subsidies is the world price.
Economics	The social science dealing with the use of scarce resources to obtain the maximum satisfaction of society's virtually unlimited economic wants is an economics.
Fixed price	Fixed price is a phrase used to mean that no bargaining is allowed over the price of a good or, less commonly, a service.
Income elasticity	Normally the income elasticity of demand; that is, the elasticity of demand with respect to income. Measured as the percentage change in demand relative to the percentage change in income.
Elasticity	In economics, elasticity is the ratio of the incremental percentage change in one variable with respect to an incremental percentage change in another variable. Elasticity is usually expressed as a positive number (i.e., an absolute value) when the sign is already clear from context.
Holding	The holding is a court's determination of a matter of law based on the issue presented in the particular case. In other words: under this law, with these facts, this result.
Labor intensive	Describing an industry or sector of the economy that relies relatively heavily on inputs of labor, usually relative to capital but sometimes to human capital or skilled labor, compared to other industries or sectors is labor intensive.

Yield	The interest rate that equates a future value or an annuity to a given present value is a yield.
Factor price	Factor price refers to the price paid for the services of a unit of a primary factor of production per unit time. Includes the wage or salary of labor and the rental prices of land and capital, and normal profits for the entrepreneur.
Expense	In accounting, an expense represents an event in which an asset is used up or a liability is incurred. In terms of the accounting equation, expenses reduce owners' equity.
Endowment	Endowment refers to the amount of something that a person or country simply has, rather than their having somehow to acquire it.
Technological progress	Technological progress causes the production possibilities frontier to shift out. More output is produced from the same inputs.
Factor intensity	Factor intensity refers to the relative importance of one factor versus others in production in an industry, usually compared across industries.
Large country	Large country refers to a country that is large enough for its international transactions to affect economic variables abroad, usually for its trade to matter for world prices.
Standard of living	Standard of living refers to the level of consumption that people enjoy, on the average, and is measured by average income per person.
Price line	A straight line representing the combinations of variables, usually two goods that cost the same at some given prices. The slope of a price line measures relative prices, and changes in prices.
Consumption possibilities	The alternative combinations of goods and services that a country could consume in a given time period are consumption possibilities.
Dutch disease	Dutch disease refers to the adverse effect on a country's other industries that occurs when one industry substantially expands its exports, causing a real appreciation of the country's currency.
Bid	A bid price is a price offered by a buyer when he/she buys a good. In the context of stock trading on a stock exchange, the bid price is the highest price a buyer of a stock is willing to pay for a share of that given stock.
Trust	An arrangement in which shareholders of independent firms agree to give up their stock in exchange for trust certificates that entitle them to a share of the trust's common profits.
Journal	Book of original entry, in which transactions are recorded in a general ledger system, is referred to as a journal.
Aid	Assistance provided by countries and by international institutions such as the World Bank to developing countries in the form of monetary grants, loans at low interest rates, in kind, or a combination of these is called aid. Aid can also refer to assistance of any type rendered to benefit some group or individual.
Immigration	Immigration refers to the migration of people into a country.
Interdependence	The extent to which departments depend on each other for resources or materials to accomplish their tasks is referred to as interdependence.
Technology	The body of knowledge and techniques that can be used to combine economic resources to produce goods and services is called technology.
Host country	The country in which the parent-country organization seeks to locate or has already located a facility is a host country.

Gastarbeiter	Gastarbeiter is a German word that literally means guest worker.
Guest worker	Guest worker refers to a foreign worker who is permitted to enter a country temporarily in order to take a job for which there is shortage of domestic labor.
Brain drain	Brain drain refers to the migration of skilled workers out of a country. First applied to the migration of British-trained scientists, physicians, and university teachers in the early 1960's, mostly to the United States.
Contribution	In business organization law, the cash or property contributed to a business by its owners is referred to as contribution.
Margin	A deposit by a buyer in stocks with a seller or a stockbroker, as security to cover fluctuations in the market in reference to stocks that the buyer has purchased but for which he has not paid is a margin. Commodities are also traded on margin.
Financial capital	Common stock, preferred stock, bonds, and retained earnings are financial capital. Financial capital appears on the corporate balance sheet under long-term liabilities and equity.
Exchange	The trade of things of value between buyer and seller so that each is better off after the trade is called the exchange.
Creditor	A person to whom a debt or legal obligation is owed, and who has the right to enforce payment of that debt or obligation is referred to as creditor.
Foreign corporation	Foreign corporation refers to a corporation incorporated in one state doing business in another state. A corporation doing business in a jurisdiction in which it was not formed.
Corporation	A legal entity chartered by a state or the Federal government that is distinct and separate from the individuals who own it is a corporation. This separation gives the corporation unique powers which other legal entities lack.
Enterprise	Enterprise refers to another name for a business organization. Other similar terms are business firm, sometimes simply business, sometimes simply firm, as well as company, and entity.
Marketing	Promoting and selling products or services to customers, or prospective customers, is referred to as marketing.
Interest	In finance and economics, interest is the price paid by a borrower for the use of a lender's money. In other words, interest is the amount of paid to "rent" money for a period of time.
Ford	Ford is an American company that manufactures and sells automobiles worldwide. Ford introduced methods for large-scale manufacturing of cars, and large-scale management of an industrial workforce, especially elaborately engineered manufacturing sequences typified by the moving assembly lines.
Parent corporation	Parent corporation refers to a corporation that owns a controlling interest of another corporation, called a subsidiary corporation.
Shares	Shares refer to an equity security, representing a shareholder's ownership of a corporation. Shares are one of a finite number of equal portions in the capital of a company, entitling the owner to a proportion of distributed, non-reinvested profits known as dividends and to a portion of the value of the company in case of liquidation.
Financial market	In economics, a financial market is a mechanism which allows people to trade money for securities or commodities such as gold or other precious metals. In general, any commodity market might be considered to be a financial market, if the usual purpose of traders is not the immediate consumption of the commodity, but rather as a means of delaying or accelerating consumption over time.

Go to **Cram101.com** for the Practice Tests for this Chapter.

Affiliates	Local television stations that are associated with a major network are called affiliates. Affiliates agree to preempt time during specified hours for programming provided by the network and carry the advertising contained in the program.
Wholesale	According to the United Nations Statistics Division Wholesale is the resale of new and used goods to retailers, to industrial, commercial, institutional or professional users, or to other wholesalers, or involves acting as an agent or broker in buying merchandise for, or selling merchandise, to such persons or companies.
Commerce	Commerce is the exchange of something of value between two entities. It is the central mechanism from which capitalism is derived.
Competitor	Other organizations in the same industry or type of business that provide a good or service to the same set of customers is referred to as a competitor.
Economic theory	Economic theory refers to a statement of a cause-effect relationship; when accepted by all economists, an economic principle.
Operation	A standardized method or technique that is performed repetitively, often on different materials resulting in different finished goods is called an operation.
Increasing returns	An increase in a firm's output by a larger percentage than the percentage increase in its inputs is increasing returns.
Returns to scale	Returns to scale refers to a technical property of production that predicts what happens to output if the quantity of all input factors is increased by some amount of scale.
Trade flow	The quantity or value of a country's bilateral trade with another country is called trade flow.
Marginal revenue	Marginal revenue refers to the change in total revenue obtained by selling one additional unit.
Marginal cost	Marginal cost refers to the increase in cost that accompanies a unit increase in output; the partial derivative of the cost function with respect to output.
Revenue	Revenue is a U.S. business term for the amount of money that a company receives from its activities, mostly from sales of products and/or services to customers.
Diminishing marginal product	The property whereby the marginal product of an input declines as the quantity of the input increases is a diminishing marginal product.
Marginal product	In a production function, the marginal product of a factor is the increase in output due to a unit increase in the input of the factor; that is, the partial derivative of the production function with respect to the factor.
Marginal product of labor	Marginal product of labor refers to the increase in the amount of output from an additional unit of labor.
Labor market	Any arrangement that brings buyers and sellers of labor services together to agree on conditions of work and pay is called a labor market.
Diminishing returns	The fall in the marginal product of a factor or factors that eventually occurs as input of that factor rises, holding the input of at least one other factor fixed, according to the Law of Diminishing Returns.
Value of the marginal product	The marginal product of an input times the price of the output is a value of the marginal product.

Go to **Cram101.com** for the Practice Tests for this Chapter.

Value marginal product	Value marginal product is defined as the change in total revenue divided by the change in total output. Depending on whether marginal revenue declines as sales increase, this may or may not equal product price.
Remainder	A remainder in property law is a future interest created in a transferee that is capable of becoming possessory upon the natural termination of a prior estate created by the same instrument.
Supply of labor	Supply of labor refers to the relationship between the quantity of labor supplied by employees and the real wage rate when all other influences on work plans remain the same.
Domestic	From or in one's own country. A domestic producer is one that produces inside the home country. A domestic price is the price inside the home country. Opposite of 'foreign' or 'world.'.
Domestic output	Domestic output refers to gross domestic product; the total output of final goods and services produced in the economy.
Emigration	Emigration is the act and the phenomenon of leaving one's native country to settle abroad. It is the same as immigration but from the perspective of the country of origin.
Full employment	Full employment refers to the unemployment rate at which there is no cyclical unemployment of the labor force; equal to between 4 and 5 percent in the United States because some frictional and structural unemployment is unavoidable.
Escalation	Regarding the structure of tariffs. In the context of a trade war, escalation refers to the increase in tariffs that occurs as countries retaliate again and again.
Trade pattern	What goods a country trades, with whom, and in what direction. Explaining the trade pattern is one of the major purposes of trade theory, especially which goods a country will export and which it will import.

Brief	Brief refers to a statement of a party's case or legal arguments, usually prepared by an attorney. Also used to make legal arguments before appellate courts.
Balance of payments	Balance of payments refers to a list, or accounting, of all of a country's international transactions for a given time period, usually one year.
Balance	In banking and accountancy, the outstanding balance is the amount of money owned, (or due), that remains in a deposit account (or a loan account) at a given date, after all past remittances, payments and withdrawal have been accounted for. It can be positive (then, in the balance sheet of a firm, it is an asset) or negative (a liability).
Public interest	The universal label that political actors wrap around the policies and programs that they advocate is referred to as public interest.
Trade surplus	A positive balance of trade is known as a trade surplus and consists of exporting more (in financial capital terms) than one imports.
Interest	In finance and economics, interest is the price paid by a borrower for the use of a lender's money. In other words, interest is the amount of paid to "rent" money for a period of time.
Deficit	The deficit is the amount by which expenditure exceed revenue.
Balance of trade	Balance of trade refers to the sum of the money gained by a given economy by selling exports, minus the cost of buying imports. They form part of the balance of payments, which also includes other transactions such as the international investment position.
Trade deficit	The amount by which imports exceed exports of goods and services is referred to as trade deficit.
Exchange rate	Exchange rate refers to the price at which one country's currency trades for another, typically on the exchange market.
Exchange	The trade of things of value between buyer and seller so that each is better off after the trade is called the exchange.
Euro	The common currency of a subset of the countries of the EU, adopted January 1, 1999 is called euro.
Foreign exchange	In finance, foreign exchange means currencies, such as U.S. Dollars and Euros. These are traded on foreign exchange markets.
Exchange market	Exchange market refers to the market on which national currencies are bought and sold.
Market	A market is, as defined in economics, a social arrangement that allows buyers and sellers to discover information and carry out a voluntary exchange of goods or services.
Foreign exchange market	A market for converting the currency of one country into that of another country is called foreign exchange market. It is by far the largest market in the world, in terms of cash value traded, and includes trading between large banks, central banks, currency speculators, multinational corporations, governments, and other financial markets and institutions.
Leadership	Management merely consists of leadership applied to business situations; or in other words: management forms a sub-set of the broader process of leadership.
Trade balance	Balance of trade in terms of exports versus imports is called trade balance.
Central Bank	Central bank refers to the institution in a country that is normally responsible for managing the supply of the country's money and the value of its currency on the foreign exchange market.
Derivative	A derivative is a generic term for specific types of investments from which payoffs over time are derived from the performance of assets (such as commodities, shares or bonds), interest

rates, exchange rates, or indices (such as a stock market index, consumer price index (CPI) or an index of weather conditions).

Merger	Merger refers to the combination of two firms into a single firm.
Domestic	From or in one's own country. A domestic producer is one that produces inside the home country. A domestic price is the price inside the home country. Opposite of 'foreign' or 'world.'.
Purchasing power	The amount of goods that money will buy, usually measured by the CPI is referred to as purchasing power.
Purchasing	Purchasing refers to the function in a firm that searches for quality material resources, finds the best suppliers, and negotiates the best price for goods and services.
Purchasing power parity	purchasing power parity is a theory based on the law of one price which says that the long-run equilibrium exchange rate of two currencies is the rate that equalizes the currencies' purchasing power.
Interest rate	The rate of return on bonds, loans, or deposits. When one speaks of 'the' interest rate, it is usually in a model where there is only one.
Federal Reserve	The Federal Reserve System was created via the Federal Reserve Act of December 23rd, 1913. All national banks were required to join the system and other banks could join. The Reserve Banks opened for business on November 16th, 1914. Federal Reserve Notes were created as part of the legislation, to provide an elastic supply of currency.
International Monetary Fund	The International Monetary Fund is the international organization entrusted with overseeing the global financial system by monitoring exchange rates and balance of payments, as well as offering technical and financial assistance when asked.
Fund	Independent accounting entity with a self-balancing set of accounts segregated for the purposes of carrying on specific activities is referred to as a fund.
Future value	Future value measures what money is worth at a specified time in the future assuming a certain interest rate. This is used in time value of money calculations.
Investment	Investment refers to spending for the production and accumulation of capital and additions to inventories. In a financial sense, buying an asset with the expectation of making a return.
Contract	A contract is a "promise" or an "agreement" that is enforced or recognized by the law. In the civil law, a contract is considered to be part of the general law of obligations.
Firm	An organization that employs resources to produce a good or service for profit and owns and operates one or more plants is referred to as a firm.
Financial assets	Financial assets refer to monetary claims or obligations by one party against another party. Examples are bonds, mortgages, bank loans, and equities.
Asset	An item of property, such as land, capital, money, a share in ownership, or a claim on others for future payment, such as a bond or a bank deposit is an asset.
Foreign subsidiary	A company owned in a foreign country by another company is referred to as foreign subsidiary.
Subsidiary	A company that is controlled by another company or corporation is a subsidiary.
Stock	In financial terminology, stock is the capital raized by a corporation, through the issuance and sale of shares.
Bond	Bond refers to a debt instrument, issued by a borrower and promising a specified stream of payments to the purchaser, usually regular interest payments plus a final repayment of

Go to **Cram101.com** for the Practice Tests for this Chapter.

principal.

Volatility	Volatility refers to the extent to which an economic variable, such as a price or an exchange rate, moves up and down over time.
International monetary system	International monetary system is a network of international commercial and government institutions that determine currency exchange rates.
Fixed exchange rate	A fixed exchange rate, sometimes is a type of exchange rate regime wherein a currency's value is matched to the value of another single currency or to a basket of other currencies, or to another measure of value, such as gold.
Gold standard	The gold standard is a monetary system in which the standard economic unit of account is a fixed weight of gold.
Creditworthiness	Creditworthiness indicates whether a borrower has in the past made loan payments when due.
Assessment	Collecting information and providing feedback to employees about their behavior, communication style, or skills is an assessment.
International macroeconomics	Same as international finance, but with more emphasis on the international determination of macroeconomic variables such as national income and the price level are called international macroeconomics.
National income	National income refers to the income generated by a country's production, and therefore the total income of its factors of production.
Macroeconomics	Macroeconomics refers to the part of economics concerned with the economy as a whole; with such major aggregates as the household, business, and government sectors; and with measures of the total economy.
Economics	The social science dealing with the use of scarce resources to obtain the maximum satisfaction of society's virtually unlimited economic wants is an economics.
Economy	The income, expenditures, and resources that affect the cost of running a business and household are called an economy.
Floating exchange rate	A system under which the exchange rate for converting one currency into another is continuously adjusted depending on the laws of supply and demand is referred to as a floating exchange rate.
Monetary policy	The use of the money supply and/or the interest rate to influence the level of economic activity and other policy objectives including the balance of payments or the exchange rate is called monetary policy.
Policy	Similar to a script in that a policy can be a less than completely rational decision-making method. Involves the use of a pre-existing set of decision steps for any problem that presents itself.
Inflation	An increase in the overall price level of an economy, usually as measured by the CPI or by the implicit price deflator is called inflation.

Firm	An organization that employs resources to produce a good or service for profit and owns and operates one or more plants is referred to as a firm.
Developed country	A developed country is one that enjoys a relatively high standard of living derived through an industrialized, diversified economy. Countries with a very high Human Development Index are generally considered developed countries.
Balance	In banking and accountancy, the outstanding balance is the amount of money owned, (or due), that remains in a deposit account (or a loan account) at a given date, after all past remittances, payments and withdrawal have been accounted for. It can be positive (then, in the balance sheet of a firm, it is an asset) or negative (a liability).
Balance of payments	Balance of payments refers to a list, or accounting, of all of a country's international transactions for a given time period, usually one year.
Bookkeeping	The recording of business transactions is called bookkeeping.
Accounting	A system that collects and processes financial information about an organization and reports that information to decision makers is referred to as accounting.
Balance sheet	A statement of the assets, liabilities, and net worth of a firm or individual at some given time often at the end of its "fiscal year," is referred to as a balance sheet.
Credit	Credit refers to a recording as positive in the balance of payments, any transaction that gives rise to a payment into the country, such as an export, the sale of an asset, or borrowing from abroad.
Debit	Debit refers to recording as negative in the balance of payments, any transaction that gives rise to a payment out of the country, such as an import, the purchase of an asset, or lending to foreigners. Opposite of credit.
Foreign exchange	In finance, foreign exchange means currencies, such as U.S. Dollars and Euros. These are traded on foreign exchange markets.
Exchange	The trade of things of value between buyer and seller so that each is better off after the trade is called the exchange.
Capital account	The capital account is one of two primary components of the balance of payments. It tracks the movement of funds for investments and loans into and out of a country.
Capital	Capital generally refers to financial wealth, especially that used to start or maintain a business. In classical economics, capital is one of four factors of production, the others being land and labor and entrepreneurship.
Export	In economics, an export is any good or commodity, shipped or otherwise transported out of a country, province, town to another part of the world in a legitimate fashion, typically for use in trade or sale.
Buyer	A buyer refers to a role in the buying center with formal authority and responsibility to select the supplier and negotiate the terms of the contract.
Deficit	The deficit is the amount by which expenditure exceed revenue.
Trade deficit	The amount by which imports exceed exports of goods and services is referred to as trade deficit.
Economics	The social science dealing with the use of scarce resources to obtain the maximum satisfaction of society's virtually unlimited economic wants is an economics.
Argument	The discussion by counsel for the respective parties of their contentions on the law and the facts of the case being tried in order to aid the jury in arriving at a correct and just conclusion is called argument.

Go to **Cram101.com** for the Practice Tests for this Chapter.

Balance of trade	Balance of trade refers to the sum of the money gained by a given economy by selling exports, minus the cost of buying imports. They form part of the balance of payments, which also includes other transactions such as the international investment position.
Policy	Similar to a script in that a policy can be a less than completely rational decision-making method. Involves the use of a pre-existing set of decision steps for any problem that presents itself.
Labor	People's physical and mental talents and efforts that are used to help produce goods and services are called labor.
Evaluation	The consumer's appraisal of the product or brand on important attributes is called evaluation.
Bilateral trade	Bilateral trade refers to the trade between two countries; that is, the value or quantity of one country's exports to the other, or the sum of exports and imports between them.
Unilateral transfer	A transfer payment is a unilateral transfer. An item in the current account of a country's accounting books that corresponds to gifts from foreigners, or pension payments to foreign residents who once worked in the host country
Current account	Current account refers to a country's international transactions arising from current flows, as opposed to changes in stocks which are part of the capital account. Includes trade in goods and services plus inflows and outflows of transfers. A current account is a deposit account in the UK and countries with a UK banking heritage.
Investment	Investment refers to spending for the production and accumulation of capital and additions to inventories. In a financial sense, buying an asset with the expectation of making a return.
Service	Service refers to a "non tangible product" that is not embodied in a physical good and that typically effects some change in another product, person, or institution. Contrasts with good.
Commodity	Could refer to any good, but in trade a commodity is usually a raw material or primary product that enters into international trade, such as metals or basic agricultural products.
Tangible	Having a physical existence is referred to as the tangible. Personal property other than real estate, such as cars, boats, stocks, or other assets.
Factors of production	Economic resources: land, capital, labor, and entrepreneurial ability are called factors of production.
Production	The creation of finished goods and services using the factors of production: land, labor, capital, entrepreneurship, and knowledge.
Insurance	Insurance refers to a system by which individuals can reduce their exposure to risk of large losses by spreading the risks among a large number of persons.
Royalties	Remuneration paid to the owners of technology, patents, or trade names for the use of same name are called royalties.
Premium	Premium refers to the fee charged by an insurance company for an insurance policy. The rate of losses must be relatively predictable: In order to set the premium (prices) insurers must be able to estimate them accurately.
Return on investment	Return on investment refers to the return a businessperson gets on the money he and other owners invest in the firm; for example, a business that earned $100 on a $1,000 investment would have a ROI of 10 percent: 100 divided by 1000.
Physical capital	Physical capital refers to the same as 'capital,' without any adjective, in the sense of plant and equipment. The word 'physical' is used only to distinguish it from human capital.

Go to **Cram101.com** for the Practice Tests for this Chapter.

Financial market	In economics, a financial market is a mechanism which allows people to trade money for securities or commodities such as gold or other precious metals. In general, any commodity market might be considered to be a financial market, if the usual purpose of traders is not the immediate consumption of the commodity, but rather as a means of delaying or accelerating consumption over time.
Dividend	Amount of corporate profits paid out for each share of stock is referred to as dividend.
Interest	In finance and economics, interest is the price paid by a borrower for the use of a lender's money. In other words, interest is the amount of paid to "rent" money for a period of time.
Market	A market is, as defined in economics, a social arrangement that allows buyers and sellers to discover information and carry out a voluntary exchange of goods or services.
Interest payment	The payment to holders of bonds payable, calculated by multiplying the stated rate on the face of the bond by the par, or face, value of the bond. If bonds are issued at a discount or premium, the interest payment does not equal the interest expense.
Government debt	The total of government obligations in the form of bonds and shorter-term borrowings. Government debt held by the public excludes bonds held by quasi-governmental agencies such as the central bank.
Pension	A pension is a steady income given to a person (usually after retirement). Pensions are typically payments made in the form of a guaranteed annuity to a retired or disabled employee.
Holding	The holding is a court's determination of a matter of law based on the issue presented in the particular case. In other words: under this law, with these facts, this result.
Aid	Assistance provided by countries and by international institutions such as the World Bank to developing countries in the form of monetary grants, loans at low interest rates, in kind, or a combination of these is called aid. Aid can also refer to assistance of any type rendered to benefit some group or individual.
Current Account deficit	Current account deficit occurs when a country imports more goods and services than it exports.
Trade surplus	A positive balance of trade is known as a trade surplus and consists of exporting more (in financial capital terms) than one imports.
Above the line	Above the line is an advertising technique using mass media to promote brands. This type of communication is conventional in nature and is considered impersonal to customers.
Below the line	Below the line is an advertising technique. It uses less conventional methods than the usual specific channels of advertising to promote products, services, etc. than ATL (Above the line) strategy.
Net borrower	A country that is borrowing more from the rest of the world than it is lending to it is called a net borrower.
Lender	Suppliers and financial institutions that lend money to companies is referred to as a lender.
Net lender	A country that is lending more to the rest of the world than it is borrowing from it is called net lender.
Current account surplus	A current account surplus is when a country exports more goods and services than it imports.
Financial assets	Financial assets refer to monetary claims or obligations by one party against another party. Examples are bonds, mortgages, bank loans, and equities.
Asset	An item of property, such as land, capital, money, a share in ownership, or a claim on others

Go to **Cram101.com** for the Practice Tests for this Chapter.
And, **NEVER** highlight a book again!

	for future payment, such as a bond or a bank deposit is an asset.
Analyst	Analyst refers to a person or tool with a primary function of information analysis, generally with a more limited, practical and short term set of goals than a researcher.
Debt security	Type of security acquired by loaning assets is called a debt security.
Security	Security refers to a claim on the borrower future income that is sold by the borrower to the lender. A security is a type of transferable interest representing financial value.
Equity	Equity is the name given to the set of legal principles, in countries following the English common law tradition, which supplement strict rules of law where their application would operate harshly, so as to achieve what is sometimes referred to as "natural justice."
Stock	In financial terminology, stock is the capital raized by a corporation, through the issuance and sale of shares.
Finance paper	Finance paper refers to a form of commercial paper that is sold directly to the lender by the finance company. It is also referred to as direct paper.
Liability	A liability is a present obligation of the enterprise arizing from past events, the settlement of which is expected to result in an outflow from the enterprise of resources embodying economic benefits.
Certificates of deposit	Certificates of deposit refer to a certificate offered by banks, savings and loans, and other financial institutions for the deposit of funds at a given interest rate over a specified time period.
Exporter	A firm that sells its product in another country is an exporter.
Consideration	Consideration in contract law, a basic requirement for an enforceable agreement under traditional contract principles, defined in this text as legal value, bargained for and given in exchange for an act or promise. In corporation law, cash or property contributed to a corporation in exchange for shares, or a promise to contribute such cash or property.
Creditor	A person to whom a debt or legal obligation is owed, and who has the right to enforce payment of that debt or obligation is referred to as creditor.
Gross domestic product	Gross domestic product refers to the total value of new goods and services produced in a given year within the borders of a country, regardless of by whom.
Government spending	Government spending refers to spending by all levels of government on goods and services.
National saving	The sum of private saving and government saving is national saving. It is the total amount of saving taking place in an economy.
National income	National income refers to the income generated by a country's production, and therefore the total income of its factors of production.
Net exports	Net exports refers to exports minus imports; same as the balance of trade. They are the sum of the money gained by a given economy by selling exports, minus the cost of buying imports. They form part of the balance of payments, which also includes other transactions such as the international investment position.
Consumption	In Keynesian economics consumption refers to personal consumption expenditure, i.e., the purchase of currently produced goods and services out of income, out of savings (net worth), or from borrowed funds. It refers to that part of disposable income that does not go to saving.
Domestic	From or in one's own country. A domestic producer is one that produces inside the home country. A domestic price is the price inside the home country. Opposite of 'foreign' or

'world.'.

National income accounting	The techniques used to measure the overall production of the economy and other related variables for the nation as a whole are called national income accounting.
Capital account surplus	Capital account surplus refers to the amount by which the purchase of domestic financial assets by foreigners exceeds the purchase of foreign financial assets by domestic consumers.
Developing country	Developing country refers to a country whose per capita income is low by world standards. Same as LDC. As usually used, it does not necessarily connote that the country's income is rising.
Debtor nation	Debtor nation refers to a country whose assets owned abroad are worth less than the assets within the country that are owned by foreigners. Contrasts with creditor nation.
Commerce	Commerce is the exchange of something of value between two entities. It is the central mechanism from which capitalism is derived.
Direct investment	Direct investment refers to a domestic firm actually investing in and owning a foreign subsidiary or division.
Foreign direct investment	Foreign direct investment refers to the buying of permanent property and businesses in foreign nations.
Creditor nation	Creditor nation refers to a country whose assets owned abroad are worth more than the assets within the country that are owned by foreigners.
Default risk	The chance that the issuer of a debt instrument will be unable to make interest payments or pay off the face value when the instrument matures is called default risk.
Debt crisis	Debt crisis refers to a situation in which a country, usually an LDC, finds itself unable to service its debts.
Default	In finance, default occurs when a debtor has not met its legal obligations according to the debt contract, e.g. it has not made a scheduled payment, or violated a covenant (condition) of the debt contract.
Budget deficit	A budget deficit occurs when an entity (often a government) spends more money than it takes
Federal budget	The annual statement of the expenditures and tax revenues of the government of the United States together with the laws and regulations that approve and support those expenditures and taxes is the federal budget.
Budget	Budget refers to an account, usually for a year, of the planned expenditures and the expected receipts of an entity. For a government, the receipts are tax revenues.
Economy	The income, expenditures, and resources that affect the cost of running a business and household are called an economy.
Fund	Independent accounting entity with a self-balancing set of accounts segregated for the purposes of carrying on specific activities is referred to as a fund.
Federal government	Federal government refers to the government of the United States, as distinct from the state and local governments.
Interest rate	The rate of return on bonds, loans, or deposits. When one speaks of 'the' interest rate, it is usually in a model where there is only one.
Standard of living	Standard of living refers to the level of consumption that people enjoy, on the average, and is measured by average income per person.
Incentive	An incentive is any factor (financial or non-financial) that provides a motive for a particular course of action, or counts as a reason for preferring one choice to the

alternatives.

Depreciate	A nation's currency is said to depreciate when exchange rates change so that a unit of its currency can buy fewer units of foreign currency.
Revenue	Revenue is a U.S. business term for the amount of money that a company receives from its activities, mostly from sales of products and/or services to customers.
Domestic output	Domestic output refers to gross domestic product; the total output of final goods and services produced in the economy.
Labor union	A group of workers organized to advance the interests of the group is called a labor union.
Union	A worker association that bargains with employers over wages and working conditions is called a union.
Trade balance	Balance of trade in terms of exports versus imports is called trade balance.
Industry	A group of firms that produce identical or similar products is an industry. It is also used specifically to refer to an area of economic production focused on manufacturing which involves large amounts of capital investment before any profit can be realized, also called "heavy industry".
Capital Outflow	Capital outflow is an economic term describing capital flowing out of (or leaving) a particular economy. Outflowing capital can be caused by any number of economic or political reasons but can often originate from instability in either sphere.
Bond	Bond refers to a debt instrument, issued by a borrower and promising a specified stream of payments to the purchaser, usually regular interest payments plus a final repayment of principal.
Government bond	A government bond is a bond issued by a national government denominated in the country's own currency. Bonds issued by national governments in foreign currencies are normally referred to as sovereign bonds.
Capital inflow	Capital inflow refers to a net flow of capital, real and/or financial, into a country, in the form of increased purchases of domestic assets by foreigners and/or reduced holdings of foreign assets by domestic residents.
Customs	Customs is an authority or agency in a country responsible for collecting customs duties and for controlling the flow of people, animals and goods (including personal effects and hazardous items) in and out of the country.
Financial transaction	A financial transaction involves a change in the status of the finances of two or more businesses or individuals.
Official settlements account	A record of the change in a country's official reserves is an official settlements account. Also referred to as reserve transaction account.
Reserve asset	Any asset that is used as international reserves, including a national currency, precious metal such as gold is referred to as a reserve asset.
Accumulation	The acquisition of an increasing quantity of something. The accumulation of factors, especially capital, is a primary mechanism for economic growth.
Special drawing right	Special drawing right refers to what was originally intended within the IMF as a sort of international money for use among central banks pegging their exchange rates. The special drawing right is a transferable right to acquire another country's currency.
Supply and demand	The partial equilibrium supply and demand economic model originally developed by Alfred Marshall attempts to describe, explain, and predict changes in the price and quantity of

goods sold in competitive markets.

Supply	Supply is the aggregate amount of any material good that can be called into being at a certain price point; it comprises one half of the equation of supply and demand. In classical economic theory, a curve representing supply is one of the factors that produce price.
Supply curve	Supply curve refers to the graph of quantity supplied as a function of price, normally upward sloping, straight or curved, and drawn with quantity on the horizontal axis and price on the vertical axis.
Exchange rate	Exchange rate refers to the price at which one country's currency trades for another, typically on the exchange market.
Flexible exchange rate	Exchange rates with a fixed parity against one or more currencies with frequent revaluation's is referred to as a flexible exchange rate.
Fixed exchange rate	A fixed exchange rate, sometimes is a type of exchange rate regime wherein a currency's value is matched to the value of another single currency or to a basket of other currencies, or to another measure of value, such as gold.
Central Bank	Central bank refers to the institution in a country that is normally responsible for managing the supply of the country's money and the value of its currency on the foreign exchange market.
Equilibrium quantity	Equilibrium quantity refers to the quantity demanded and supplied at the equilibrium price in a competitive market; the profit-maximizing output of a firm.
Appreciation	Appreciation refers to a rise in the value of a country's currency on the exchange market, relative either to a particular other currency or to a weighted average of other currencies. The currency is said to appreciate. Opposite of 'depreciation.' Appreciation can also refer to the increase in value of any asset.
Excess supply	Supply minus demand. Thus a country's supply of exports of a homogeneous good is its excess supply of that good.
International trade	The export of goods and services from a country and the import of goods and services into a country is referred to as the international trade.
Disequilibrium	Inequality or imbalance of supply and demand is referred to as disequilibrium.
Demand curve	Demand curve refers to the graph of quantity demanded as a function of price, normally downward sloping, straight or curved, and drawn with quantity on the horizontal axis and price on the vertical axis.
Quota	A government-imposed restriction on quantity, or sometimes on total value, used to restrict the import of something to a specific quantity is called a quota.
Floating exchange rate	A system under which the exchange rate for converting one currency into another is continuously adjusted depending on the laws of supply and demand is referred to as a floating exchange rate.
Devaluation	Lowering the value of a nation's currency relative to other currencies is called devaluation.
Trade credit	Trade credit refers to an amount that is loaned to an exporter to be repaid when the exports are paid for by the foreign importer.
International Monetary Fund	The International Monetary Fund is the international organization entrusted with overseeing the global financial system by monitoring exchange rates and balance of payments, as well as offering technical and financial assistance when asked.
Federal Reserve	The Federal Reserve System was created via the Federal Reserve Act of December 23rd, 1913. All national banks were required to join the system and other banks could join. The Reserve

	Banks opened for business on November 16th, 1914. Federal Reserve Notes were created as part of the legislation, to provide an elastic supply of currency.
Forward exchange	When two parties agree to exchange currency and execute a deal at some specific date in the future, we have forward exchange.
Forward premium	The difference between a forward exchange rate and the spot exchange rate, expressed as an annualized percentage return on buying foreign currency spot and selling it forward is a forward premium.
Exchange market	Exchange market refers to the market on which national currencies are bought and sold.
Exercise price	Exercise price refers to the price at which the purchaser of an option has the right to buy or sell the underlying financial instrument. Also known as the strike price.
Black market	Black market refers to an illegal market, in which something is bought and sold outside of official government-sanctioned channels. Black markets tend to arise when a government tries to fix a price without providing an alternative allocation method
Forward rate	Forward rate refers to the forward exchange rate, this is the exchange rate on a forward market transaction.
Intervention	Intervention refers to an activity in which a government buys or sells its currency in the foreign exchange market in order to affect its currency's exchange rate.
Spot market	Spot market refers to a market in which commodities are bought and sold for cash and immediate delivery.
Call option	Call option refers to an option contract that provides the right to buy a security at a specified price within a certain time period.
Put option	An option contract that provides the right to sell a security at a specified price within a specified period of time is a put option.
Spot rate	Spot rate refers to the rate at which the currency is traded for immediate delivery. It is the existing cash price.
Arbitrage	An arbitrage is a combination of nearly simultaneous transactions designed to profit from an existing discrepancy among prices, exchange rates, and/or interest rates on different markets without assuming risk.
Discount	The difference between the face value of a bond and its selling price, when a bond is sold for less than its face value it's referred to as a discount.
Hedging	A technique for avoiding a risk by making a counteracting transaction is referred to as hedging.
Futures	Futures refer to contracts for the sale and future delivery of stocks or commodities, wherein either party may waive delivery, and receive or pay, as the case may be, the difference in market price at the time set for delivery.
Option	A contract that gives the purchaser the option to buy or sell the underlying financial instrument at a specified price, called the exercise price or strike price, within a specific period of time.
Swap	In finance a swap is a derivative, where two counterparties exchange one stream of cash flows against another stream. These streams are called the legs of the swap. The cash flows are calculated over a notional principal amount. Swaps are often used to hedge certain risks, for instance interest rate risk. Another use is speculation.

Exchange	The trade of things of value between buyer and seller so that each is better off after the trade is called the exchange.
Supply and demand	The partial equilibrium supply and demand economic model originally developed by Alfred Marshall attempts to describe, explain, and predict changes in the price and quantity of goods sold in competitive markets.
Supply	Supply is the aggregate amount of any material good that can be called into being at a certain price point; it comprises one half of the equation of supply and demand. In classical economic theory, a curve representing supply is one of the factors that produce price.
Foreign exchange	In finance, foreign exchange means currencies, such as U.S. Dollars and Euros. These are traded on foreign exchange markets.
Exporter	A firm that sells its product in another country is an exporter.
Exchange rate	Exchange rate refers to the price at which one country's currency trades for another, typically on the exchange market.
Bid	A bid price is a price offered by a buyer when he/she buys a good. In the context of stock trading on a stock exchange, the bid price is the highest price a buyer of a stock is willing to pay for a share of that given stock.
Market	A market is, as defined in economics, a social arrangement that allows buyers and sellers to discover information and carry out a voluntary exchange of goods or services.
Free market	A free market is a market where price is determined by the unregulated interchange of supply and demand rather than set by artificial means.
Spot market	Spot market refers to a market in which commodities are bought and sold for cash and immediate delivery.
Arbitrage	An arbitrage is a combination of nearly simultaneous transactions designed to profit from an existing discrepancy among prices, exchange rates, and/or interest rates on different markets without assuming risk.
Homogeneous	In the context of procurement/purchasing, homogeneous is used to describe goods that do not vary in their essential characteristic irrespective of the source of supply.
Euro	The common currency of a subset of the countries of the EU, adopted January 1, 1999 is called euro.
Domestic	From or in one's own country. A domestic producer is one that produces inside the home country. A domestic price is the price inside the home country. Opposite of 'foreign' or 'world.'.
Profit	Profit refers to the return to the resource entrepreneurial ability; total revenue minus total cost.
Transaction cost	A transaction cost is a cost incurred in making an economic exchange. For example, most people, when buying or selling a stock, must pay a commission to their broker; that commission is a transaction cost of doing the stock deal.
Numeraire	The unit in which prices are measured. This may be a currency, but in real models, such as most trade models, the numeraire is usually one of the goods, whose price is then set at one.
Cross rates	The exchange rate of two foreign currencies expressed in terms of a third currency, neither of which is the US Dollar are called cross rates.
Contract	A contract is a "promise" or an "agreement" that is enforced or recognized by the law. In the civil law, a contract is considered to be part of the general law of obligations.

Go to **Cram101.com** for the Practice Tests for this Chapter.

Option	A contract that gives the purchaser the option to buy or sell the underlying financial instrument at a specified price, called the exercise price or strike price, within a specific period of time.
Depreciate	A nation's currency is said to depreciate when exchange rates change so that a unit of its currency can buy fewer units of foreign currency.
Forward exchange	When two parties agree to exchange currency and execute a deal at some specific date in the future, we have forward exchange.
Exchange market	Exchange market refers to the market on which national currencies are bought and sold.
Forward market	A market for exchange of currencies in the future is the forward market. Participants in a forward market enter into a contract to exchange currencies, not today, but at a specified date in the future, typically 30, 60, or 90 days from now, and at a price that is agreed upon.
Forward premium	The difference between a forward exchange rate and the spot exchange rate, expressed as an annualized percentage return on buying foreign currency spot and selling it forward is a forward premium.
Premium	Premium refers to the fee charged by an insurance company for an insurance policy. The rate of losses must be relatively predictable: In order to set the premium (prices) insurers must be able to estimate them accurately.
Forward rate	Forward rate refers to the forward exchange rate, this is the exchange rate on a forward market transaction.
Spot rate	Spot rate refers to the rate at which the currency is traded for immediate delivery. It is the existing cash price.
Discount	The difference between the face value of a bond and its selling price, when a bond is sold for less than its face value it's referred to as a discount.
Commercial bank	A firm that engages in the business of banking is a commercial bank.
Swap	In finance a swap is a derivative, where two counterparties exchange one stream of cash flows against another stream. These streams are called the legs of the swap. The cash flows are calculated over a notional principal amount. Swaps are often used to hedge certain risks, for instance interest rate risk. Another use is speculation.
Citibank	In April of 2006, Citibank struck a deal with 7-Eleven to put its ATMs in over 5,500 convenience stores in the U.S. In the same month, it also announced it would sell all of its Buffalo and Rochester New York branches and accounts to M&T Bank.
Swap rate	Swap rate is the difference between the spot and forward exchange rates.
Points	Loan origination fees that may be deductible as interest by a buyer of property. A seller of property who pays points reduces the selling price by the amount of the points paid for the buyer.
Yield	The interest rate that equates a future value or an annuity to a given present value is a yield.
Spot transaction	The predominant type of exchange rate transaction, involving the immediate exchange of bank deposits denominated in different currencies is a spot transaction.
Shares	Shares refer to an equity security, representing a shareholder's ownership of a corporation. Shares are one of a finite number of equal portions in the capital of a company, entitling the owner to a proportion of distributed, non-reinvested profits known as dividends and to a portion of the value of the company in case of liquidation.

Go to **Cram101.com** for the Practice Tests for this Chapter.

Broker	In commerce, a broker is a party that mediates between a buyer and a seller. A broker who also acts as a seller or as a buyer becomes a principal party to the deal.
Firm	An organization that employs resources to produce a good or service for profit and owns and operates one or more plants is referred to as a firm.
Buyer	A buyer refers to a role in the buying center with formal authority and responsibility to select the supplier and negotiate the terms of the contract.
Matching	Matching refers to an accounting concept that establishes when expenses are recognized. Expenses are matched with the revenues they helped to generate and are recognized when those revenues are recognized.
Service	Service refers to a "non tangible product" that is not embodied in a physical good and that typically effects some change in another product, person, or institution. Contrasts with good.
Futures market	Futures market refers to a market for exchange in futures contracts. That is, participants contract to exchange currencies, not today, but at a specified calendar date in the future, and at a price that is agreed upon today.
Futures	Futures refer to contracts for the sale and future delivery of stocks or commodities, wherein either party may waive delivery, and receive or pay, as the case may be, the difference in market price at the time set for delivery.
Chicago Mercantile Exchange	The Chicago Mercantile Exchange is the largest futures exchange in the United States. It has four major product areas: short term interest rates, stock market indexes, foreign exchange, and commodities. It has the largest options and futures contracts open interest (number of contracts outstanding) of any futures exchange in the world, which indicates a very high liquidity. This is vital to the success of any stock or futures exchange.
Maturity date	The date on which the final payment on a bond is due from the bond issuer to the investor is a maturity date.
Maturity	Maturity refers to the final payment date of a loan or other financial instrument, after which point no further interest or principal need be paid.
Writ	Writ refers to a commandment of a court given for the purpose of compelling certain action from the defendant, and usually executed by a sheriff or other judicial officer.
International trade	The export of goods and services from a country and the import of goods and services into a country is referred to as the international trade.
Hedging	A technique for avoiding a risk by making a counteracting transaction is referred to as hedging.
Futures contract	In finance, a futures contract is a standardized contract, traded on a futures exchange, to buy or sell a certain underlying instrument at a certain date in the future, at a pre-set price. The
Financial institution	A financial institution acts as an agent that provides financial services for its clients. Financial institutions generally fall under financial regulation from a government authority.
Wholesale	According to the United Nations Statistics Division Wholesale is the resale of new and used goods to retailers, to industrial, commercial, institutional or professional users, or to other wholesalers, or involves acting as an agent or broker in buying merchandise for, or selling merchandise, to such persons or companies.
Liability	A liability is a present obligation of the enterprise arizing from past events, the settlement of which is expected to result in an outflow from the enterprise of resources embodying economic benefits.

Go to **Cram101.com** for the Practice Tests for this Chapter.

Asset	An item of property, such as land, capital, money, a share in ownership, or a claim on others for future payment, such as a bond or a bank deposit is an asset.
Fixed exchange rate	A fixed exchange rate, sometimes is a type of exchange rate regime wherein a currency's value is matched to the value of another single currency or to a basket of other currencies, or to another measure of value, such as gold.
European option	An option that can be exercized only at the expiration date of the contract is referred to as european option.
American option	A stock option that can be exercized at any time up to the expiration date of the contract is referred to as American option.
Call option	Call option refers to an option contract that provides the right to buy a security at a specified price within a certain time period.
Put option	An option contract that provides the right to sell a security at a specified price within a specified period of time is a put option.
Exercise price	Exercise price refers to the price at which the purchaser of an option has the right to buy or sell the underlying financial instrument. Also known as the strike price.
Appreciation	Appreciation refers to a rise in the value of a country's currency on the exchange market, relative either to a particular other currency or to a weighted average of other currencies. The currency is said to appreciate. Opposite of 'depreciation.' Appreciation can also refer to the increase in value of any asset.
Hedge	Hedge refers to a process of offsetting risk. In the foreign exchange market, hedgers use the forward market to cover a transaction or open position and thereby reduce exchange risk. The term applies most commonly to trade.
Insurance	Insurance refers to a system by which individuals can reduce their exposure to risk of large losses by spreading the risks among a large number of persons.
Stock exchange	A stock exchange is a corporation or mutual organization which provides facilities for stock brokers and traders, to trade company stocks and other securities.
Stock	In financial terminology, stock is the capital raized by a corporation, through the issuance and sale of shares.
Central Bank	Central bank refers to the institution in a country that is normally responsible for managing the supply of the country's money and the value of its currency on the foreign exchange market.
Intervention	Intervention refers to an activity in which a government buys or sells its currency in the foreign exchange market in order to affect its currency's exchange rate.
Federal Reserve	The Federal Reserve System was created via the Federal Reserve Act of December 23rd, 1913. All national banks were required to join the system and other banks could join. The Reserve Banks opened for business on November 16th, 1914. Federal Reserve Notes were created as part of the legislation, to provide an elastic supply of currency.
Foreign exchange market	A market for converting the currency of one country into that of another country is called foreign exchange market. It is by far the largest market in the world, in terms of cash value traded, and includes trading between large banks, central banks, currency speculators, multinational corporations, governments, and other financial markets and institutions.
Financial assets	Financial assets refer to monetary claims or obligations by one party against another party. Examples are bonds, mortgages, bank loans, and equities.
Supply curve	Supply curve refers to the graph of quantity supplied as a function of price, normally upward

sloping, straight or curved, and drawn with quantity on the horizontal axis and price on the vertical axis.

Depreciation	Depreciation is an accounting and finance term for the method of attributing the cost of an asset across the useful life of the asset. Depreciation is a reduction in the value of a currency in floating exchange rate.
Bank of England	The Bank of England is the central bank of the United Kingdom, sometimes known as "The Old Lady of Threadneedle Street" or "The Old Lady".
Balance	In banking and accountancy, the outstanding balance is the amount of money owned, (or due), that remains in a deposit account (or a loan account) at a given date, after all past remittances, payments and withdrawal have been accounted for. It can be positive (then, in the balance sheet of a firm, it is an asset) or negative (a liability).
Operation	A standardized method or technique that is performed repetitively, often on different materials resulting in different finished goods is called an operation.
Black market	Black market refers to an illegal market, in which something is bought and sold outside of official government-sanctioned channels. Black markets tend to arise when a government tries to fix a price without providing an alternative allocation method
Prohibition	Prohibition refers to denial of the right to import or export, applying to particular products and/or particular countries. Includes embargo.
Official rate	Official rate refers to the par value of a pegged exchange rate.
Policy	Similar to a script in that a policy can be a less than completely rational decision-making method. Involves the use of a pre-existing set of decision steps for any problem that presents itself.
Developed country	A developed country is one that enjoys a relatively high standard of living derived through an industrialized, diversified economy. Countries with a very high Human Development Index are generally considered developed countries.
Developing country	Developing country refers to a country whose per capita income is low by world standards. Same as LDC. As usually used, it does not necessarily connote that the country's income is rising.
Economy	The income, expenditures, and resources that affect the cost of running a business and household are called an economy.
Wall Street Journal	Dow Jones & Company was founded in 1882 by reporters Charles Dow, Edward Jones and Charles Bergstresser. Jones converted the small Customers' Afternoon Letter into The Wall Street Journal, first published in 1889, and began delivery of the Dow Jones News Service via telegraph. The Journal featured the Jones 'Average', the first of several indexes of stock and bond prices on the New York Stock Exchange.
Journal	Book of original entry, in which transactions are recorded in a general ledger system, is referred to as a journal.
United Nations	An international organization created by multilateral treaty in 1945 to promote social and economic cooperation among nations and to protect human rights is the United Nations.
Assessment	Collecting information and providing feedback to employees about their behavior, communication style, or skills is an assessment.
Analyst	Analyst refers to a person or tool with a primary function of information analysis, generally with a more limited, practical and short term set of goals than a researcher.
Money market	The money market, in macroeconomics and international finance, refers to the equilibration of

demand for a country's domestic money to its money supply; market for short-term financial instruments.

Export	In economics, an export is any good or commodity, shipped or otherwise transported out of a country, province, town to another part of the world in a legitimate fashion, typically for use in trade or sale.
Merchant	Under the Uniform Commercial Code, one who regularly deals in goods of the kind sold in the contract at issue, or holds himself out as having special knowledge or skill relevant to such goods, or who makes the sale through an agent who regularly deals in such goods or claims such knowledge or skill is referred to as merchant.
Dealer	People who link buyers with sellers by buying and selling securities at stated prices are referred to as a dealer.
Regulation	Regulation refers to restrictions state and federal laws place on business with regard to the conduct of its activities.
Corporation	A legal entity chartered by a state or the Federal government that is distinct and separate from the individuals who own it is a corporation. This separation gives the corporation unique powers which other legal entities lack.
Treasurer	In many governments, a treasurer is the person responsible for running the treasury. Treasurers are also employed by organizations to look after funds.
Cash flow	In finance, cash flow refers to the amounts of cash being received and spent by a business during a defined period of time, sometimes tied to a specific project. Most of the time they are being used to determine gaps in the liquid position of a company.
Derivatives market	The derivatives market is the financial market for derivatives. The market can be divided into two, that for exchange traded derivatives and that for over-the-counter derivatives. The legal nature of these products is very different as well as the way they are traded, though many market participants are active in both.
Derivative	A derivative is a generic term for specific types of investments from which payoffs over time are derived from the performance of assets (such as commodities, shares or bonds), interest rates, exchange rates, or indices (such as a stock market index, consumer price index (CPI) or an index of weather conditions).
Business Week	Business Week is a business magazine published by McGraw-Hill. It was first published in 1929 under the direction of Malcolm Muir, who was serving as president of the McGraw-Hill Publishing company at the time. It is considered to be the standard both in industry and among students.
Bilateral exchange rate	The exchange rate between two countries' currencies, defined as the number of units of either currency needed to purchase one unit of the other is referred to as the bilateral exchange rate.
Weighted average	The weighted average unit cost of the goods available for sale for both cost of goods sold and ending inventory.
Economics	The social science dealing with the use of scarce resources to obtain the maximum satisfaction of society's virtually unlimited economic wants is an economics.
Economic theory	Economic theory refers to a statement of a cause-effect relationship; when accepted by all economists, an economic principle.
Endogenous variable	Endogenous variable refers to an economic variable that is determined within a model. It is therefore not subject to direct manipulation by the modeler, since that would override the model.

Go to **Cram101.com** for the Practice Tests for this Chapter.

Exogenous variable	Exogenous variable refers to a variable that is taken as given by an economic model. It therefore is subject to direct manipulation by the modeler. In most models, policy variables such as tariffs and par values of pegged exchange rates are exogenous.
Real exchange rate	The nominal exchange rate adjusted for inflation is the real exchange rate. Unlike most other real variables, this adjustment requires accounting for price levels in two currencies.
Purchasing power	The amount of goods that money will buy, usually measured by the CPI is referred to as purchasing power.
Law of one price	The principle that identical goods should sell for the same price throughout the world if trade were free and frictionless is referred to as the law of one price.
Relative price	Relative price refers to the price of one thing in terms of another; i.e., the ratio of two prices.
Nominal value	Nominal value is the value of anything expressed in money of the day.
Purchasing	Purchasing refers to the function in a firm that searches for quality material resources, finds the best suppliers, and negotiates the best price for goods and services.
Inflation	An increase in the overall price level of an economy, usually as measured by the CPI or by the implicit price deflator is called inflation.
Variable	A variable is something measured by a number; it is used to analyze what happens to other things when the size of that number changes.
Purchasing power parity	purchasing power parity is a theory based on the law of one price which says that the long-run equilibrium exchange rate of two currencies is the rate that equalizes the currencies' purchasing power.

Transaction cost	A transaction cost is a cost incurred in making an economic exchange. For example, most people, when buying or selling a stock, must pay a commission to their broker; that commission is a transaction cost of doing the stock deal.
Market	A market is, as defined in economics, a social arrangement that allows buyers and sellers to discover information and carry out a voluntary exchange of goods or services.
Common currency	A situation where several countries form a monetary union with a single currency and a unified central bank is referred to as common currency.
Exchange rate	Exchange rate refers to the price at which one country's currency trades for another, typically on the exchange market.
Exchange	The trade of things of value between buyer and seller so that each is better off after the trade is called the exchange.
Purchasing power	The amount of goods that money will buy, usually measured by the CPI is referred to as purchasing power.
Purchasing	Purchasing refers to the function in a firm that searches for quality material resources, finds the best suppliers, and negotiates the best price for goods and services.
Purchasing power parity	purchasing power parity is a theory based on the law of one price which says that the long-run equilibrium exchange rate of two currencies is the rate that equalizes the currencies' purchasing power.
Price index	A measure of the average prices of a group of goods relative to a base year. A typical price index for a vector of quantities q and prices pb, pg in the base and given years respectively would be I = 100 Pgq / Pbq.
Gross domestic product	Gross domestic product refers to the total value of new goods and services produced in a given year within the borders of a country, regardless of by whom.
Spot exchange rate	The exchange rate at which a foreign exchange dealer will convert one currency into another that particular day is the spot exchange rate.
Domestic price	The price of a good or service within a country, determined by domestic demand and supply is referred to as domestic price.
GDP deflator	In economics, the GDP deflator is a measure of the change in prices of all new, domestically produced, final goods and services in an economy.
Domestic	From or in one's own country. A domestic producer is one that produces inside the home country. A domestic price is the price inside the home country. Opposite of 'foreign' or 'world.'.
Economy	The income, expenditures, and resources that affect the cost of running a business and household are called an economy.
Service	Service refers to a "non tangible product" that is not embodied in a physical good and that typically effects some change in another product, person, or institution. Contrasts with good.
Weighted average	The weighted average unit cost of the goods available for sale for both cost of goods sold and ending inventory.
Consumer price index	Consumer price index refers to a price index for the goods purchased by consumers in an economy, usually based on only a representative sample of typical consumer goods and services. Commonly used to measure inflation. Contrasts with the implicit price deflator.
Nominal value	Nominal value is the value of anything expressed in money of the day.

Price level	The overall level of prices in a country, as usually measured empirically by a price index, but often captured in theoretical models by a single variable is a price level.
Base year	The year used as the basis for comparison by a price index such as the CPI. The index for any year is the average of prices for that year compared to the base year; e.g., 110 means that prices are 10% higher than in the base year.
Household	An economic unit that provides the economy with resources and uses the income received to purchase goods and services that satisfy economic wants is called household.
Budget	Budget refers to an account, usually for a year, of the planned expenditures and the expected receipts of an entity. For a government, the receipts are tax revenues.
Differentiated product	A firm's product that is not identical to products of other firms in the same industry is a differentiated product.
Law of one price	The principle that identical goods should sell for the same price throughout the world if trade were free and frictionless is referred to as the law of one price.
Homogeneous	In the context of procurement/purchasing, homogeneous is used to describe goods that do not vary in their essential characteristic irrespective of the source of supply.
Commodity	Could refer to any good, but in trade a commodity is usually a raw material or primary product that enters into international trade, such as metals or basic agricultural products.
International trade	The export of goods and services from a country and the import of goods and services into a country is referred to as the international trade.
Tariff	A tax imposed by a nation on an imported good is called a tariff.
Relative price	Relative price refers to the price of one thing in terms of another; i.e., the ratio of two prices.
Inflation	An increase in the overall price level of an economy, usually as measured by the CPI or by the implicit price deflator is called inflation.
Analogy	Analogy is either the cognitive process of transferring information from a particular subject to another particular subject (the target), or a linguistic expression corresponding to such a process. In a narrower sense, analogy is an inference or an argument from a particular to another particular, as opposed to deduction, induction, and abduction, where at least one of the premises or the conclusion is general.
Points	Loan origination fees that may be deductible as interest by a buyer of property. A seller of property who pays points reduces the selling price by the amount of the points paid for the buyer.
Variable	A variable is something measured by a number; it is used to analyze what happens to other things when the size of that number changes.
Hyperinflation	Hyperinflation refers to a very rapid rise in the price level; an extremely high rate of inflation.
Real exchange rate	The nominal exchange rate adjusted for inflation is the real exchange rate. Unlike most other real variables, this adjustment requires accounting for price levels in two currencies.
Inflation rate	The percentage increase in the price level per year is an inflation rate. Alternatively, the inflation rate is the rate of decrease in the purchasing power of money.
Economics	The social science dealing with the use of scarce resources to obtain the maximum satisfaction of society's virtually unlimited economic wants is an economics.
Journal	Book of original entry, in which transactions are recorded in a general ledger system, is

referred to as a journal.

Depreciate	A nation's currency is said to depreciate when exchange rates change so that a unit of its currency can buy fewer units of foreign currency.
Depreciation	Depreciation is an accounting and finance term for the method of attributing the cost of an asset across the useful life of the asset. Depreciation is a reduction in the value of a currency in floating exchange rate.
Policy	Similar to a script in that a policy can be a less than completely rational decision-making method. Involves the use of a pre-existing set of decision steps for any problem that presents itself.
Toyota	Toyota is a Japanese multinational corporation that manufactures automobiles, trucks and buses. Toyota is the world's second largest automaker by sales. Toyota also provides financial services through its subsidiary, Toyota Financial Services, and participates in other lines of business.
Arbitrage	An arbitrage is a combination of nearly simultaneous transactions designed to profit from an existing discrepancy among prices, exchange rates, and/or interest rates on different markets without assuming risk.
Short run	Short run refers to a period of time that permits an increase or decrease in current production volume with existing capacity, but one that is too short to permit enlargement of that capacity itself (eg, the building of new plants, training of additional workers, etc.).
Long run	In economic models, the long run time frame assumes no fixed factors of production. Firms can enter or leave the marketplace, and the cost (and availability) of land, labor, raw materials, and capital goods can be assumed to vary.
Endogenous variable	Endogenous variable refers to an economic variable that is determined within a model. It is therefore not subject to direct manipulation by the modeler, since that would override the model.
Exogenous variable	Exogenous variable refers to a variable that is taken as given by an economic model. It therefore is subject to direct manipulation by the modeler. In most models, policy variables such as tariffs and par values of pegged exchange rates are exogenous.
Economic system	Economic system refers to a particular set of institutional arrangements and a coordinating mechanism for solving the economizing problem; a method of organizing an economy, of which the market system and the command system are the two general types.
Foreign exchange	In finance, foreign exchange means currencies, such as U.S. Dollars and Euros. These are traded on foreign exchange markets.
Supply	Supply is the aggregate amount of any material good that can be called into being at a certain price point; it comprises one half of the equation of supply and demand. In classical economic theory, a curve representing supply is one of the factors that produce price.
Asset	An item of property, such as land, capital, money, a share in ownership, or a claim on others for future payment, such as a bond or a bank deposit is an asset.
Money supply	There are several formal definitions, but all include the quantity of currency in circulation plus the amount of demand deposits. The money supply, together with the amount of real economic activity in a country, is an important determinant of price.
Demand curve	Demand curve refers to the graph of quantity demanded as a function of price, normally downward sloping, straight or curved, and drawn with quantity on the horizontal axis and price on the vertical axis.
Supply curve	Supply curve refers to the graph of quantity supplied as a function of price, normally upward

Go to **Cram101.com** for the Practice Tests for this Chapter.

201

sloping, straight or curved, and drawn with quantity on the horizontal axis and price on the vertical axis.

Contract	A contract is a "promise" or an "agreement" that is enforced or recognized by the law. In the civil law, a contract is considered to be part of the general law of obligations.
Economic policy	Economic policy refers to the actions that governments take in the economic field. It covers the systems for setting interest rates and government deficit as well as the labor market, national ownership, and many other areas of government.
Basket	A basket is an economic term for a group of several securities created for the purpose of simultaneous buying or selling. Baskets are frequently used for program trading.
Developed country	A developed country is one that enjoys a relatively high standard of living derived through an industrialized, diversified economy. Countries with a very high Human Development Index are generally considered developed countries.
Supply and demand	The partial equilibrium supply and demand economic model originally developed by Alfred Marshall attempts to describe, explain, and predict changes in the price and quantity of goods sold in competitive markets.
Demand factor	A demand factor is a factor that determines consumers' willingness and ability to pay for goods and services.
Industry	A group of firms that produce identical or similar products is an industry. It is also used specifically to refer to an area of economic production focused on manufacturing which involves large amounts of capital investment before any profit can be realized, also called "heavy industry".
Export	In economics, an export is any good or commodity, shipped or otherwise transported out of a country, province, town to another part of the world in a legitimate fashion, typically for use in trade or sale.
Balance	In banking and accountancy, the outstanding balance is the amount of money owned, (or due), that remains in a deposit account (or a loan account) at a given date, after all past remittances, payments and withdrawal have been accounted for. It can be positive (then, in the balance sheet of a firm, it is an asset) or negative (a liability).
Floating exchange rate	A system under which the exchange rate for converting one currency into another is continuously adjusted depending on the laws of supply and demand is referred to as a floating exchange rate.
Federal Reserve	The Federal Reserve System was created via the Federal Reserve Act of December 23rd, 1913. All national banks were required to join the system and other banks could join. The Reserve Banks opened for business on November 16th, 1914. Federal Reserve Notes were created as part of the legislation, to provide an elastic supply of currency.
Central Bank	Central bank refers to the institution in a country that is normally responsible for managing the supply of the country's money and the value of its currency on the foreign exchange market.
Deficit	The deficit is the amount by which expenditure exceed revenue.
Intervention	Intervention refers to an activity in which a government buys or sells its currency in the foreign exchange market in order to affect its currency's exchange rate.
Developing country	Developing country refers to a country whose per capita income is low by world standards. Same as LDC. As usually used, it does not necessarily connote that the country's income is rising.
Balance of trade	Balance of trade refers to the sum of the money gained by a given economy by selling exports,

Go to **Cram101.com** for the Practice Tests for this Chapter.

	minus the cost of buying imports. They form part of the balance of payments, which also includes other transactions such as the international investment position.
Labor productivity	In labor economics labor productivity is a measure of the efficiency of the labor force. It is usually measured as output per hour of all people. When comparing labor productivity one mostly looks at the change over time.
Productivity	Productivity refers to the total output of goods and services in a given period of time divided by work hours.
Traded good	A good that is exported or imported or -- sometimes -- a good that could be exported or imported if it weren't tariffs, or quotas, is referred to as traded good.
Labor	People's physical and mental talents and efforts that are used to help produce goods and services are called labor.
Nontraded good	Nontraded good refers to a good that is not traded, either because it cannot be or because trade barriers are too high. Except when services are being distinguished from goods, they are often mentioned as examples of nontraded goods.
Euro	The common currency of a subset of the countries of the EU, adopted January 1, 1999 is called euro.
Wage differential	The difference between the wage received by one worker or group of workers and that received by another worker or group of workers is a wage differential.
Wage	The payment for the service of a unit of labor, per unit time. In trade theory, it is the only payment to labor, usually unskilled labor. In empirical work, wage data may exclude other compenzation, which must be added to get the total cost of employment.
Per capita income	The per capita income for a group of people may be defined as their total personal income, divided by the total population. Per capita income is usually reported in units of currency per year.
Per capita	Per capita refers to per person. Usually used to indicate the average per person of any given statistic, commonly income.
Black market	Black market refers to an illegal market, in which something is bought and sold outside of official government-sanctioned channels. Black markets tend to arise when a government tries to fix a price without providing an alternative allocation method
Nominal exchange rate	Nominal exchange rate refers to the actual exchange rate at which currencies are exchanged on an exchange market. Contrasts with real exchange rate.
Consumption	In Keynesian economics consumption refers to personal consumption expenditure, i.e., the purchase of currently produced goods and services out of income, out of savings (net worth), or from borrowed funds. It refers to that part of disposable income that does not go to saving.
Term structure of interest rates	The relationship among interest rates on bonds with different terms to maturity is referred to as term structure of interest rates.
Nominal interest rate	The interest rate actually observed in the market, in contrast to the real interest rate is a nominal interest rate.
Interest Rate Parity	The Interest Rate Parity is the basic identity that relates interest rates and exchange rates. The identity is theoretical, and usually follows from assumptions imposed in economics models.
Real interest	The real interest rate is the nominal interest rate minus the inflation rate. It is a better

Go to **Cram101.com** for the Practice Tests for this Chapter.

rate	measure of the return that a lender receives (or the cost to the borrower) because it takes into account the fact that the value of money changes due to inflation over the course of the loan period.
Financial assets	Financial assets refer to monetary claims or obligations by one party against another party. Examples are bonds, mortgages, bank loans, and equities.
Interest parity	Interest parity refers to equality of returns on otherwise identical financial assets denominated in different currencies.
Interest rate	The rate of return on bonds, loans, or deposits. When one speaks of 'the' interest rate, it is usually in a model where there is only one.
Interest	In finance and economics, interest is the price paid by a borrower for the use of a lender's money. In other words, interest is the amount of paid to "rent" money for a period of time.
Uncovered interest parity	Equality of expected returns on otherwise comparable financial assets denominated in two currencies, without any cover against exchange risk is uncovered interest parity.

Covered interest arbitrage	Covered interest arbitrage is the investment strategy where an investor buys a financial instrument denominated in a foreign currency, and hedges his foreign exchange risk by selling a forward contract in the amount of the proceeds of the investment back into his base currency.
Interest parity	Interest parity refers to equality of returns on otherwise identical financial assets denominated in different currencies.
Arbitrage	An arbitrage is a combination of nearly simultaneous transactions designed to profit from an existing discrepancy among prices, exchange rates, and/or interest rates on different markets without assuming risk.
Interest	In finance and economics, interest is the price paid by a borrower for the use of a lender's money. In other words, interest is the amount of paid to "rent" money for a period of time.
Profit	Profit refers to the return to the resource entrepreneurial ability; total revenue minus total cost.
Investment	Investment refers to spending for the production and accumulation of capital and additions to inventories. In a financial sense, buying an asset with the expectation of making a return.
Forward market	A market for exchange of currencies in the future is the forward market. Participants in a forward market enter into a contract to exchange currencies, not today, but at a specified date in the future, typically 30, 60, or 90 days from now, and at a price that is agreed upon.
Market	A market is, as defined in economics, a social arrangement that allows buyers and sellers to discover information and carry out a voluntary exchange of goods or services.
Spot exchange rate	The exchange rate at which a foreign exchange dealer will convert one currency into another that particular day is the spot exchange rate.
Interest rate	The rate of return on bonds, loans, or deposits. When one speaks of 'the' interest rate, it is usually in a model where there is only one.
Exchange rate	Exchange rate refers to the price at which one country's currency trades for another, typically on the exchange market.
Forward rate	Forward rate refers to the forward exchange rate, this is the exchange rate on a forward market transaction.
Exchange	The trade of things of value between buyer and seller so that each is better off after the trade is called the exchange.
Domestic	From or in one's own country. A domestic producer is one that produces inside the home country. A domestic price is the price inside the home country. Opposite of 'foreign' or 'world.'.
Interest Rate Parity	The Interest Rate Parity is the basic identity that relates interest rates and exchange rates. The identity is theoretical, and usually follows from assumptions imposed in economics models.
Forward premium	The difference between a forward exchange rate and the spot exchange rate, expressed as an annualized percentage return on buying foreign currency spot and selling it forward is a forward premium.
Discount	The difference between the face value of a bond and its selling price, when a bond is sold for less than its face value it's referred to as a discount.
Premium	Premium refers to the fee charged by an insurance company for an insurance policy. The rate of losses must be relatively predictable: In order to set the premium (prices) insurers must

Go to **Cram101.com** for the Practice Tests for this Chapter.

be able to estimate them accurately.

Fund	Independent accounting entity with a self-balancing set of accounts segregated for the purposes of carrying on specific activities is referred to as a fund.
Bond	Bond refers to a debt instrument, issued by a borrower and promising a specified stream of payments to the purchaser, usually regular interest payments plus a final repayment of principal.
Forward exchange rate	The exchange rates governing forward exchange transactions is called the forward exchange rate.
Forward exchange	When two parties agree to exchange currency and execute a deal at some specific date in the future, we have forward exchange.
Spot rate	Spot rate refers to the rate at which the currency is traded for immediate delivery. It is the existing cash price.
Uncovered interest parity	Equality of expected returns on otherwise comparable financial assets denominated in two currencies, without any cover against exchange risk is uncovered interest parity.
Yield	The interest rate that equates a future value or an annuity to a given present value is a yield.
Foreign exchange	In finance, foreign exchange means currencies, such as U.S. Dollars and Euros. These are traded on foreign exchange markets.
Transaction cost	A transaction cost is a cost incurred in making an economic exchange. For example, most people, when buying or selling a stock, must pay a commission to their broker; that commission is a transaction cost of doing the stock deal.
Security	Security refers to a claim on the borrower future income that is sold by the borrower to the lender. A security is a type of transferable interest representing financial value.
Asset	An item of property, such as land, capital, money, a share in ownership, or a claim on others for future payment, such as a bond or a bank deposit is an asset.
Political risk	Refers to the many different actions of people, subgroups, and whole countries that have the potential to affect the financial status of a firm is called political risk.
International capital flows	International capital flows are purchases and sales of financial assets across national borders. Flows of physical capital goods are typically treated as ordinary trade flows, not capital flows, in the balance of payments accounts.
Economy	The income, expenditures, and resources that affect the cost of running a business and household are called an economy.
Political economy	Early name for the discipline of economics. A field within economics encompassing several alternatives to neoclassical economics, including Marxist economics. Also called radical political economy.
Transactions cost	Any cost associated with bringing buyers and sellers together is referred to as transactions cost.
Currency swap	Currency swap refers to the exchange of a set of payments in one currency for a set of payments in another currency.
Capital flow	International capital movement is referred to as capital flow.
Inflation	An increase in the overall price level of an economy, usually as measured by the CPI or by the implicit price deflator is called inflation.
Journal	Book of original entry, in which transactions are recorded in a general ledger system, is

Go to **Cram101.com** for the Practice Tests for this Chapter.

	referred to as a journal.
Capital	Capital generally refers to financial wealth, especially that used to start or maintain a business. In classical economics, capital is one of four factors of production, the others being land and labor and entrepreneurship.
Swap	In finance a swap is a derivative, where two counterparties exchange one stream of cash flows against another stream. These streams are called the legs of the swap. The cash flows are calculated over a notional principal amount. Swaps are often used to hedge certain risks, for instance interest rate risk. Another use is speculation.
Nominal interest rate	The interest rate actually observed in the market, in contrast to the real interest rate is a nominal interest rate.
Inflation rate	The percentage increase in the price level per year is an inflation rate. Alternatively, the inflation rate is the rate of decrease in the purchasing power of money.
Real interest rate	The real interest rate is the nominal interest rate minus the inflation rate. It is a better measure of the return that a lender receives (or the cost to the borrower) because it takes into account the fact that the value of money changes due to inflation over the course of the loan period.
Price index	A measure of the average prices of a group of goods relative to a base year. A typical price index for a vector of quantities q and prices pb, pg in the base and given years respectively would be I = 100 Pgq / Pbq.
Consumer price index	Consumer price index refers to a price index for the goods purchased by consumers in an economy, usually based on only a representative sample of typical consumer goods and services. Commonly used to measure inflation. Contrasts with the implicit price deflator.
Simple interest	Simple interest is interest that accrues linearly. In other words, it grows by a certain fraction of the principal per time period.
Principal	In agency law, one under whose direction an agent acts and for whose benefit that agent acts is a principal.
Service	Service refers to a "non tangible product" that is not embodied in a physical good and that typically effects some change in another product, person, or institution. Contrasts with good.
Value of money	Value of money refers to the quantity of goods and services for which a unit of money can be exchanged; the purchasing power of a unit of money; the reciprocal of the price level.
Gain	In finance, gain is a profit or an increase in value of an investment such as a stock or bond. Gain is calculated by fair market value or the proceeds from the sale of the investment minus the sum of the purchase price and all costs associated with it.
Consumption	In Keynesian economics consumption refers to personal consumption expenditure, i.e., the purchase of currently produced goods and services out of income, out of savings (net worth), or from borrowed funds. It refers to that part of disposable income that does not go to saving.
Purchasing power	The amount of goods that money will buy, usually measured by the CPI is referred to as purchasing power.
Purchasing	Purchasing refers to the function in a firm that searches for quality material resources, finds the best suppliers, and negotiates the best price for goods and services.
Lender	Suppliers and financial institutions that lend money to companies is referred to as a lender.
Analyst	Analyst refers to a person or tool with a primary function of information analysis, generally

Go to **Cram101.com** for the Practice Tests for this Chapter.

	with a more limited, practical and short term set of goals than a researcher.
Creditor	A person to whom a debt or legal obligation is owed, and who has the right to enforce payment of that debt or obligation is referred to as creditor.
Expense	In accounting, an expense represents an event in which an asset is used up or a liability is incurred. In terms of the accounting equation, expenses reduce owners' equity.
Long run	In economic models, the long run time frame assumes no fixed factors of production. Firms can enter or leave the marketplace, and the cost (and availability) of land, labor, raw materials, and capital goods can be assumed to vary.
Interest parity condition	Interest parity condition refers to the observation that the domestic interest rate equals the foreign interest rate plus the expected appreciation or depreciation in the foreign currency.
Purchasing power parity	purchasing power parity is a theory based on the law of one price which says that the long-run equilibrium exchange rate of two currencies is the rate that equalizes the currencies' purchasing power.
Policy	Similar to a script in that a policy can be a less than completely rational decision-making method. Involves the use of a pre-existing set of decision steps for any problem that presents itself.
Term structure of interest rates	The relationship among interest rates on bonds with different terms to maturity is referred to as term structure of interest rates.
Maturity date	The date on which the final payment on a bond is due from the bond issuer to the investor is a maturity date.
Maturity	Maturity refers to the final payment date of a loan or other financial instrument, after which point no further interest or principal need be paid.
Risk premium	In finance, the risk premium can be the expected rate of return above the risk-free interest rate.
Holding period	The period of time during which property has been held for income tax purposes. The holding period is significant in determining whether gain or loss from the sale or exchange of a capital asset is long term or short term.
Holding	The holding is a court's determination of a matter of law based on the issue presented in the particular case. In other words: under this law, with these facts, this result.
Points	Loan origination fees that may be deductible as interest by a buyer of property. A seller of property who pays points reduces the selling price by the amount of the points paid for the buyer.
Depreciate	A nation's currency is said to depreciate when exchange rates change so that a unit of its currency can buy fewer units of foreign currency.
Spot market	Spot market refers to a market in which commodities are bought and sold for cash and immediate delivery.
Credit market	A credit market is where borrowers come together with lenders to determine conditions of exchange such as interest rates and the duration of a loan.
Credit	Credit refers to a recording as positive in the balance of payments, any transaction that gives rise to a payment into the country, such as an export, the sale of an asset, or borrowing from abroad.
Interest income	Interest income refers to payments of income to those who supply the economy with capital.

Incentive	An incentive is any factor (financial or non-financial) that provides a motive for a particular course of action, or counts as a reason for preferring one choice to the alternatives.
Diversified portfolio	Diversified portfolio refers to a portfolio that includes a variety of assets whose prices are not likely all to change together. In international economics, this usually means holding assets denominated in different currencies.
Efficient market	Efficient market refers to a market in which, at a minimum, current price changes are independent of past price changes, or, more strongly, price reflects all available information.
Systematic risk	Movements in a stock portfolio's value that are attributable to macroeconomic forces affecting all firms in an economy, rather than factors specific to an individual firm are referred to as systematic risk.
Diversification	Investing in a collection of assets whose returns do not always move together, with the result that overall risk is lower than for individual assets is referred to as diversification.
Capital flight	Large financial capital outflows from a country prompted by fear of default or, especially, by fear of devaluation is called capital flight.
Capital inflow	Capital inflow refers to a net flow of capital, real and/or financial, into a country, in the form of increased purchases of domestic assets by foreigners and/or reduced holdings of foreign assets by domestic residents.
Short position	In finance, a short position in a security, such as a stock or a Bond, means the holder of the position has sold a security that he does not own, with the intention to buy it back at a later time at a lower price.
Long position	In finance, a long position in a security, such as a stock or a bond, means the holder of the position owns the security.
Risk aversion	Risk aversion is the reluctance of a person to accept a bargain with an uncertain payoff rather than another bargain with a more certain but possibly lower expected payoff.
Portfolio	In finance, a portfolio is a collection of investments held by an institution or a private individual. Holding but not always a portfolio is part of an investment and risk-limiting strategy called diversification. By owning several assets, certain types of risk (in particular specific risk) can be reduced.
Home bias	Home bias refers to a preference, by consumers or other demanders, for products produced in their own country compared to otherwise identical imports. This was proposed by Trefler as a possible explanation for the mystery of the missing trade.
Contagion	The phenomenon of a financial crisis in one country spilling over to another, which then suffers many of the same problems, is known as contagion.
Variance	Variance refers to a measure of how much an economic or statistical variable varies across values or observations. Its calculation is the same as that of the covariance, being the covariance of the variable with itself.

Exchange rate	Exchange rate refers to the price at which one country's currency trades for another, typically on the exchange market.
Treasurer	In many governments, a treasurer is the person responsible for running the treasury. Treasurers are also employed by organizations to look after funds.
Exchange	The trade of things of value between buyer and seller so that each is better off after the trade is called the exchange.
International capital flows	International capital flows are purchases and sales of financial assets across national borders. Flows of physical capital goods are typically treated as ordinary trade flows, not capital flows, in the balance of payments accounts.
Capital flow	International capital movement is referred to as capital flow.
Investment	Investment refers to spending for the production and accumulation of capital and additions to inventories. In a financial sense, buying an asset with the expectation of making a return.
Capital	Capital generally refers to financial wealth, especially that used to start or maintain a business. In classical economics, capital is one of four factors of production, the others being land and labor and entrepreneurship.
Firm	An organization that employs resources to produce a good or service for profit and owns and operates one or more plants is referred to as a firm.
Translation exposure	The foreign-located assets and liabilities of a multinational corporation, which are denominated in foreign currency units, and are exposed to losses and gains due to changing exchange rates is called accounting or translation exposure.
Economic exposure	The extent to which a firm's future international earning power is affected by changes in exchange rates is referred to as the economic exposure.
Present value	The value today of a stream of payments and/or receipts over time in the future and/or the past, converted to the present using an interest rate. If X_t is the amount in period t and r the interest rate, then present value at time $t=0$ is $V = ?T/t$.
Cash flow	In finance, cash flow refers to the amounts of cash being received and spent by a business during a defined period of time, sometimes tied to a specific project. Most of the time they are being used to determine gaps in the liquid position of a company.
Domestic	From or in one's own country. A domestic producer is one that produces inside the home country. A domestic price is the price inside the home country. Opposite of 'foreign' or 'world.'.
Liability	A liability is a present obligation of the enterprise arizing from past events, the settlement of which is expected to result in an outflow from the enterprise of resources embodying economic benefits.
Residual	Residual payments can refer to an ongoing stream of payments in respect of the completion of past achievements.
Equity	Equity is the name given to the set of legal principles, in countries following the English common law tradition, which supplement strict rules of law where their application would operate harshly, so as to achieve what is sometimes referred to as "natural justice."
Asset	An item of property, such as land, capital, money, a share in ownership, or a claim on others for future payment, such as a bond or a bank deposit is an asset.
Balance sheet	A statement of the assets, liabilities, and net worth of a firm or individual at some given time often at the end of its "fiscal year," is referred to as a balance sheet.
Balance	In banking and accountancy, the outstanding balance is the amount of money owned, (or due),

	that remains in a deposit account (or a loan account) at a given date, after all past remittances, payments and withdrawal have been accounted for. It can be positive (then, in the balance sheet of a firm, it is an asset) or negative (a liability).
Depreciate	A nation's currency is said to depreciate when exchange rates change so that a unit of its currency can buy fewer units of foreign currency.
Transaction exposure	Transaction exposure refers to foreign exchange gains and losses resulting from actual international transactions. These may be hedged through the foreign exchange market, the money market, or the currency futures market.
Contract	A contract is a "promise" or an "agreement" that is enforced or recognized by the law. In the civil law, a contract is considered to be part of the general law of obligations.
Writ	Writ refers to a commandment of a court given for the purpose of compelling certain action from the defendant, and usually executed by a sheriff or other judicial officer.
Forward exchange	When two parties agree to exchange currency and execute a deal at some specific date in the future, we have forward exchange.
Exchange market	Exchange market refers to the market on which national currencies are bought and sold.
Market	A market is, as defined in economics, a social arrangement that allows buyers and sellers to discover information and carry out a voluntary exchange of goods or services.
Hedge	Hedge refers to a process of offsetting risk. In the foreign exchange market, hedgers use the forward market to cover a transaction or open position and thereby reduce exchange risk. The term applies most commonly to trade.
Forward market	A market for exchange of currencies in the future is the forward market. Participants in a forward market enter into a contract to exchange currencies, not today, but at a specified date in the future, typically 30, 60, or 90 days from now, and at a price that is agreed upon.
Operation	A standardized method or technique that is performed repetitively, often on different materials resulting in different finished goods is called an operation.
Swap	In finance a swap is a derivative, where two counterparties exchange one stream of cash flows against another stream. These streams are called the legs of the swap. The cash flows are calculated over a notional principal amount. Swaps are often used to hedge certain risks, for instance interest rate risk. Another use is speculation.
Hedging	A technique for avoiding a risk by making a counteracting transaction is referred to as hedging.
Accounts receivable	Accounts receivable is one of a series of accounting transactions dealing with the billing of customers which owe money to a person, company or organization for goods and services that have been provided to the customer. This is typically done in a one person organization by writing an invoice and mailing or delivering it to each customer.
Accounts payable	A written record of all vendors to whom the business firm owes money is referred to as accounts payable.
Credit	Credit refers to a recording as positive in the balance of payments, any transaction that gives rise to a payment into the country, such as an export, the sale of an asset, or borrowing from abroad.
Payables	Obligations to make future economic sacrifices, usually cash payments, are referred to as payables. Same as current liabilities.
Policy	Similar to a script in that a policy can be a less than completely rational decision-making

Go to **Cram101.com** for the Practice Tests for this Chapter.

	method. Involves the use of a pre-existing set of decision steps for any problem that presents itself.
Premium	Premium refers to the fee charged by an insurance company for an insurance policy. The rate of losses must be relatively predictable: In order to set the premium (prices) insurers must be able to estimate them accurately.
Futures	Futures refer to contracts for the sale and future delivery of stocks or commodities, wherein either party may waive delivery, and receive or pay, as the case may be, the difference in market price at the time set for delivery.
Option	A contract that gives the purchaser the option to buy or sell the underlying financial instrument at a specified price, called the exercise price or strike price, within a specific period of time.
Forward rate	Forward rate refers to the forward exchange rate, this is the exchange rate on a forward market transaction.
Spot rate	Spot rate refers to the rate at which the currency is traded for immediate delivery. It is the existing cash price.
Long run	In economic models, the long run time frame assumes no fixed factors of production. Firms can enter or leave the marketplace, and the cost (and availability) of land, labor, raw materials, and capital goods can be assumed to vary.
Property	Assets defined in the broadest legal sense. Property includes the unrealized receivables of a cash basis taxpayer, but not services rendered.
Forward exchange rate	The exchange rates governing forward exchange transactions is called the forward exchange rate.
Risk premium	In finance, the risk premium can be the expected rate of return above the risk-free interest rate.
Foreign exchange	In finance, foreign exchange means currencies, such as U.S. Dollars and Euros. These are traded on foreign exchange markets.
Discount	The difference between the face value of a bond and its selling price, when a bond is sold for less than its face value it's referred to as a discount.
Journal	Book of original entry, in which transactions are recorded in a general ledger system, is referred to as a journal.
Foreign exchange market	A market for converting the currency of one country into that of another country is called foreign exchange market. It is by far the largest market in the world, in terms of cash value traded, and includes trading between large banks, central banks, currency speculators, multinational corporations, governments, and other financial markets and institutions.
Risk aversion	Risk aversion is the reluctance of a person to accept a bargain with an uncertain payoff rather than another bargain with a more certain but possibly lower expected payoff.
Contribution	In business organization law, the cash or property contributed to a business by its owners is referred to as contribution.
Portfolio	In finance, a portfolio is a collection of investments held by an institution or a private individual. Holding but not always a portfolio is part of an investment and risk-limiting strategy called diversification. By owning several assets, certain types of risk (in particular specific risk) can be reduced.
Interest rate	The rate of return on bonds, loans, or deposits. When one speaks of 'the' interest rate, it is usually in a model where there is only one.

Interest	In finance and economics, interest is the price paid by a borrower for the use of a lender's money. In other words, interest is the amount of paid to "rent" money for a period of time.
Corporation	A legal entity chartered by a state or the Federal government that is distinct and separate from the individuals who own it is a corporation. This separation gives the corporation unique powers which other legal entities lack.
Credit risk	The risk of loss due to a counterparty defaulting on a contract, or more generally the risk of loss due to some "credit event" is called credit risk.
Creditor	A person to whom a debt or legal obligation is owed, and who has the right to enforce payment of that debt or obligation is referred to as creditor.
Security	Security refers to a claim on the borrower future income that is sold by the borrower to the lender. A security is a type of transferable interest representing financial value.
Spot exchange rate	The exchange rate at which a foreign exchange dealer will convert one currency into another that particular day is the spot exchange rate.
Holding	The holding is a court's determination of a matter of law based on the issue presented in the particular case. In other words: under this law, with these facts, this result.
Bond	Bond refers to a debt instrument, issued by a borrower and promising a specified stream of payments to the purchaser, usually regular interest payments plus a final repayment of principal.
Expected return	Expected return refers to the return on an asset expected over the next period.
Efficient market	Efficient market refers to a market in which, at a minimum, current price changes are independent of past price changes, or, more strongly, price reflects all available information.
Economic policy	Economic policy refers to the actions that governments take in the economic field. It covers the systems for setting interest rates and government deficit as well as the labor market, national ownership, and many other areas of government.
Depreciation	Depreciation is an accounting and finance term for the method of attributing the cost of an asset across the useful life of the asset. Depreciation is a reduction in the value of a currency in floating exchange rate.
Profit	Profit refers to the return to the resource entrepreneurial ability; total revenue minus total cost.
Speculation	The purchase or sale of an asset in hopes that its price will rise or fall respectively, in order to make a profit is called speculation.
Financial market	In economics, a financial market is a mechanism which allows people to trade money for securities or commodities such as gold or other precious metals. In general, any commodity market might be considered to be a financial market, if the usual purpose of traders is not the immediate consumption of the commodity, but rather as a means of delaying or accelerating consumption over time.
Empirical finding	Something that is observed from real-world observation or data, in contrast to something that is deduced from theory is an empirical finding.
Accounting	A system that collects and processes financial information about an organization and reports that information to decision makers is referred to as accounting.
Economics	The social science dealing with the use of scarce resources to obtain the maximum satisfaction of society's virtually unlimited economic wants is an economics.
Trend	Trend refers to the long-term movement of an economic variable, such as its average rate of

Go to **Cram101.com** for the Practice Tests for this Chapter.

225

	increase or decrease over enough years to encompass several business cycles.
Spot market	Spot market refers to a market in which commodities are bought and sold for cash and immediate delivery.
Yield	The interest rate that equates a future value or an annuity to a given present value is a yield.
Long position	In finance, a long position in a security, such as a stock or a bond, means the holder of the position owns the security.
Fixture	Fixture refers to a thing that was originally personal property and that has been actually or constructively affixed to the soil itself or to some structure legally a part of the land.
Short position	In finance, a short position in a security, such as a stock or a Bond, means the holder of the position has sold a security that he does not own, with the intention to buy it back at a later time at a lower price.
Service	Service refers to a "non tangible product" that is not embodied in a physical good and that typically effects some change in another product, person, or institution. Contrasts with good.
Transaction cost	A transaction cost is a cost incurred in making an economic exchange. For example, most people, when buying or selling a stock, must pay a commission to their broker; that commission is a transaction cost of doing the stock deal.
Abnormal profit	Abnormal profit is an economic term of profit exceeding the normal profit. Normal profit equals the opportunity cost of labor and capital, while supernormal profit is the amount exceeds the normal return from these input factors in production.
Diversification	Investing in a collection of assets whose returns do not always move together, with the result that overall risk is lower than for individual assets is referred to as diversification.
Financial capital	Common stock, preferred stock, bonds, and retained earnings are financial capital. Financial capital appears on the corporate balance sheet under long-term liabilities and equity.
Incentive	An incentive is any factor (financial or non-financial) that provides a motive for a particular course of action, or counts as a reason for preferring one choice to the alternatives.
Fund	Independent accounting entity with a self-balancing set of accounts segregated for the purposes of carrying on specific activities is referred to as a fund.
Diversified portfolio	Diversified portfolio refers to a portfolio that includes a variety of assets whose prices are not likely all to change together. In international economics, this usually means holding assets denominated in different currencies.
Weighted average	The weighted average unit cost of the goods available for sale for both cost of goods sold and ending inventory.
Expected value	A representative value from a probability distribution arrived at by multiplying each outcome by the associated probability and summing up the values is called the expected value.
Variable	A variable is something measured by a number; it is used to analyze what happens to other things when the size of that number changes.
Variance	Variance refers to a measure of how much an economic or statistical variable varies across values or observations. Its calculation is the same as that of the covariance, being the covariance of the variable with itself.
Systematic risk	Movements in a stock portfolio's value that are attributable to macroeconomic forces

Go to **Cram101.com** for the Practice Tests for this Chapter.

affecting all firms in an economy, rather than factors specific to an individual firm are referred to as systematic risk.

Industry	A group of firms that produce identical or similar products is an industry. It is also used specifically to refer to an area of economic production focused on manufacturing which involves large amounts of capital investment before any profit can be realized, also called "heavy industry".
Business cycle	Business cycle refers to the pattern followed by macroeconommic variables, such as GDP and unemployment that rise and fall irregularly over time, relative to trend.
Recession	A significant decline in economic activity. In the U.S., recession is approximately defined as two successive quarters of falling GDP, as judged by NBER.
Home bias	Home bias refers to a preference, by consumers or other demanders, for products produced in their own country compared to otherwise identical imports. This was proposed by Trefler as a possible explanation for the mystery of the missing trade.
Implicit cost	Implicit cost refers to the monetary income a firm sacrifices when it uses a resource it owns rather than supplying the resource in the market; equal to what the resource could have earned in the best-paying alternative employment.
Regulation	Regulation refers to restrictions state and federal laws place on business with regard to the conduct of its activities.
Bid	A bid price is a price offered by a buyer when he/she buys a good. In the context of stock trading on a stock exchange, the bid price is the highest price a buyer of a stock is willing to pay for a share of that given stock.
Explicit cost	The monetary payment a firm must make to an outsider to obtain a resource is an explicit cost. It is an easy accounted cost, such as wage, rent and materials.
International diversification	Achieving diversification through many different foreign investments that are influenced by a variety of factors is referred to as international diversification. By diversifying across nations whose economic cycles are not perfectly correlated, investors can typically reduce the variability of their returns.
Gain	In finance, gain is a profit or an increase in value of an investment such as a stock or bond. Gain is calculated by fair market value or the proceeds from the sale of the investment minus the sum of the purchase price and all costs associated with it.
Mutual fund	A mutual fund is a form of collective investment that pools money from many investors and invests the money in stocks, bonds, short-term money market instruments, and/or other securities. In a mutual fund, the fund manager trades the fund's underlying securities, realizing capital gains or loss, and collects the dividend or interest income.
Shares	Shares refer to an equity security, representing a shareholder's ownership of a corporation. Shares are one of a finite number of equal portions in the capital of a company, entitling the owner to a proportion of distributed, non-reinvested profits known as dividends and to a portion of the value of the company in case of liquidation.
Production	The creation of finished goods and services using the factors of production: land, labor, capital, entrepreneurship, and knowledge.
Country risk	Country risk relates to the likelihood that changes in the business environment will occur that reduce the profitability of doing business in a country. These changes can adversely affect operating profits as well as the value of assets.
Portfolio investment	Portfolio investment refers to the acquisition of portfolio capital. Usually refers to such transactions across national borders and/or across currencies.

229

Stock	In financial terminology, stock is the capital raized by a corporation, through the issuance and sale of shares.
Turnover	Turnover in a financial context refers to the rate at which a provider of goods cycles through its average inventory. Turnover in a human resources context refers to the characteristic of a given company or industry, relative to rate at which an employer gains and loses staff.
Direct investment	Direct investment refers to a domestic firm actually investing in and owning a foreign subsidiary or division.
Factors of production	Economic resources: land, capital, labor, and entrepreneurial ability are called factors of production.
International trade	The export of goods and services from a country and the import of goods and services into a country is referred to as the international trade.
Consideration	Consideration in contract law, a basic requirement for an enforceable agreement under traditional contract principles, defined in this text as legal value, bargained for and given in exchange for an act or promise. In corporation law, cash or property contributed to a corporation in exchange for shares, or a promise to contribute such cash or property.
Perfectly competitive	Perfectly competitive is an economic agent, group of agents, model or analysis that is characterized by perfect competition. Contrasts with imperfectly competitive.
Stockholder	A stockholder is an individual or company (including a corporation) that legally owns one or more shares of stock in a joined stock company. The shareholders are the owners of a corporation. Companies listed at the stock market strive to enhance shareholder value.
Internationa-ization	Internationalization refers to another term for fragmentation. Used by Grossman and Helpman.
Market research	Market research is the process of systematic gathering, recording and analyzing of data about customers, competitors and the market. Market research can help create a business plan, launch a new product or service, fine tune existing products and services, expand into new markets etc. It can be used to determine which portion of the population will purchase the product/service, based on variables like age, gender, location and income level. It can be found out what market characteristics your target market has.
Assessment	Collecting information and providing feedback to employees about their behavior, communication style, or skills is an assessment.
Enterprise	Enterprise refers to another name for a business organization. Other similar terms are business firm, sometimes simply business, sometimes simply firm, as well as company, and entity.
Merger	Merger refers to the combination of two firms into a single firm.
Multinational enterprise	Multinational enterprise refers to a firm, usually a corporation, that operates in two or more countries.
Capital structure	Capital Structure refers to the way a corporation finances itself through some combination of equity sales, equity options, bonds, and loans. Optimal capital structure refers to the particular combination that minimizes the cost of capital while maximizing the stock price.
Capital structure theory	A theory that addresses the relative importance of debt and equity in the overall financing of the firm is called capital structure theory.
Subsidiary	A company that is controlled by another company or corporation is a subsidiary.

Go to **Cram101.com** for the Practice Tests for this Chapter.

Export	In economics, an export is any good or commodity, shipped or otherwise transported out of a country, province, town to another part of the world in a legitimate fashion, typically for use in trade or sale.
Tariff	A tax imposed by a nation on an imported good is called a tariff.
Cost advantage	Possession of a lower cost of production or operation than a competing firm or country is cost advantage.
Economy	The income, expenditures, and resources that affect the cost of running a business and household are called an economy.
Economies of scale	In economics, returns to scale and economies of scale are related terms that describe what happens as the scale of production increases. They are different terms and not to be used interchangeably.
Financial management	The job of managing a firm's resources so it can meet its goals and objectives is called financial management.
Management	Management characterizes the process of leading and directing all or part of an organization, often a business, through the deployment and manipulation of resources. Early twentieth-century management writer Mary Parker Follett defined management as "the art of getting things done through people."
Marketing	Promoting and selling products or services to customers, or prospective customers, is referred to as marketing.
Expense	In accounting, an expense represents an event in which an asset is used up or a liability is incurred. In terms of the accounting equation, expenses reduce owners' equity.
Research and development	The use of resources for the deliberate discovery of new information and ways of doing things, together with the application of that information in inventing new products or processes is referred to as research and development.
Competitor	Other organizations in the same industry or type of business that provide a good or service to the same set of customers is referred to as a competitor.
Technology	The body of knowledge and techniques that can be used to combine economic resources to produce goods and services is called technology.
Potential competition	Potential competition refers to the new competitors that may be induced to enter an industry if firms now in that industry are receiving large economic profits.
Complement	A good that is used in conjunction with another good is a complement. For example, cameras and film would complement eachother.
Developing country	Developing country refers to a country whose per capita income is low by world standards. Same as LDC. As usually used, it does not necessarily connote that the country's income is rising.
Exporter	A firm that sells its product in another country is an exporter.
Volatility	Volatility refers to the extent to which an economic variable, such as a price or an exchange rate, moves up and down over time.
Emerging market	The term emerging market is commonly used to describe business and market activity in industrializing or emerging regions of the world.
Financial assets	Financial assets refer to monetary claims or obligations by one party against another party. Examples are bonds, mortgages, bank loans, and equities.
Contagion	The phenomenon of a financial crisis in one country spilling over to another, which then

233

suffers many of the same problems, is known as contagion.

International Monetary Fund	The International Monetary Fund is the international organization entrusted with overseeing the global financial system by monitoring exchange rates and balance of payments, as well as offering technical and financial assistance when asked.
Capital market	A financial market in which long-term debt and equity instruments are traded is referred to as a capital market. The capital market includes the stock market and the bond market.
Financial crisis	A loss of confidence in a country's currency or other financial assets causing international investors to withdraw their funds from the country is referred to as a financial crisis.
Host country	The country in which the parent-country organization seeks to locate or has already located a facility is a host country.
Consumption	In Keynesian economics consumption refers to personal consumption expenditure, i.e., the purchase of currently produced goods and services out of income, out of savings (net worth), or from borrowed funds. It refers to that part of disposable income that does not go to saving.
Devaluation	Lowering the value of a nation's currency relative to other currencies is called devaluation.
Default	In finance, default occurs when a debtor has not met its legal obligations according to the debt contract, e.g. it has not made a scheduled payment, or violated a covenant (condition) of the debt contract.
Capital flight	Large financial capital outflows from a country prompted by fear of default or, especially, by fear of devaluation is called capital flight.
Capital account	The capital account is one of two primary components of the balance of payments. It tracks the movement of funds for investments and loans into and out of a country.
Deficit	The deficit is the amount by which expenditure exceed revenue.
Capital account deficit	Capital account deficit refers to the amount by which the purchase of foreign financial assets by consumers exceeds the purchase of domestic financial assets by foreigners .
Capital controls	Capital controls refer to restrictions on cross-border capital flows that segment different stock markets; limit amount of a firm's stock a foreigner can own; and limit a citizen's ability to invest outside the country.
Capital control	Any policy intended to restrict the free movement of capital, especially financial capital, into or out of a country is referred to as capital control.
Developed country	A developed country is one that enjoys a relatively high standard of living derived through an industrialized, diversified economy. Countries with a very high Human Development Index are generally considered developed countries.
Debtor nation	Debtor nation refers to a country whose assets owned abroad are worth less than the assets within the country that are owned by foreigners. Contrasts with creditor nation.
Debt crisis	Debt crisis refers to a situation in which a country, usually an LDC, finds itself unable to service its debts.
Pleading	In the law, a pleading is one of the papers filed with a court in a civil action, such as a complaint, a demurrer, or an answer.
Capital Outflow	Capital outflow is an economic term describing capital flowing out of (or leaving) a particular economy. Outflowing capital can be caused by any number of economic or political reasons but can often originate from instability in either sphere.
International	International reserves refers to the assets denominated in foreign currency, plus gold, held

235

reserves	by a central bank, sometimes for the purpose of intervening in the exchange market to influence or peg the exchange rate.
Aid	Assistance provided by countries and by international institutions such as the World Bank to developing countries in the form of monetary grants, loans at low interest rates, in kind, or a combination of these is called aid. Aid can also refer to assistance of any type rendered to benefit some group or individual.
Capital inflow	Capital inflow refers to a net flow of capital, real and/or financial, into a country, in the form of increased purchases of domestic assets by foreigners and/or reduced holdings of foreign assets by domestic residents.
External debt	The amount that a country owes to foreigners, including the debts of both the country's government and its private sector is an external debt.
World Bank	The World Bank is a group of five international organizations responsible for providing finance and advice to countries for the purposes of economic development and poverty reduction, and for encouraging and safeguarding international investment.
Guaranty	An undertaking by one person to be answerable for the payment of some debt, or the due performance of some contract or duty by another person, who remains liable to pay or perform the same is called guaranty.
Trust	An arrangement in which shareholders of independent firms agree to give up their stock in exchange for trust certificates that entitle them to a share of the trust's common profits.
Appreciation	Appreciation refers to a rise in the value of a country's currency on the exchange market, relative either to a particular other currency or to a weighted average of other currencies. The currency is said to appreciate. Opposite of 'depreciation.' Appreciation can also refer to the increase in value of any asset.
Current account	Current account refers to a country's international transactions arising from current flows, as opposed to changes in stocks which are part of the capital account. Includes trade in goods and services plus inflows and outflows of transfers. A current account is a deposit account in the UK and countries with a UK banking heritage.
Current Account deficit	Current account deficit occurs when a country imports more goods and services than it exports.
Capital account surplus	Capital account surplus refers to the amount by which the purchase of domestic financial assets by foreigners exceeds the purchase of foreign financial assets by domestic consumers.
Contractionary fiscal policy	A decrease in government purchases for goods and services, an increase in net taxes, or some combination of the two, for the purpose of decreasing aggregate demand and thus controlling inflation is referred to as contractionary fiscal policy.
Fiscal policy	Fiscal policy refers to any macroeconomic policy involving the levels of government purchases, transfers, or taxes, usually implicitly focused on domestic goods, residents, or firms.
Monetary policy	The use of the money supply and/or the interest rate to influence the level of economic activity and other policy objectives including the balance of payments or the exchange rate is called monetary policy.
Money supply	There are several formal definitions, but all include the quantity of currency in circulation plus the amount of demand deposits. The money supply, together with the amount of real economic activity in a country, is an important determinant of price.
Supply	Supply is the aggregate amount of any material good that can be called into being at a certain price point; it comprises one half of the equation of supply and demand. In classical

Go to **Cram101.com** for the Practice Tests for this Chapter.

economic theory, a curve representing supply is one of the factors that produce price.

Lender	Suppliers and financial institutions that lend money to companies is referred to as a lender.
National income	National income refers to the income generated by a country's production, and therefore the total income of its factors of production.
Manufacturing	Production of goods primarily by the application of labor and capital to raw materials and other intermediate inputs, in contrast to agriculture, mining, forestry, fishing, and services a manufacturing.
Real property	Real property is a legal term encompassing real estate and ownership interests in real estate (immovable property).
Collateral	Property that is pledged to the lender to guarantee payment in the event that the borrower is unable to make debt payments is called collateral.
Fixed exchange rate	A fixed exchange rate, sometimes is a type of exchange rate regime wherein a currency's value is matched to the value of another single currency or to a basket of other currencies, or to another measure of value, such as gold.
Pegged exchange rate	A pegged exchange rate, is a type of exchange rate regime wherein a currency's value is matched to the value of another single currency or to a basket of other currencies, or to another measure of value, such as gold.
Central Bank	Central bank refers to the institution in a country that is normally responsible for managing the supply of the country's money and the value of its currency on the foreign exchange market.
Intervention	Intervention refers to an activity in which a government buys or sells its currency in the foreign exchange market in order to affect its currency's exchange rate.
Bail	Bail refers to an amount of money the defendant pays to the court upon release from custody as security that he or she will return for trial.
Moral hazard	Moral hazard arises when people behave recklessly because they know they will be saved if things go wrong.
Exchange rate regime	Exchange rate regime refers to the rules under which a country's exchange rate is determined, especially the way the monetary or other government authorities do or do not intervene in the exchange market.
Fixed exchange rate regime	A regime in which central banks buy and sell their own currencies to keep their exchange rates fixed at a certain level is referred to as fixed exchange rate regime.
Transparency	Transparency refers to a concept that describes a company being so open to other companies working with it that the once-solid barriers between them become see-through and electronic information is shared as if the companies were one.
Disclosure	Disclosure means the giving out of information, either voluntarily or to be in compliance with legal regulations or workplace rules.
Euro	The common currency of a subset of the countries of the EU, adopted January 1, 1999 is called euro.

Balance of trade	Balance of trade refers to the sum of the money gained by a given economy by selling exports, minus the cost of buying imports. They form part of the balance of payments, which also includes other transactions such as the international investment position.
Unlimited wants	The insatiable desire of consumers for goods and services that will give them satisfaction or utility are called unlimited wants. Unlimited wants and needs are one half of the fundamental problem of scarcity that has plagued humanity since the beginning of time. The other half of the scarcity problem is limited resources.
Elasticity	In economics, elasticity is the ratio of the incremental percentage change in one variable with respect to an incremental percentage change in another variable. Elasticity is usually expressed as a positive number (i.e., an absolute value) when the sign is already clear from context.
Balance	In banking and accountancy, the outstanding balance is the amount of money owned, (or due), that remains in a deposit account (or a loan account) at a given date, after all past remittances, payments and withdrawal have been accounted for. It can be positive (then, in the balance sheet of a firm, it is an asset) or negative (a liability).
Budget constraint	Budget constraint refers to the maximum quantity of goods that could be purchased for a given level of income and a given set of prices.
Budget	Budget refers to an account, usually for a year, of the planned expenditures and the expected receipts of an entity. For a government, the receipts are tax revenues.
Firm	An organization that employs resources to produce a good or service for profit and owns and operates one or more plants is referred to as a firm.
Consumption	In Keynesian economics consumption refers to personal consumption expenditure, i.e., the purchase of currently produced goods and services out of income, out of savings (net worth), or from borrowed funds. It refers to that part of disposable income that does not go to saving.
International trade	The export of goods and services from a country and the import of goods and services into a country is referred to as the international trade.
Trade pattern	What goods a country trades, with whom, and in what direction. Explaining the trade pattern is one of the major purposes of trade theory, especially which goods a country will export and which it will import.
Relative price	Relative price refers to the price of one thing in terms of another; i.e., the ratio of two prices.
Domestic	From or in one's own country. A domestic producer is one that produces inside the home country. A domestic price is the price inside the home country. Opposite of 'foreign' or 'world.'.
Exchange rate	Exchange rate refers to the price at which one country's currency trades for another, typically on the exchange market.
Exchange	The trade of things of value between buyer and seller so that each is better off after the trade is called the exchange.
Common currency	A situation where several countries form a monetary union with a single currency and a unified central bank is referred to as common currency.
Devaluation	Lowering the value of a nation's currency relative to other currencies is called devaluation.
Buyer	A buyer refers to a role in the buying center with formal authority and responsibility to select the supplier and negotiate the terms of the contract.

Go to **Cram101.com** for the Practice Tests for this Chapter.

Quantity demanded	The amount of a good or service that buyers desire to purchase at a particular price during some period is a quantity demanded.
Economics	The social science dealing with the use of scarce resources to obtain the maximum satisfaction of society's virtually unlimited economic wants is an economics.
Supply and demand	The partial equilibrium supply and demand economic model originally developed by Alfred Marshall attempts to describe, explain, and predict changes in the price and quantity of goods sold in competitive markets.
Foreign exchange	In finance, foreign exchange means currencies, such as U.S. Dollars and Euros. These are traded on foreign exchange markets.
Supply	Supply is the aggregate amount of any material good that can be called into being at a certain price point; it comprises one half of the equation of supply and demand. In classical economic theory, a curve representing supply is one of the factors that produce price.
Inelastic demand	Inelastic demand refers to product or resource demand for which the elasticity coefficient for price is less than 1. This means the resulting percentage change in quantity demanded is less than the percentage change in price. In other words, consumers are relatively less sensitive to changes in price.
Inelastic	Inelastic refers to having an elasticity less than one. For a price elasticity of demand, this means that expenditure falls as price falls. For an income elasticity, it means that expenditure share falls with income.
Change in the quantity supplied	Change in the quantity supplied refers to a change in sellers' plans that occurs when the price of a good changes but all other influences on sellers' plans remain unchanged. It is illustrated by a movement along the supply curve.
Elasticity of supply	Elasticity of supply refers to a measure of the response of quantity of a good supplied to a change in price of that good. Likely to be positive in output markets.
Quantity supplied	The amount of a good or service that producers offer to sell at a particular price during a given time period is called quantity supplied.
Total revenue	Total revenue refers to the total number of dollars received by a firm from the sale of a product; equal to the total expenditures for the product produced by the firm; equal to the quantity sold multiplied by the price at which it is sold.
Revenue	Revenue is a U.S. business term for the amount of money that a company receives from its activities, mostly from sales of products and/or services to customers.
Elastic demand	Elastic demand refers to product or resource demand whose price elasticity is greater than 1. This means the resulting change in quantity demanded is greater than the percentage change in price.
Export	In economics, an export is any good or commodity, shipped or otherwise transported out of a country, province, town to another part of the world in a legitimate fashion, typically for use in trade or sale.
Demand curve	Demand curve refers to the graph of quantity demanded as a function of price, normally downward sloping, straight or curved, and drawn with quantity on the horizontal axis and price on the vertical axis.
Slope	The slope of a line in the plane containing the x and y axes is generally represented by the letter m, and is defined as the change in the y coordinate divided by the corresponding change in the x coordinate, between two distinct points on the line.
Supply curve	Supply curve refers to the graph of quantity supplied as a function of price, normally upward sloping, straight or curved, and drawn with quantity on the horizontal axis and price on the

Go to **Cram101.com** for the Practice Tests for this Chapter.

vertical axis.

Market	A market is, as defined in economics, a social arrangement that allows buyers and sellers to discover information and carry out a voluntary exchange of goods or services.
Central Bank	Central bank refers to the institution in a country that is normally responsible for managing the supply of the country's money and the value of its currency on the foreign exchange market.
Quota	A government-imposed restriction on quantity, or sometimes on total value, used to restrict the import of something to a specific quantity is called a quota.
Tariff	A tax imposed by a nation on an imported good is called a tariff.
Equilibrium quantity	Equilibrium quantity refers to the quantity demanded and supplied at the equilibrium price in a competitive market; the profit-maximizing output of a firm.
Balance of payments	Balance of payments refers to a list, or accounting, of all of a country's international transactions for a given time period, usually one year.
Capital flow	International capital movement is referred to as capital flow.
Capital	Capital generally refers to financial wealth, especially that used to start or maintain a business. In classical economics, capital is one of four factors of production, the others being land and labor and entrepreneurship.
Increase in demand	Increase in demand refers to an increase in the quantity demanded of a good or service at every price; a shift of the demand curve to the right.
Federal Reserve	The Federal Reserve System was created via the Federal Reserve Act of December 23rd, 1913. All national banks were required to join the system and other banks could join. The Reserve Banks opened for business on November 16th, 1914. Federal Reserve Notes were created as part of the legislation, to provide an elastic supply of currency.
Short run	Short run refers to a period of time that permits an increase or decrease in current production volume with existing capacity, but one that is too short to permit enlargement of that capacity itself (eg, the building of new plants, training of additional workers, etc.).
Contract	A contract is a "promise" or an "agreement" that is enforced or recognized by the law. In the civil law, a contract is considered to be part of the general law of obligations.
Exporter	A firm that sells its product in another country is an exporter.
Gain	In finance, gain is a profit or an increase in value of an investment such as a stock or bond. Gain is calculated by fair market value or the proceeds from the sale of the investment minus the sum of the purchase price and all costs associated with it.
Consideration	Consideration in contract law, a basic requirement for an enforceable agreement under traditional contract principles, defined in this text as legal value, bargained for and given in exchange for an act or promise. In corporation law, cash or property contributed to a corporation in exchange for shares, or a promise to contribute such cash or property.
Depreciate	A nation's currency is said to depreciate when exchange rates change so that a unit of its currency can buy fewer units of foreign currency.
Trade balance	Balance of trade in terms of exports versus imports is called trade balance.
Trade surplus	A positive balance of trade is known as a trade surplus and consists of exporting more (in financial capital terms) than one imports.
Trade deficit	The amount by which imports exceed exports of goods and services is referred to as trade deficit.

Deficit	The deficit is the amount by which expenditure exceed revenue.
Inelastic supply	Inelastic supply refers to product or resource supply for which the price elasticity coefficient is less than 1. The percentage change in quantity supplied is less than the percentage change in price.
Perfectly inelastic supply	Perfectly inelastic supply refers to product or resource supply in which price can be of any amount at a particular quantity of the product or resource demanded; quantity supplied does not respond to a change in price; graphs as a vertical supply curve.
Contribution	In business organization law, the cash or property contributed to a business by its owners is referred to as contribution.
Industry	A group of firms that produce identical or similar products is an industry. It is also used specifically to refer to an area of economic production focused on manufacturing which involves large amounts of capital investment before any profit can be realized, also called "heavy industry".
Profit margin	Profit margin is a measure of profitability. It is calculated using a formula and written as a percentage or a number. Profit margin = Net income before tax and interest / Revenue.
Profit	Profit refers to the return to the resource entrepreneurial ability; total revenue minus total cost.
Margin	A deposit by a buyer in stocks with a seller or a stockbroker, as security to cover fluctuations in the market in reference to stocks that the buyer has purchased but for which he has not paid is a margin. Commodities are also traded on margin.
Appreciation	Appreciation refers to a rise in the value of a country's currency on the exchange market, relative either to a particular other currency or to a weighted average of other currencies. The currency is said to appreciate. Opposite of 'depreciation.' Appreciation can also refer to the increase in value of any asset.
Cost of capital	Cost of capital refers to the percentage cost of funds used for acquiring resources for an organization, typically a weighted average of the firms cost of equity and cost of debt.
Long run	In economic models, the long run time frame assumes no fixed factors of production. Firms can enter or leave the marketplace, and the cost (and availability) of land, labor, raw materials, and capital goods can be assumed to vary.
Labor	People's physical and mental talents and efforts that are used to help produce goods and services are called labor.
Commodity	Could refer to any good, but in trade a commodity is usually a raw material or primary product that enters into international trade, such as metals or basic agricultural products.
Forbes	David Churbuck founded online Forbes in 1996. The site drew attention when it uncovered Stephen Glass' journalistic fraud in The New Republic in 1998, a scoop that gave credibility to internet journalism.
Competitiveness	Competitiveness usually refers to characteristics that permit a firm to compete effectively with other firms due to low cost or superior technology, perhaps internationally.
Depreciation	Depreciation is an accounting and finance term for the method of attributing the cost of an asset across the useful life of the asset. Depreciation is a reduction in the value of a currency in floating exchange rate.
Economy	The income, expenditures, and resources that affect the cost of running a business and household are called an economy.
Flexible	Exchange rates with a fixed parity against one or more currencies with frequent revaluation's

exchange rate	is referred to as a flexible exchange rate.
Political economy	Early name for the discipline of economics. A field within economics encompassing several alternatives to neoclassical economics, including Marxist economics. Also called radical political economy.
Oligopoly	A market structure in which there are a small number of sellers, at least some of whose individual decisions about price or quantity matter to the others is an oligopoly.
Journal	Book of original entry, in which transactions are recorded in a general ledger system, is referred to as a journal.
Federal reserve system	The central banking authority responsible for monetary policy in the United States is called federal reserve system or the Fed.
Board of Governors	A board of governors is usually the governing board of a public entity; the Board of Governors of the Federal Reserve System; the Federal Reserve Board.
Macroeconomics	Macroeconomics refers to the part of economics concerned with the economy as a whole; with such major aggregates as the household, business, and government sectors; and with measures of the total economy.
Absorption approach	Absorption approach refers to a way of understanding the determinants of the balance of trade, noting that it is equal to income minus absorption.
Absorption	Total demand for goods and services by all residents of a country is absorption. The term was introduced as part of the Absorption Approach.
Production	The creation of finished goods and services using the factors of production: land, labor, capital, entrepreneurship, and knowledge.
Economic growth	Economic growth refers to the increase over time in the capacity of an economy to produce goods and services and to improve the well-being of its citizens.
Service	Service refers to a "non tangible product" that is not embodied in a physical good and that typically effects some change in another product, person, or institution. Contrasts with good.
Full employment	Full employment refers to the unemployment rate at which there is no cyclical unemployment of the labor force; equal to between 4 and 5 percent in the United States because some frictional and structural unemployment is unavoidable.
Domestic output	Domestic output refers to gross domestic product; the total output of final goods and services produced in the economy.
Government spending	Government spending refers to spending by all levels of government on goods and services.
Investment	Investment refers to spending for the production and accumulation of capital and additions to inventories. In a financial sense, buying an asset with the expectation of making a return.
Net exports	Net exports refers to exports minus imports; same as the balance of trade. They are the sum of the money gained by a given economy by selling exports, minus the cost of buying imports. They form part of the balance of payments, which also includes other transactions such as the international investment position.
Inflation	An increase in the overall price level of an economy, usually as measured by the CPI or by the implicit price deflator is called inflation.
Financial assets	Financial assets refer to monetary claims or obligations by one party against another party. Examples are bonds, mortgages, bank loans, and equities.

Asset	An item of property, such as land, capital, money, a share in ownership, or a claim on others for future payment, such as a bond or a bank deposit is an asset.
Interdependence	The extent to which departments depend on each other for resources or materials to accomplish their tasks is referred to as interdependence.
Exchange market	Exchange market refers to the market on which national currencies are bought and sold.
Portfolio	In finance, a portfolio is a collection of investments held by an institution or a private individual. Holding but not always a portfolio is part of an investment and risk-limiting strategy called diversification. By owning several assets, certain types of risk (in particular specific risk) can be reduced.
Economic interdependence	Economic interdependence describes countries/nation-states and/or supranational states such as the European Union (EU) or North American Free Trade Agreement (NAFTA) that are interdependent for any (or all) of the following: food , energy, minerals,manufactured goods, multinational/transnational corporations , financial institutions and foreign debt.
International Monetary Fund	The International Monetary Fund is the international organization entrusted with overseeing the global financial system by monitoring exchange rates and balance of payments, as well as offering technical and financial assistance when asked.
Capital account	The capital account is one of two primary components of the balance of payments. It tracks the movement of funds for investments and loans into and out of a country.
Special drawing right	Special drawing right refers to what was originally intended within the IMF as a sort of international money for use among central banks pegging their exchange rates. The special drawing right is a transferable right to acquire another country's currency.
Above the line	Above the line is an advertising technique using mass media to promote brands. This type of communication is conventional in nature and is considered impersonal to customers.
Below the line	Below the line is an advertising technique. It uses less conventional methods than the usual specific channels of advertising to promote products, services, etc. than ATL (Above the line) strategy.
Money supply	There are several formal definitions, but all include the quantity of currency in circulation plus the amount of demand deposits. The money supply, together with the amount of real economic activity in a country, is an important determinant of price.
Holding	The holding is a court's determination of a matter of law based on the issue presented in the particular case. In other words: under this law, with these facts, this result.
Fund	Independent accounting entity with a self-balancing set of accounts segregated for the purposes of carrying on specific activities is referred to as a fund.
Disequilibrium	Inequality or imbalance of supply and demand is referred to as disequilibrium.
Authority	Authority in agency law, refers to an agent's ability to affect his principal's legal relations with third parties. Also used to refer to an actor's legal power or ability to do something. In addition, sometimes used to refer to a statute, case, or other legal source that justifies a particular result.
Excess demand	Demand minus supply. Thus a country's demand for imports of a homogeneous good is its excess demand for that good.
Innovation	Innovation refers to the first commercially successful introduction of a new product, the use of a new method of production, or the creation of a new form of business organization.
Price level	The overall level of prices in a country, as usually measured empirically by a price index, but often captured in theoretical models by a single variable is a price level.

Go to **Cram101.com** for the Practice Tests for this Chapter.

Stock	In financial terminology, stock is the capital raized by a corporation, through the issuance and sale of shares.
Competitor	Other organizations in the same industry or type of business that provide a good or service to the same set of customers is referred to as a competitor.
Floating exchange rate	A system under which the exchange rate for converting one currency into another is continuously adjusted depending on the laws of supply and demand is referred to as a floating exchange rate.
Adjustment mechanism	The theoretical process by which a market moves from disequilibrium toward equilibrium is the adjustment mechanism.
Fixed exchange rate	A fixed exchange rate, sometimes is a type of exchange rate regime wherein a currency's value is matched to the value of another single currency or to a basket of other currencies, or to another measure of value, such as gold.
Economic model	Economic model refers to a simplified picture of economic reality; an abstract generalization.
Commercial bank	A firm that engages in the business of banking is a commercial bank.
Domestic credit	Domestic credit refers to credit extended by a country's central bank to domestic borrowers, including the government and commercial banks. In the United States, the largest component by far is the Fed's holdings of U.S. government bonds.
Credit	Credit refers to a recording as positive in the balance of payments, any transaction that gives rise to a payment into the country, such as an export, the sale of an asset, or borrowing from abroad.
International reserves	International reserves refers to the assets denominated in foreign currency, plus gold, held by a central bank, sometimes for the purpose of intervening in the exchange market to influence or peg the exchange rate.
Excess supply	Supply minus demand. Thus a country's supply of exports of a homogeneous good is its excess supply of that good.
Remainder	A remainder in property law is a future interest created in a transferee that is capable of becoming possessory upon the natural termination of a prior estate created by the same instrument.
Open economy	Open economy refers to an economy that permits transactions with the outside world, at least including trade of some goods. Contrasts with closed economy.
Interest rate	The rate of return on bonds, loans, or deposits. When one speaks of 'the' interest rate, it is usually in a model where there is only one.
Interest	In finance and economics, interest is the price paid by a borrower for the use of a lender's money. In other words, interest is the amount of paid to "rent" money for a period of time.
Openness	Openness refers to the extent to which an economy is open, often measured by the ratio of its trade to GDP.
Exchange rate regime	Exchange rate regime refers to the rules under which a country's exchange rate is determined, especially the way the monetary or other government authorities do or do not intervene in the exchange market.
Law of one price	The principle that identical goods should sell for the same price throughout the world if trade were free and frictionless is referred to as the law of one price.
Domestic price	The price of a good or service within a country, determined by domestic demand and supply is referred to as domestic price.

Money market	The money market, in macroeconomics and international finance, refers to the equilibration of demand for a country's domestic money to its money supply; market for short-term financial instruments.
Managed float	An exchange rate regime in which the rate is allowed to be determined in the exchange market without an announced par value as the goal of intervention, but the authorities do nonetheless intervene at their discretion to influence the rate is a managed float.
Variable	A variable is something measured by a number; it is used to analyze what happens to other things when the size of that number changes.
Monetary policy	The use of the money supply and/or the interest rate to influence the level of economic activity and other policy objectives including the balance of payments or the exchange rate is called monetary policy.
Policy	Similar to a script in that a policy can be a less than completely rational decision-making method. Involves the use of a pre-existing set of decision steps for any problem that presents itself.
Currency exchange rate	The rate between two currencies that specifies how much one country's currency is worth expressed in terms of the other country's currency is the currency exchange rate.
Drawback	Drawback refers to rebate of import duties when the imported good is re-exported or used as input to the production of an exported good.
Economic policy	Economic policy refers to the actions that governments take in the economic field. It covers the systems for setting interest rates and government deficit as well as the labor market, national ownership, and many other areas of government.
Developing country	Developing country refers to a country whose per capita income is low by world standards. Same as LDC. As usually used, it does not necessarily connote that the country's income is rising.
Price elasticity	The responsiveness of the market to change in price is called price elasticity. If price elasticity is low, a large change in price will lead to a small change in supply.
Perfectly elastic	Perfectly elastic refers to a supply or demand curve with a price elasticity of infinity, implying that the supply or demand curve as usually drawn is horizontal. A small open economy faces perfectly elastic demand for its exports and supply of its imports.
Elastic supply	Elastic supply refers to product or resource supply whose price elasticity is greater than 1. This means the resulting change in quantity supplied is greater than the percentage change in price.
Perfectly elastic supply	Perfectly elastic supply refers to product or resource supply in which quantity supplied can be of any amount at a particular product or resource price; graphs as a horizontal supply curve.
Total supply	Total supply refers to the supply schedule or the supply curve of all sellers of a good or service.

Go to **Cram101.com** for the Practice Tests for this Chapter.

Exchange rate	Exchange rate refers to the price at which one country's currency trades for another, typically on the exchange market.
Exchange	The trade of things of value between buyer and seller so that each is better off after the trade is called the exchange.
Market	A market is, as defined in economics, a social arrangement that allows buyers and sellers to discover information and carry out a voluntary exchange of goods or services.
Asset	An item of property, such as land, capital, money, a share in ownership, or a claim on others for future payment, such as a bond or a bank deposit is an asset.
Financial assets	Financial assets refer to monetary claims or obligations by one party against another party. Examples are bonds, mortgages, bank loans, and equities.
Supply	Supply is the aggregate amount of any material good that can be called into being at a certain price point; it comprises one half of the equation of supply and demand. In classical economic theory, a curve representing supply is one of the factors that produce price.
Variable	A variable is something measured by a number; it is used to analyze what happens to other things when the size of that number changes.
Volatility	Volatility refers to the extent to which an economic variable, such as a price or an exchange rate, moves up and down over time.
Capital mobility	The ability of capital to move internationally. The degree of capital mobility depends on government policies restricting or taxing capital inflows and/or outflows, plus the risk that investors in one country associate with assets in another.
Capital	Capital generally refers to financial wealth, especially that used to start or maintain a business. In classical economics, capital is one of four factors of production, the others being land and labor and entrepreneurship.
Perfect capital mobility	The absence of any barriers to international capital movements is referred to as perfect capital mobility. Under this scenario a practically unlimited amount of lending shifts between countries in response to the slightest change in one country's interest rate.
Covered interest arbitrage	Covered interest arbitrage is the investment strategy where an investor buys a financial instrument denominated in a foreign currency, and hedges his foreign exchange risk by selling a forward contract in the amount of the proceeds of the investment back into his base currency.
Covered interest rate	The covered interest rate, in a currency other than your own, is the nominal interest rate plus the forward premium on the currency.
Interest Rate Parity	The Interest Rate Parity is the basic identity that relates interest rates and exchange rates. The identity is theoretical, and usually follows from assumptions imposed in economics models.
Interest rate	The rate of return on bonds, loans, or deposits. When one speaks of 'the' interest rate, it is usually in a model where there is only one.
Arbitrage	An arbitrage is a combination of nearly simultaneous transactions designed to profit from an existing discrepancy among prices, exchange rates, and/or interest rates on different markets without assuming risk.
Domestic	From or in one's own country. A domestic producer is one that produces inside the home country. A domestic price is the price inside the home country. Opposite of 'foreign' or 'world.'.
Interest	In finance and economics, interest is the price paid by a borrower for the use of a lender's

Go to **Cram101.com** for the Practice Tests for this Chapter.

	money. In other words, interest is the amount of paid to "rent" money for a period of time.
Forward exchange rate	The exchange rates governing forward exchange transactions is called the forward exchange rate.
Forward exchange	When two parties agree to exchange currency and execute a deal at some specific date in the future, we have forward exchange.
Portfolio	In finance, a portfolio is a collection of investments held by an institution or a private individual. Holding but not always a portfolio is part of an investment and risk-limiting strategy called diversification. By owning several assets, certain types of risk (in particular specific risk) can be reduced.
Balance of payments	Balance of payments refers to a list, or accounting, of all of a country's international transactions for a given time period, usually one year.
Money supply	There are several formal definitions, but all include the quantity of currency in circulation plus the amount of demand deposits. The money supply, together with the amount of real economic activity in a country, is an important determinant of price.
Balance	In banking and accountancy, the outstanding balance is the amount of money owned, (or due), that remains in a deposit account (or a loan account) at a given date, after all past remittances, payments and withdrawal have been accounted for. It can be positive (then, in the balance sheet of a firm, it is an asset) or negative (a liability).
Relative supply	The ratio of the supply of one good to the supply of another, most useful in representing general equilibrium in a two-good economy, where relative price adjusts to equate relative supply and relative demand.
Foreign bonds	Bonds sold in a foreign country and denominated in that country's currency are foreign bonds. Many domestic markets are also open to foreign borrowers who, although domiciled outside the country, can issue bonds in the domestic currency for sale to local investors as long as they comply with the same local regulations as their domestic counterparts.
Bond	Bond refers to a debt instrument, issued by a borrower and promising a specified stream of payments to the purchaser, usually regular interest payments plus a final repayment of principal.
Perfect substitute	A good that is regarded by its demanders as identical to another good, so that the elasticity of substitution between them is infinite is referred to as perfect substitute.
Expected return	Expected return refers to the return on an asset expected over the next period.
International adjustment process	International adjustment process refers to any mechanism for change in international markets. Similar to the specie flow mechanism, exchange-market intervention causes money supplies of surplus countries to expand and vice versa, leading to price and interest rate changes that correct the current and capital account imbalances.
International capital flows	International capital flows are purchases and sales of financial assets across national borders. Flows of physical capital goods are typically treated as ordinary trade flows, not capital flows, in the balance of payments accounts.
Economic integration	Occurs when two or more nations join to form a free-trade zone are called economic integration. As economic integration increases, the barriers of trade between markets diminishes.
Flexible exchange rate	Exchange rates with a fixed parity against one or more currencies with frequent revaluation's is referred to as a flexible exchange rate.
Fiscal policy	Fiscal policy refers to any macroeconomic policy involving the levels of government purchases, transfers, or taxes, usually implicitly focused on domestic goods, residents, or

	firms.
Capital flow	International capital movement is referred to as capital flow.
Money market	The money market, in macroeconomics and international finance, refers to the equilibration of demand for a country's domestic money to its money supply; market for short-term financial instruments.
Integration	Economic integration refers to reducing barriers among countries to transactions and to movements of goods, capital, and labor, including harmonization of laws, regulations, and standards. Integrated markets theoretically function as a unified market.
Short run	Short run refers to a period of time that permits an increase or decrease in current production volume with existing capacity, but one that is too short to permit enlargement of that capacity itself (eg, the building of new plants, training of additional workers, etc.).
Economics	The social science dealing with the use of scarce resources to obtain the maximum satisfaction of society's virtually unlimited economic wants is an economics.
Journal	Book of original entry, in which transactions are recorded in a general ledger system, is referred to as a journal.
Policy	Similar to a script in that a policy can be a less than completely rational decision-making method. Involves the use of a pre-existing set of decision steps for any problem that presents itself.
Risk premium	In finance, the risk premium can be the expected rate of return above the risk-free interest rate.
Premium	Premium refers to the fee charged by an insurance company for an insurance policy. The rate of losses must be relatively predictable: In order to set the premium (prices) insurers must be able to estimate them accurately.
Forward market	A market for exchange of currencies in the future is the forward market. Participants in a forward market enter into a contract to exchange currencies, not today, but at a specified date in the future, typically 30, 60, or 90 days from now, and at a price that is agreed upon.
Fixed exchange rate	A fixed exchange rate, sometimes is a type of exchange rate regime wherein a currency's value is matched to the value of another single currency or to a basket of other currencies, or to another measure of value, such as gold.
Disequilibrium	Inequality or imbalance of supply and demand is referred to as disequilibrium.
Floating exchange rate	A system under which the exchange rate for converting one currency into another is continuously adjusted depending on the laws of supply and demand is referred to as a floating exchange rate.
Export	In economics, an export is any good or commodity, shipped or otherwise transported out of a country, province, town to another part of the world in a legitimate fashion, typically for use in trade or sale.
Economic model	Economic model refers to a simplified picture of economic reality; an abstract generalization.
Federal Reserve	The Federal Reserve System was created via the Federal Reserve Act of December 23rd, 1913. All national banks were required to join the system and other banks could join. The Reserve Banks opened for business on November 16th, 1914. Federal Reserve Notes were created as part of the legislation, to provide an elastic supply of currency.
Commercial bank	A firm that engages in the business of banking is a commercial bank.

Macroeconomics	Macroeconomics refers to the part of economics concerned with the economy as a whole; with such major aggregates as the household, business, and government sectors; and with measures of the total economy.
Bank reserves	Bank reserves are banks' holdings of deposits in accounts with their central bank, plus currency that is physically held in bank vaults (vault cash). The central bank sets minimum reserve requirements.
Contract	A contract is a "promise" or an "agreement" that is enforced or recognized by the law. In the civil law, a contract is considered to be part of the general law of obligations.
International reserves	International reserves refers to the assets denominated in foreign currency, plus gold, held by a central bank, sometimes for the purpose of intervening in the exchange market to influence or peg the exchange rate.
Foreign exchange	In finance, foreign exchange means currencies, such as U.S. Dollars and Euros. These are traded on foreign exchange markets.
Domestic credit	Domestic credit refers to credit extended by a country's central bank to domestic borrowers, including the government and commercial banks. In the United States, the largest component by far is the Fed's holdings of U.S. government bonds.
Excess demand	Demand minus supply. Thus a country's demand for imports of a homogeneous good is its excess demand for that good.
Excess supply	Supply minus demand. Thus a country's supply of exports of a homogeneous good is its excess supply of that good.
Remainder	A remainder in property law is a future interest created in a transferee that is capable of becoming possessory upon the natural termination of a prior estate created by the same instrument.
Credit	Credit refers to a recording as positive in the balance of payments, any transaction that gives rise to a payment into the country, such as an export, the sale of an asset, or borrowing from abroad.
Economy	The income, expenditures, and resources that affect the cost of running a business and household are called an economy.
Open economy	Open economy refers to an economy that permits transactions with the outside world, at least including trade of some goods. Contrasts with closed economy.
Openness	Openness refers to the extent to which an economy is open, often measured by the ratio of its trade to GDP.
International trade	The export of goods and services from a country and the import of goods and services into a country is referred to as the international trade.
Price level	The overall level of prices in a country, as usually measured empirically by a price index, but often captured in theoretical models by a single variable is a price level.
Adjustment mechanism	The theoretical process by which a market moves from disequilibrium toward equilibrium is the adjustment mechanism.
Exchange rate regime	Exchange rate regime refers to the rules under which a country's exchange rate is determined, especially the way the monetary or other government authorities do or do not intervene in the exchange market.
Law of one price	The principle that identical goods should sell for the same price throughout the world if trade were free and frictionless is referred to as the law of one price.
Domestic price	The price of a good or service within a country, determined by domestic demand and supply is

referred to as domestic price.

Central Bank	Central bank refers to the institution in a country that is normally responsible for managing the supply of the country's money and the value of its currency on the foreign exchange market.
Managed float	An exchange rate regime in which the rate is allowed to be determined in the exchange market without an announced par value as the goal of intervention, but the authorities do nonetheless intervene at their discretion to influence the rate is a managed float.
Inflation rate	The percentage increase in the price level per year is an inflation rate. Alternatively, the inflation rate is the rate of decrease in the purchasing power of money.
Real income	Real income refers to the amount of goods and services that can be purchased with nominal income during some period of time; nominal income adjusted for inflation.
Inflation	An increase in the overall price level of an economy, usually as measured by the CPI or by the implicit price deflator is called inflation.
Monetary policy	The use of the money supply and/or the interest rate to influence the level of economic activity and other policy objectives including the balance of payments or the exchange rate is called monetary policy.
Appreciation	Appreciation refers to a rise in the value of a country's currency on the exchange market, relative either to a particular other currency or to a weighted average of other currencies. The currency is said to appreciate. Opposite of 'depreciation.' Appreciation can also refer to the increase in value of any asset.
Depreciation	Depreciation is an accounting and finance term for the method of attributing the cost of an asset across the useful life of the asset. Depreciation is a reduction in the value of a currency in floating exchange rate.
Holding	The holding is a court's determination of a matter of law based on the issue presented in the particular case. In other words: under this law, with these facts, this result.
Spot market	Spot market refers to a market in which commodities are bought and sold for cash and immediate delivery.
Depreciate	A nation's currency is said to depreciate when exchange rates change so that a unit of its currency can buy fewer units of foreign currency.
Spot exchange rate	The exchange rate at which a foreign exchange dealer will convert one currency into another that particular day is the spot exchange rate.
Spot rate	Spot rate refers to the rate at which the currency is traded for immediate delivery. It is the existing cash price.
Deficit	The deficit is the amount by which expenditure exceed revenue.
Authority	Authority in agency law, refers to an agent's ability to affect his principal's legal relations with third parties. Also used to refer to an actor's legal power or ability to do something. In addition, sometimes used to refer to a statute, case, or other legal source that justifies a particular result.
Long run	In economic models, the long run time frame assumes no fixed factors of production. Firms can enter or leave the marketplace, and the cost (and availability) of land, labor, raw materials, and capital goods can be assumed to vary.
Sterilize	Sterilize refers to the use of offsetting open market actions to prevent an act of exchange market intervention from changing the monetary base. Any purchase of foreign exchange is accompanied by an equal-value sale of domestic bonds, and vice versa.

Go to **Cram101.com** for the Practice Tests for this Chapter.

Foreign exchange intervention	An international 'financial transaction in which a central bank buys or sells currency to influence foreign exchange rates a foreign exchange intervention.
International Monetary Fund	The International Monetary Fund is the international organization entrusted with overseeing the global financial system by monitoring exchange rates and balance of payments, as well as offering technical and financial assistance when asked.
Intervention	Intervention refers to an activity in which a government buys or sells its currency in the foreign exchange market in order to affect its currency's exchange rate.
Fund	Independent accounting entity with a self-balancing set of accounts segregated for the purposes of carrying on specific activities is referred to as a fund.
Operation	A standardized method or technique that is performed repetitively, often on different materials resulting in different finished goods is called an operation.
Exchange market	Exchange market refers to the market on which national currencies are bought and sold.
Foreign exchange market	A market for converting the currency of one country into that of another country is called foreign exchange market. It is by far the largest market in the world, in terms of cash value traded, and includes trading between large banks, central banks, currency speculators, multinational corporations, governments, and other financial markets and institutions.
Stock	In financial terminology, stock is the capital raized by a corporation, through the issuance and sale of shares.
Trade surplus	A positive balance of trade is known as a trade surplus and consists of exporting more (in financial capital terms) than one imports.
Balance of trade	Balance of trade refers to the sum of the money gained by a given economy by selling exports, minus the cost of buying imports. They form part of the balance of payments, which also includes other transactions such as the international investment position.
Trade flow	The quantity or value of a country's bilateral trade with another country is called trade flow.
Expected value	A representative value from a probability distribution arrived at by multiplying each outcome by the associated probability and summing up the values is called the expected value.
Balanced trade	Balanced trade is an alternative economic model to free trade. Under balanced trade nations are required to provide a fairly even reciprocal trade pattern; they cannot run large trade deficits.
Cartel	Cartel refers to a group of firms that seeks to raise the price of a good by restricting its supply. The term is usually used for international groups, especially involving state-owned firms and/or governments.
Trade deficit	The amount by which imports exceed exports of goods and services is referred to as trade deficit.
Trade balance	Balance of trade in terms of exports versus imports is called trade balance.
Anticipation	In finance, anticipation is where debts are paid off early, generally in order to pay less interest.
Financial market	In economics, a financial market is a mechanism which allows people to trade money for securities or commodities such as gold or other precious metals. In general, any commodity market might be considered to be a financial market, if the usual purpose of traders is not the immediate consumption of the commodity, but rather as a means of delaying or accelerating consumption over time.

Opportunity cost	The cost of something in terms of opportunity foregone. The opportunity cost to a country of producing a unit more of a good, such as for export or to replace an import, is the quantity of some other good that could have been produced instead.
Forward premium	The difference between a forward exchange rate and the spot exchange rate, expressed as an annualized percentage return on buying foreign currency spot and selling it forward is a forward premium.
Writ	Writ refers to a commandment of a court given for the purpose of compelling certain action from the defendant, and usually executed by a sheriff or other judicial officer.
Equilibrium price	Equilibrium price refers to the price in a competitive market at which the quantity demanded and the quantity supplied are equal, there is neither a shortage nor a surplus, and there is no tendency for price to rise or fall.
Interest parity	Interest parity refers to equality of returns on otherwise identical financial assets denominated in different currencies.
Fixed price	Fixed price is a phrase used to mean that no bargaining is allowed over the price of a good or, less commonly, a service.
Capital inflow	Capital inflow refers to a net flow of capital, real and/or financial, into a country, in the form of increased purchases of domestic assets by foreigners and/or reduced holdings of foreign assets by domestic residents.
Purchasing power	The amount of goods that money will buy, usually measured by the CPI is referred to as purchasing power.
Purchasing	Purchasing refers to the function in a firm that searches for quality material resources, finds the best suppliers, and negotiates the best price for goods and services.
Currency union	A group of countries that agree to peg their exchange rates and to coordinate their monetary policies so as to avoid the need for currency realignments is called a currency union.
Union	A worker association that bargains with employers over wages and working conditions is called a union.
Medium of exchange	Medium of exchange refers to any item sellers generally accept and buyers generally use to pay for a good or service; money; a convenient means of exchanging goods and services without engaging in barter.
Store of value	To act as a store of value, a commodity, a form of money, or financial capital must be able to be reliably saved, stored, and retrieved - and be predictably useful when it is so retrieved.
Economic development	Increase in the economic standard of living of a country's population, normally accomplished by increasing its stocks of physical and human capital and improving its technology is an economic development.
Transactions cost	Any cost associated with bringing buyers and sellers together is referred to as transactions cost.
Dollarization	Dollarization refers to the official adoption by a country other than the United States of the U.S. dollar as its local currency.
Economic policy	Economic policy refers to the actions that governments take in the economic field. It covers the systems for setting interest rates and government deficit as well as the labor market, national ownership, and many other areas of government.
Realization	Realization is the sale of assets when an entity is being liquidated.
Purchasing	purchasing power parity is a theory based on the law of one price which says that the long-

power parity	run equilibrium exchange rate of two currencies is the rate that equalizes the currencies' purchasing power.
Service	Service refers to a "non tangible product" that is not embodied in a physical good and that typically effects some change in another product, person, or institution. Contrasts with good.
Unemployment rate	The unemployment rate is the number of unemployed workers divided by the total civilian labor force, which includes both the unemployed and those with jobs (all those willing and able to work for pay).
Euro	The common currency of a subset of the countries of the EU, adopted January 1, 1999 is called euro.
Management control	That aspect of management concerned with the comparison of actual versus planned performance as well as the development and implementation of procedures to correct substandard performance is called management control.
Management	Management characterizes the process of leading and directing all or part of an organization, often a business, through the deployment and manipulation of resources. Early twentieth-century management writer Mary Parker Follett defined management as "the art of getting things done through people."
Long position	In finance, a long position in a security, such as a stock or a bond, means the holder of the position owns the security.
Profit	Profit refers to the return to the resource entrepreneurial ability; total revenue minus total cost.
Short position	In finance, a short position in a security, such as a stock or a Bond, means the holder of the position has sold a security that he does not own, with the intention to buy it back at a later time at a lower price.
Inventory	Tangible property held for sale in the normal course of business or used in producing goods or services for sale is an inventory.
Deutsche Bank	Deutsche Bank was founded in Germany on January 22, 1870 as a specialist bank for foreign trade. Major projects in its first decades included the Northern Pacific Railroad in the United States (1883) and the Baghdad Railway (1888). It also financed bond offerings of the steel concern Krupp (1885) and introduced the chemical company Bayer on the Berlin stock market.
DaimlerChrysler	In 2002, the merged company, DaimlerChrysler, appeared to run two independent product lines, with few signs of corporate integration. In 2003, however, it was alleged by the Detroit News that the "merger of equals" was, in fact, a takeover.
Counterparty	A counterparty is a legal and financial term. It means a party to a contract. Any legal entity can be a counterparty.
Bid	A bid price is a price offered by a buyer when he/she buys a good. In the context of stock trading on a stock exchange, the bid price is the highest price a buyer of a stock is willing to pay for a share of that given stock.
Asymmetric information	Asymmetric information refers to the failure of two parties to a transaction to have the same relevant information. Examples are buyers who know less about product quality than sellers, and lenders who know less about likely default than borrowers.
Inventory control	Inventory control, in the field of loss prevention, are systems designed to introduce technical barriers to shoplifting.
Dealer	People who link buyers with sellers by buying and selling securities at stated prices are

referred to as a dealer.

Complaint	The pleading in a civil case in which the plaintiff states his claim and requests relief is called complaint. In the common law, it is a formal legal document that sets out the basic facts and legal reasons that the filing party (the plaintiffs) believes are sufficient to support a claim against another person, persons, entity or entities (the defendants) that entitles the plaintiff(s) to a remedy (either money damages or injunctive relief).
Wall Street Journal	Dow Jones & Company was founded in 1882 by reporters Charles Dow, Edward Jones and Charles Bergstresser. Jones converted the small Customers' Afternoon Letter into The Wall Street Journal, first published in 1889, and began delivery of the Dow Jones News Service via telegraph. The Journal featured the Jones 'Average', the first of several indexes of stock and bond prices on the New York Stock Exchange.
Developing country	Developing country refers to a country whose per capita income is low by world standards. Same as LDC. As usually used, it does not necessarily connote that the country's income is rising.
Channel	Channel, in communications (sometimes called communications channel), refers to the medium used to convey information from a sender (or transmitter) to a receiver.
Reserve currency	A reserve currency is a currency which is held in significant quantities by many governments and institutions as part of their foreign exchange reserves.
Commodity money	Commodity money is an object in use as a medium of exchange, but which also has a substantial value in alternative uses. Gold coins would be an example of commodity money.
Currency board	A currency board is a system, popular in emerging economies, in which the exchange rate of a local currency and a foreign currency can be controlled by law.
Public policy	Decision making by government. Governments are constantly concerned about what they should or should not do. And whatever they do or do not do is public policy. public program All those activities designed to implement a public policy; often this calls for the creation of organizations, public agencies, and bureaus.
Gold standard	The gold standard is a monetary system in which the standard economic unit of account is a fixed weight of gold.
Currency area	Currency area refers to a group of countries that share a common currency. Originally defined by Mundell as a group that has fixed exchange rates among their national currencies.
Speculation	The purchase or sale of an asset in hopes that its price will rise or fall respectively, in order to make a profit is called speculation.
Commodity	Could refer to any good, but in trade a commodity is usually a raw material or primary product that enters into international trade, such as metals or basic agricultural products.
Optimum	Optimum refers to the best. Usually refers to a most preferred choice by consumers subject to a budget constraint or a profit maximizing choice by firms or industry subject to a technological constraint.
International monetary system	International monetary system is a network of international commercial and government institutions that determine currency exchange rates.

Gold standard	The gold standard is a monetary system in which the standard economic unit of account is a fixed weight of gold.
Fixed exchange rate	A fixed exchange rate, sometimes is a type of exchange rate regime wherein a currency's value is matched to the value of another single currency or to a basket of other currencies, or to another measure of value, such as gold.
Exchange rate	Exchange rate refers to the price at which one country's currency trades for another, typically on the exchange market.
Exchange	The trade of things of value between buyer and seller so that each is better off after the trade is called the exchange.
Fixed price	Fixed price is a phrase used to mean that no bargaining is allowed over the price of a good or, less commonly, a service.
Supply	Supply is the aggregate amount of any material good that can be called into being at a certain price point; it comprises one half of the equation of supply and demand. In classical economic theory, a curve representing supply is one of the factors that produce price.
Homogeneous	In the context of procurement/purchasing, homogeneous is used to describe goods that do not vary in their essential characteristic irrespective of the source of supply.
Commodity	Could refer to any good, but in trade a commodity is usually a raw material or primary product that enters into international trade, such as metals or basic agricultural products.
Wholesale	According to the United Nations Statistics Division Wholesale is the resale of new and used goods to retailers, to industrial, commercial, institutional or professional users, or to other wholesalers, or involves acting as an agent or broker in buying merchandise for, or selling merchandise, to such persons or companies.
Economic growth	Economic growth refers to the increase over time in the capacity of an economy to produce goods and services and to improve the well-being of its citizens.
Money supply	There are several formal definitions, but all include the quantity of currency in circulation plus the amount of demand deposits. The money supply, together with the amount of real economic activity in a country, is an important determinant of price.
Stock	In financial terminology, stock is the capital raized by a corporation, through the issuance and sale of shares.
Price level	The overall level of prices in a country, as usually measured empirically by a price index, but often captured in theoretical models by a single variable is a price level.
Argument	The discussion by counsel for the respective parties of their contentions on the law and the facts of the case being tried in order to aid the jury in arriving at a correct and just conclusion is called argument.
Disequilibrium	Inequality or imbalance of supply and demand is referred to as disequilibrium.
Balance	In banking and accountancy, the outstanding balance is the amount of money owned, (or due), that remains in a deposit account (or a loan account) at a given date, after all past remittances, payments and withdrawal have been accounted for. It can be positive (then, in the balance sheet of a firm, it is an asset) or negative (a liability).
Deficit	The deficit is the amount by which expenditure exceed revenue.
Net exports	Net exports refers to exports minus imports; same as the balance of trade. They are the sum of the money gained by a given economy by selling exports, minus the cost of buying imports. They form part of the balance of payments, which also includes other transactions such as the international investment position.

Go to **Cram101.com** for the Practice Tests for this Chapter.

Export	In economics, an export is any good or commodity, shipped or otherwise transported out of a country, province, town to another part of the world in a legitimate fashion, typically for use in trade or sale.
Financial capital	Common stock, preferred stock, bonds, and retained earnings are financial capital. Financial capital appears on the corporate balance sheet under long-term liabilities and equity.
Capital	Capital generally refers to financial wealth, especially that used to start or maintain a business. In classical economics, capital is one of four factors of production, the others being land and labor and entrepreneurship.
International trade	The export of goods and services from a country and the import of goods and services into a country is referred to as the international trade.
International capital flows	International capital flows are purchases and sales of financial assets across national borders. Flows of physical capital goods are typically treated as ordinary trade flows, not capital flows, in the balance of payments accounts.
Capital flow	International capital movement is referred to as capital flow.
Merchant	Under the Uniform Commercial Code, one who regularly deals in goods of the kind sold in the contract at issue, or holds himself out as having special knowledge or skill relevant to such goods, or who makes the sale through an agent who regularly deals in such goods or claims such knowledge or skill is referred to as merchant.
International reserves	International reserves refers to the assets denominated in foreign currency, plus gold, held by a central bank, sometimes for the purpose of intervening in the exchange market to influence or peg the exchange rate.
Foreign exchange	In finance, foreign exchange means currencies, such as U.S. Dollars and Euros. These are traded on foreign exchange markets.
Holding	The holding is a court's determination of a matter of law based on the issue presented in the particular case. In other words: under this law, with these facts, this result.
Holder	A person in possession of a document of title or an instrument payable or indorsed to him, his order, or to bearer is a holder.
Inflation	An increase in the overall price level of an economy, usually as measured by the CPI or by the implicit price deflator is called inflation.
Purchasing power	The amount of goods that money will buy, usually measured by the CPI is referred to as purchasing power.
Consideration	Consideration in contract law, a basic requirement for an enforceable agreement under traditional contract principles, defined in this text as legal value, bargained for and given in exchange for an act or promise. In corporation law, cash or property contributed to a corporation in exchange for shares, or a promise to contribute such cash or property.
Purchasing	Purchasing refers to the function in a firm that searches for quality material resources, finds the best suppliers, and negotiates the best price for goods and services.
Purchasing power parity	purchasing power parity is a theory based on the law of one price which says that the long-run equilibrium exchange rate of two currencies is the rate that equalizes the currencies' purchasing power.
Deflation	Deflation is an increase in the market value of money which is equivalent to a decrease in the general price level, over a period of time. The term is also used to refer to a decrease in the size of the money supply
Keynes	English economist Keynes (1883-1946) radical ideas impacted modern economics as well as

political theory. He is most noted for his advocation of interventionist government policy in which the government fiscal and monetary measures to handle the effects of economic recessions, depressions, and booms.

Wage	The payment for the service of a unit of labor, per unit time. In trade theory, it is the only payment to labor, usually unskilled labor. In empirical work, wage data may exclude other compenzation, which must be added to get the total cost of employment.
Brief	Brief refers to a statement of a party's case or legal arguments, usually prepared by an attorney. Also used to make legal arguments before appellate courts.
Policy	Similar to a script in that a policy can be a less than completely rational decision-making method. Involves the use of a pre-existing set of decision steps for any problem that presents itself.
Depression	Depression refers to a prolonged period characterized by high unemployment, low output and investment, depressed business confidence, falling prices, and widespread business failures. A milder form of business downturn is a recession.
Economy	The income, expenditures, and resources that affect the cost of running a business and household are called an economy.
Devaluation	Lowering the value of a nation's currency relative to other currencies is called devaluation.
Domestic	From or in one's own country. A domestic producer is one that produces inside the home country. A domestic price is the price inside the home country. Opposite of 'foreign' or 'world.'.
Aid	Assistance provided by countries and by international institutions such as the World Bank to developing countries in the form of monetary grants, loans at low interest rates, in kind, or a combination of these is called aid. Aid can also refer to assistance of any type rendered to benefit some group or individual.
Freely convertible currency	A country's currency is freely convertible when the government of that country allows both residents and nonresidents to purchase unlimited amounts of foreign currency with the domestic currency is referred to as freely convertible currency.
Convertible currency	Convertible currency refers to a currency that can legally be exchanged for another or for gold.
Bretton Woods	A 1944 conference in which representatives of 40 countries met to design a new international monetary system is referred to as the Bretton Woods conference.
Par value	The central value of a pegged exchange rate, around which the actual rate is permitted to fluctuate within set bounds is a par value.
Central Bank	Central bank refers to the institution in a country that is normally responsible for managing the supply of the country's money and the value of its currency on the foreign exchange market.
Market	A market is, as defined in economics, a social arrangement that allows buyers and sellers to discover information and carry out a voluntary exchange of goods or services.
International Monetary Fund	The International Monetary Fund is the international organization entrusted with overseeing the global financial system by monitoring exchange rates and balance of payments, as well as offering technical and financial assistance when asked.
Operation	A standardized method or technique that is performed repetitively, often on different materials resulting in different finished goods is called an operation.
Fund	Independent accounting entity with a self-balancing set of accounts segregated for the

purposes of carrying on specific activities is referred to as a fund.

Bretton Woods conference	The United Nations Monetary and Financial Conference, commonly known as Bretton Woods conference, was a gathering of 730 delegates from all 45 Allied nations at the Mount Washington Hotel. The conference was held from 1 July to 22 July 1944, when the Agreements were signed to set up the International Bank for Reconstruction and Development, GATT and the International Monetary Fund, to regulate the international monetary and financial order after World War II.
Balance of payments	Balance of payments refers to a list, or accounting, of all of a country's international transactions for a given time period, usually one year.
Conditionality	A conditionality in international development is a condition attached to a loan or to debt relief, typically by the International Monetary Fund or World Bank. They may involve relatively uncontroversial requirements to enhance aid effectiveness, such as anti-corruption measures, but they may involve highly controversial ones, such as austerity or the privatization of key public services, which may provoke strong political opposition in the recipient country. These are often grouped under the label structural adjustment.
Leverage	Leverage is using given resources in such a way that the potential positive or negative outcome is magnified. In finance, this generally refers to borrowing.
Gain	In finance, gain is a profit or an increase in value of an investment such as a stock or bond. Gain is calculated by fair market value or the proceeds from the sale of the investment minus the sum of the purchase price and all costs associated with it.
Payments imbalance	An imbalance in the balance of payments, normally including both current and capital accounts is a payments imbalance.
Consumer good	Products and services that are ultimately consumed rather than used in the production of another good are a consumer good.
Free market	A free market is a market where price is determined by the unregulated interchange of supply and demand rather than set by artificial means.
Subsidy	Subsidy refers to government financial assistance to a domestic producer.
Government spending	Government spending refers to spending by all levels of government on goods and services.
Special drawing right	Special drawing right refers to what was originally intended within the IMF as a sort of international money for use among central banks pegging their exchange rates. The special drawing right is a transferable right to acquire another country's currency.
Unit of account	Unit of account refers to a basic function of money, providing a unit of measurement for defining, recording, and comparing value.
Asset	An item of property, such as land, capital, money, a share in ownership, or a claim on others for future payment, such as a bond or a bank deposit is an asset.
Rate of exchange	Rate of exchange refers to the price paid in one's own money to acquire 1 unit of a foreign currency; the rate at which the money of one nation is exchanged for the money of another nation.
Bretton Woods system	The Bretton Woods system of international monetary management established the rules for commercial and financial relations among the world's major industrial states. The Bretton Woods system was the first example of a fully-negotiated monetary order intended to govern monetary relations among independent nation-states.
Pegged exchange rate	A pegged exchange rate, is a type of exchange rate regime wherein a currency's value is matched to the value of another single currency or to a basket of other currencies, or to

Go to **Cram101.com** for the Practice Tests for this Chapter.

	another measure of value, such as gold.
Adjustable peg	Adjustable peg refers to an exchange rate that is pegged, but for which it is understood that the par value will be changed occasionally.
Official rate	Official rate refers to the par value of a pegged exchange rate.
Liability	A liability is a present obligation of the enterprise arizing from past events, the settlement of which is expected to result in an outflow from the enterprise of resources embodying economic benefits.
Floating exchange rate	A system under which the exchange rate for converting one currency into another is continuously adjusted depending on the laws of supply and demand is referred to as a floating exchange rate.
Supply and demand	The partial equilibrium supply and demand economic model originally developed by Alfred Marshall attempts to describe, explain, and predict changes in the price and quantity of goods sold in competitive markets.
Managed float	An exchange rate regime in which the rate is allowed to be determined in the exchange market without an announced par value as the goal of intervention, but the authorities do nonetheless intervene at their discretion to influence the rate is a managed float.
Basket	A basket is an economic term for a group of several securities created for the purpose of simultaneous buying or selling. Baskets are frequently used for program trading.
Cooperative	A business owned and controlled by the people who use it, producers, consumers, or workers with similar needs who pool their resources for mutual gain is called cooperative.
Tender	An unconditional offer of payment, consisting in the actual production in money or legal tender of a sum not less than the amount due.
Exchange market	Exchange market refers to the market on which national currencies are bought and sold.
Intervention	Intervention refers to an activity in which a government buys or sells its currency in the foreign exchange market in order to affect its currency's exchange rate.
Authority	Authority in agency law, refers to an agent's ability to affect his principal's legal relations with third parties. Also used to refer to an actor's legal power or ability to do something. In addition, sometimes used to refer to a statute, case, or other legal source that justifies a particular result.
Foreign exchange market	A market for converting the currency of one country into that of another country is called foreign exchange market. It is by far the largest market in the world, in terms of cash value traded, and includes trading between large banks, central banks, currency speculators, multinational corporations, governments, and other financial markets and institutions.
Currency board	A currency board is a system, popular in emerging economies, in which the exchange rate of a local currency and a foreign currency can be controlled by law.
Monetary union	An arrangement by which several nations adopt a common currency as a unit of account and medium of exchange. The European Monetary Union is scheduled to adopt the 'Euro' as the common currency in 1999.
Legal tender	Legal tender is payment that, by law, cannot be refused in settlement of a debt denominated in the same currency.
Union	A worker association that bargains with employers over wages and working conditions is called a union.
Euro	The common currency of a subset of the countries of the EU, adopted January 1, 1999 is called euro.

Depreciate	A nation's currency is said to depreciate when exchange rates change so that a unit of its currency can buy fewer units of foreign currency.
Monetary policy	The use of the money supply and/or the interest rate to influence the level of economic activity and other policy objectives including the balance of payments or the exchange rate is called monetary policy.
Inflation rate	The percentage increase in the price level per year is an inflation rate. Alternatively, the inflation rate is the rate of decrease in the purchasing power of money.
Relative price	Relative price refers to the price of one thing in terms of another; i.e., the ratio of two prices.
Depreciation	Depreciation is an accounting and finance term for the method of attributing the cost of an asset across the useful life of the asset. Depreciation is a reduction in the value of a currency in floating exchange rate.
Flexible exchange rate	Exchange rates with a fixed parity against one or more currencies with frequent revaluation's is referred to as a flexible exchange rate.
Speculation	The purchase or sale of an asset in hopes that its price will rise or fall respectively, in order to make a profit is called speculation.
Destabilizing speculation	Destabilizing speculation refers to speculation that increases the movements of the price in the market where the speculation occurs. Movement may be defined by amplitude, frequency, or some other measure.
Mistake	In contract law a mistake is incorrect understanding by one or more parties to a contract and may be used as grounds to invalidate the agreement. Common law has identified three different types of mistake in contract: unilateral mistake, mutual mistake, and common mistake.
Large country	Large country refers to a country that is large enough for its international transactions to affect economic variables abroad, usually for its trade to matter for world prices.
Openness	Openness refers to the extent to which an economy is open, often measured by the ratio of its trade to GDP.
Closed economy	Closed economy refers to an economy that does not permit economic transactions with the outside world; a country in autarky.
Domestic price	The price of a good or service within a country, determined by domestic demand and supply is referred to as domestic price.
Open economy	Open economy refers to an economy that permits transactions with the outside world, at least including trade of some goods. Contrasts with closed economy.
Capital Outflow	Capital outflow is an economic term describing capital flowing out of (or leaving) a particular economy. Outflowing capital can be caused by any number of economic or political reasons but can often originate from instability in either sphere.
Excess supply	Supply minus demand. Thus a country's supply of exports of a homogeneous good is its excess supply of that good.
Currency area	Currency area refers to a group of countries that share a common currency. Originally defined by Mundell as a group that has fixed exchange rates among their national currencies.
Optimum	Optimum refers to the best. Usually refers to a most preferred choice by consumers subject to a budget constraint or a profit maximizing choice by firms or industry subject to a technological constraint.
Increase in demand	Increase in demand refers to an increase in the quantity demanded of a good or service at every price; a shift of the demand curve to the right.

Go to **Cram101.com** for the Practice Tests for this Chapter.

Supply of labor	Supply of labor refers to the relationship between the quantity of labor supplied by employees and the real wage rate when all other influences on work plans remain the same.
Trade deficit	The amount by which imports exceed exports of goods and services is referred to as trade deficit.
Excess demand	Demand minus supply. Thus a country's demand for imports of a homogeneous good is its excess demand for that good.
Labor	People's physical and mental talents and efforts that are used to help produce goods and services are called labor.
Factors of production	Economic resources: land, capital, labor, and entrepreneurial ability are called factors of production.
Equilibrium wage	The wage rate at which the quantity of labor supplied in a given time period equals the quantity of labor demanded is an equilibrium wage.
Production	The creation of finished goods and services using the factors of production: land, labor, capital, entrepreneurship, and knowledge.
Economics	The social science dealing with the use of scarce resources to obtain the maximum satisfaction of society's virtually unlimited economic wants is an economics.
Switching costs	Switching costs is a term used in microeconomics, strategic management, and marketing to describe any impediment to a customer's changing of suppliers. In many markets, consumers are forced to incur costs when switching from one supplier to another. These costs are called switching costs and can come in many different shapes.
Currency union	A group of countries that agree to peg their exchange rates and to coordinate their monetary policies so as to avoid the need for currency realignments is called a currency union.
Integration	Economic integration refers to reducing barriers among countries to transactions and to movements of goods, capital, and labor, including harmonization of laws, regulations, and standards. Integrated markets theoretically function as a unified market.
Externality	Externality refers to an effect of one economic agent's actions on another, such that one agent's decisions make another better or worse off by changing their utility or cost.
Journal	Book of original entry, in which transactions are recorded in a general ledger system, is referred to as a journal.
Adoption	In corporation law, a corporation's acceptance of a pre-incorporation contract by action of its board of directors, by which the corporation becomes liable on the contract, is referred to as adoption.
Exchange rate mechanism	Mechanism for aligning the exchange rates of EU currencies against each other is referred to as exchange rate mechanism.
Financial transaction	A financial transaction involves a change in the status of the finances of two or more businesses or individuals.
Capital controls	Capital controls refer to restrictions on cross-border capital flows that segment different stock markets; limit amount of a firm's stock a foreigner can own; and limit a citizen's ability to invest outside the country.
Financial market	In economics, a financial market is a mechanism which allows people to trade money for securities or commodities such as gold or other precious metals. In general, any commodity market might be considered to be a financial market, if the usual purpose of traders is not the immediate consumption of the commodity, but rather as a means of delaying or accelerating consumption over time.

Capital control	Any policy intended to restrict the free movement of capital, especially financial capital, into or out of a country is referred to as capital control.
Management	Management characterizes the process of leading and directing all or part of an organization, often a business, through the deployment and manipulation of resources. Early twentieth-century management writer Mary Parker Follett defined management as "the art of getting things done through people."
Capital mobility	The ability of capital to move internationally. The degree of capital mobility depends on government policies restricting or taxing capital inflows and/or outflows, plus the risk that investors in one country associate with assets in another.
Expense	In accounting, an expense represents an event in which an asset is used up or a liability is incurred. In terms of the accounting equation, expenses reduce owners' equity.
Fiscal policy	Fiscal policy refers to any macroeconomic policy involving the levels of government purchases, transfers, or taxes, usually implicitly focused on domestic goods, residents, or firms.
Preparation	Preparation refers to usually the first stage in the creative process. It includes education and formal training.
Government debt	The total of government obligations in the form of bonds and shorter-term borrowings. Government debt held by the public excludes bonds held by quasi-governmental agencies such as the central bank.
Government bond	A government bond is a bond issued by a national government denominated in the country's own currency. Bonds issued by national governments in foreign currencies are normally referred to as sovereign bonds.
Budget deficit	A budget deficit occurs when an entity (often a government) spends more money than it takes
Interest rate	The rate of return on bonds, loans, or deposits. When one speaks of 'the' interest rate, it is usually in a model where there is only one.
Convergence	The blending of various facets of marketing functions and communication technology to create more efficient and expanded synergies is a convergence.
Interest	In finance and economics, interest is the price paid by a borrower for the use of a lender's money. In other words, interest is the amount of paid to "rent" money for a period of time.
Budget	Budget refers to an account, usually for a year, of the planned expenditures and the expected receipts of an entity. For a government, the receipts are tax revenues.
Points	Loan origination fees that may be deductible as interest by a buyer of property. A seller of property who pays points reduces the selling price by the amount of the points paid for the buyer.
Bond	Bond refers to a debt instrument, issued by a borrower and promising a specified stream of payments to the purchaser, usually regular interest payments plus a final repayment of principal.
Credit	Credit refers to a recording as positive in the balance of payments, any transaction that gives rise to a payment into the country, such as an export, the sale of an asset, or borrowing from abroad.
Payments system	The method of conducting transactions in the economy is referred to as the payments system. Collective term for mechanisms (both paper-backed and electronic) for moving funds, payments and money among financial institutions throughout the nation.
Regulation	Regulation refers to restrictions state and federal laws place on business with regard to the

conduct of its activities.

Federal reserve system	The central banking authority responsible for monetary policy in the United States is called federal reserve system or the Fed.
Federal Reserve	The Federal Reserve System was created via the Federal Reserve Act of December 23rd, 1913. All national banks were required to join the system and other banks could join. The Reserve Banks opened for business on November 16th, 1914. Federal Reserve Notes were created as part of the legislation, to provide an elastic supply of currency.
Appreciation	Appreciation refers to a rise in the value of a country's currency on the exchange market, relative either to a particular other currency or to a weighted average of other currencies. The currency is said to appreciate. Opposite of 'depreciation.' Appreciation can also refer to the increase in value of any asset.
Credibility	The extent to which a source is perceived as having knowledge, skill, or experience relevant to a communication topic and can be trusted to give an unbiased opinion or present objective information on the issue is called credibility.
Bank run	A bank run is a type of financial crisis. It is a panic which occurs when a large number of customers of a bank fear it is insolvent and withdraw their deposits.
Speculative attack	A speculative attack involves massive selling of domestic currency assets by both domestic and foreign investors.
Financial crisis	A loss of confidence in a country's currency or other financial assets causing international investors to withdraw their funds from the country is referred to as a financial crisis.
Service	Service refers to a "non tangible product" that is not embodied in a physical good and that typically effects some change in another product, person, or institution. Contrasts with good.
Expansionary fiscal policy	An increase in government purchases of goods and services, a decrease in net taxes, or some combination of the two for the purpose of increasing aggregate demand and expanding real output is an expansionary fiscal policy.
Reserve currency	A reserve currency is a currency which is held in significant quantities by many governments and institutions as part of their foreign exchange reserves.
Commerce	Commerce is the exchange of something of value between two entities. It is the central mechanism from which capitalism is derived.
Monetary theory	The theory that relates changes in the quantity of money to changes in economic activity a monetary theory.
Manufactured good	A manufactured good refers to goods that have been processed in any way.
Contract	A contract is a "promise" or an "agreement" that is enforced or recognized by the law. In the civil law, a contract is considered to be part of the general law of obligations.
Medium of exchange	Medium of exchange refers to any item sellers generally accept and buyers generally use to pay for a good or service; money; a convenient means of exchanging goods and services without engaging in barter.
Transaction cost	A transaction cost is a cost incurred in making an economic exchange. For example, most people, when buying or selling a stock, must pay a commission to their broker; that commission is a transaction cost of doing the stock deal.
Vehicle currency	A currency that plays a central role in the foreign exchange market is a vehicle currency.
Store of value	To act as a store of value, a commodity, a form of money, or financial capital must be able

Go to **Cram101.com** for the Practice Tests for this Chapter.

	to be reliably saved, stored, and retrieved - and be predictably useful when it is so retrieved.
Official reserves	The reserves of foreign-currency-denominated assets that a central bank holds, sometimes as backing for its own currency, but usually only for the purpose of possible future exchange market intervention are official reserves.
Standing	Standing refers to the legal requirement that anyone seeking to challenge a particular action in court must demonstrate that such action substantially affects his legitimate interests before he will be entitled to bring suit.
Financial assets	Financial assets refer to monetary claims or obligations by one party against another party. Examples are bonds, mortgages, bank loans, and equities.
Issuer	The company that borrows money from investors by issuing bonds is referred to as issuer. They are legally responsible for the obligations of the issue and for reporting financial conditions, material developments and any other operational activities as required by the regulations of their jurisdictions.
Seigniorage	The difference between what money can buy and its cost of production. Therefore, seigniorage is the benefit that a government or other monetary authority derives from the ability to create money; profits from minting, printing, or coining money.
Market share	That fraction of an industry's output accounted for by an individual firm or group of firms is called market share.
Capital account	The capital account is one of two primary components of the balance of payments. It tracks the movement of funds for investments and loans into and out of a country.
Current account	Current account refers to a country's international transactions arising from current flows, as opposed to changes in stocks which are part of the capital account. Includes trade in goods and services plus inflows and outflows of transfers. A current account is a deposit account in the UK and countries with a UK banking heritage.
Traded good	A good that is exported or imported or -- sometimes -- a good that could be exported or imported if it weren't tariffs, or quotas, is referred to as traded good.
Profit	Profit refers to the return to the resource entrepreneurial ability; total revenue minus total cost.
Favorable exchange rate	An exchange rate different from the market or official rate, provided by the government on a transaction as an indirect way of providing a subsidy is a favorable exchange rate.
Protectionism	Protectionism refers to advocacy of protection. The word has a negative connotation, and few advocates of protection in particular situations will acknowledge being protectionists.
Developed country	A developed country is one that enjoys a relatively high standard of living derived through an industrialized, diversified economy. Countries with a very high Human Development Index are generally considered developed countries.
Crawling peg	The crawling peg is an exchange rate that is pegged, but for which the par value is changed frequently in a pre-announced fashion in response to changes in a country's balance of payments.
International banking facilities	Banking establishments in the United States that can accept time deposits from foreigners but are not subject to either reserve requirements or restrictions on interest payments are international banking facilities.
London interbank offered rate	London Interbank Offered Rate is a daily reference rate based on the interest rates at which banks offer to lend unsecured funds to other banks in the London wholesale (or "interbank") money market.

Go to **Cram101.com** for the Practice Tests for this Chapter.

Debt/equity swap	Debt/equity swap refers to an exchange of debt for equity, in which a lender is given a share of ownership to replace a loan. Used as a method of resolving debt crises.
Eurocurrency	Eurocurrency is the term used to describe deposits residing in banks that are located outside the borders of the country that issues the currency the deposit is denominated in.
Corruption	The unauthorized use of public office for private gain. The most common forms of corruption are bribery, extortion, and the misuse of inside information.
Swap	In finance a swap is a derivative, where two counterparties exchange one stream of cash flows against another stream. These streams are called the legs of the swap. The cash flows are calculated over a notional principal amount. Swaps are often used to hedge certain risks, for instance interest rate risk. Another use is speculation.

Go to **Cram101.com** for the Practice Tests for this Chapter.

Market	A market is, as defined in economics, a social arrangement that allows buyers and sellers to discover information and carry out a voluntary exchange of goods or services.
Eurocurrency	Eurocurrency is the term used to describe deposits residing in banks that are located outside the borders of the country that issues the currency the deposit is denominated in.
Domestic	From or in one's own country. A domestic producer is one that produces inside the home country. A domestic price is the price inside the home country. Opposite of 'foreign' or 'world.'.
Regulation	Regulation refers to restrictions state and federal laws place on business with regard to the conduct of its activities.
Money market	The money market, in macroeconomics and international finance, refers to the equilibration of demand for a country's domestic money to its money supply; market for short-term financial instruments.
Balance	In banking and accountancy, the outstanding balance is the amount of money owned, (or due), that remains in a deposit account (or a loan account) at a given date, after all past remittances, payments and withdrawal have been accounted for. It can be positive (then, in the balance sheet of a firm, it is an asset) or negative (a liability).
Consideration	Consideration in contract law, a basic requirement for an enforceable agreement under traditional contract principles, defined in this text as legal value, bargained for and given in exchange for an act or promise. In corporation law, cash or property contributed to a corporation in exchange for shares, or a promise to contribute such cash or property.
Profit	Profit refers to the return to the resource entrepreneurial ability; total revenue minus total cost.
Interest rate	The rate of return on bonds, loans, or deposits. When one speaks of 'the' interest rate, it is usually in a model where there is only one.
Interest	In finance and economics, interest is the price paid by a borrower for the use of a lender's money. In other words, interest is the amount of paid to "rent" money for a period of time.
Fund	Independent accounting entity with a self-balancing set of accounts segregated for the purposes of carrying on specific activities is referred to as a fund.
Competitor	Other organizations in the same industry or type of business that provide a good or service to the same set of customers is referred to as a competitor.
Reserve requirement	The reserve requirement is a bank regulation, that sets the minimum reserves each bank must hold to customer deposits and notes.
Deposit insurance	Deposit insurance is a measure taken by banks in many countries to protect their clients' savings, either fully or in part, against any possible situation that would prevent the bank from returning said savings.
Insurance	Insurance refers to a system by which individuals can reduce their exposure to risk of large losses by spreading the risks among a large number of persons.
Credit	Credit refers to a recording as positive in the balance of payments, any transaction that gives rise to a payment into the country, such as an export, the sale of an asset, or borrowing from abroad.
Perfectly elastic	Perfectly elastic refers to a supply or demand curve with a price elasticity of infinity, implying that the supply or demand curve as usually drawn is horizontal. A small open economy faces perfectly elastic demand for its exports and supply of its imports.
Points	Loan origination fees that may be deductible as interest by a buyer of property. A seller of

Go to **Cram101.com** for the Practice Tests for this Chapter.

	property who pays points reduces the selling price by the amount of the points paid for the buyer.
Commercial paper	Commercial paper is a money market security issued by large banks and corporations. It is generally not used to finance long-term investments but rather for purchases of inventory or to manage working capital. It is commonly bought by money funds (the issuing amounts are often too high for individual investors), and is generally regarded as a very safe investment.
Certificate of deposit	An acknowledgment by a bank of the receipt of money with an engagement to pay it back is referred to as certificate of deposit.
Bank of America	In 2004, a California jury decided that Bank of America had illegally raided the Social Security benefits of a million customers. The jury awarded damages that could exceed $1 billion. Bank of America had been accused of withholding customers' direct deposit social security benefit payments to cover debts in cases where a debt is owed to the bank by the customer (e.g.: due to an overdrawn account, various service fees, etc.), this is in direct violation of California state law.
Deutsche Bank	Deutsche Bank was founded in Germany on January 22, 1870 as a specialist bank for foreign trade. Major projects in its first decades included the Northern Pacific Railroad in the United States (1883) and the Baghdad Railway (1888). It also financed bond offerings of the steel concern Krupp (1885) and introduced the chemical company Bayer on the Berlin stock market.
Corporation	A legal entity chartered by a state or the Federal government that is distinct and separate from the individuals who own it is a corporation. This separation gives the corporation unique powers which other legal entities lack.
National bank	A National bank refers to federally chartered banks. They are an ordinary private bank which operates nationally (as opposed to regionally or locally or even internationally).
Citibank	In April of 2006, Citibank struck a deal with 7-Eleven to put its ATMs in over 5,500 convenience stores in the U.S. In the same month, it also announced it would sell all of its Buffalo and Rochester New York branches and accounts to M&T Bank.
Commerce	Commerce is the exchange of something of value between two entities. It is the central mechanism from which capitalism is derived.
Euro	The common currency of a subset of the countries of the EU, adopted January 1, 1999 is called euro.
Credit Suisse First Boston	Credit Suisse First Boston is a leading global investment bank serving institutional, corporate, government and high net worth clients. The Firm operates under a "One-Bank" policy as part of the Zurich-based Credit Suisse Group, a leading global financial services company.
Capital controls	Capital controls refer to restrictions on cross-border capital flows that segment different stock markets; limit amount of a firm's stock a foreigner can own; and limit a citizen's ability to invest outside the country.
Capital control	Any policy intended to restrict the free movement of capital, especially financial capital, into or out of a country is referred to as capital control.
Capital	Capital generally refers to financial wealth, especially that used to start or maintain a business. In classical economics, capital is one of four factors of production, the others being land and labor and entrepreneurship.
International capital flows	International capital flows are purchases and sales of financial assets across national borders. Flows of physical capital goods are typically treated as ordinary trade flows, not capital flows, in the balance of payments accounts.

Capital flow	International capital movement is referred to as capital flow.
Quota	A government-imposed restriction on quantity, or sometimes on total value, used to restrict the import of something to a specific quantity is called a quota.
Financial institution	A financial institution acts as an agent that provides financial services for its clients. Financial institutions generally fall under financial regulation from a government authority.
Central Bank	Central bank refers to the institution in a country that is normally responsible for managing the supply of the country's money and the value of its currency on the foreign exchange market.
Investment	Investment refers to spending for the production and accumulation of capital and additions to inventories. In a financial sense, buying an asset with the expectation of making a return.
International banking facilities	Banking establishments in the United States that can accept time deposits from foreigners but are not subject to either reserve requirements or restrictions on interest payments are international banking facilities.
Federal Reserve	The Federal Reserve System was created via the Federal Reserve Act of December 23rd, 1913. All national banks were required to join the system and other banks could join. The Reserve Banks opened for business on November 16th, 1914. Federal Reserve Notes were created as part of the legislation, to provide an elastic supply of currency.
Shell	One of the original Seven Sisters, Royal Dutch/Shell is the world's third-largest oil company by revenue, and a major player in the petrochemical industry and the solar energy business. Shell has six core businesses: Exploration and Production, Gas and Power, Downstream, Chemicals, Renewables, and Trading/Shipping, and operates in more than 140 countries.
Asset	An item of property, such as land, capital, money, a share in ownership, or a claim on others for future payment, such as a bond or a bank deposit is an asset.
Balance sheet	A statement of the assets, liabilities, and net worth of a firm or individual at some given time often at the end of its "fiscal year," is referred to as a balance sheet.
Liability	A liability is a present obligation of the enterprise arizing from past events, the settlement of which is expected to result in an outflow from the enterprise of resources embodying economic benefits.
Financial management	The job of managing a firm's resources so it can meet its goals and objectives is called financial management.
Accounting	A system that collects and processes financial information about an organization and reports that information to decision makers is referred to as accounting.
Management	Management characterizes the process of leading and directing all or part of an organization, often a business, through the deployment and manipulation of resources. Early twentieth-century management writer Mary Parker Follett defined management as "the art of getting things done through people."
Journal	Book of original entry, in which transactions are recorded in a general ledger system, is referred to as a journal.
Users	Users refer to people in the organization who actually use the product or service purchased by the buying center.
Money supply	There are several formal definitions, but all include the quantity of currency in circulation plus the amount of demand deposits. The money supply, together with the amount of real economic activity in a country, is an important determinant of price.
Supply	Supply is the aggregate amount of any material good that can be called into being at a

certain price point; it comprises one half of the equation of supply and demand. In classical economic theory, a curve representing supply is one of the factors that produce price.

Time deposit	The technical name for a savings account is a time deposit; the bank can require prior notice before the owner withdraws money from a time deposit.
Intermediaries	Intermediaries specialize in information either to bring together two parties to a transaction or to buy in order to sell again.
Eurodollars	Eurodollars refers to u.S. dollars that are deposited in foreign banks outside the United States or in foreign branches of U.S. banks.
Certificates of deposit	Certificates of deposit refer to a certificate offered by banks, savings and loans, and other financial institutions for the deposit of funds at a given interest rate over a specified time period.
London interbank offered rate	London Interbank Offered Rate is a daily reference rate based on the interest rates at which banks offer to lend unsecured funds to other banks in the London wholesale (or "interbank") money market.
Diversification	Investing in a collection of assets whose returns do not always move together, with the result that overall risk is lower than for individual assets is referred to as diversification.
Financial instrument	Formal or legal documents in writing, such as contracts, deeds, wills, bonds, leases, and mortgages is referred to as a financial instrument.
Instrument	Instrument refers to an economic variable that is controlled by policy makers and can be used to influence other variables, called targets. Examples are monetary and fiscal policies used to achieve external and internal balance.
Petrodollar	Petrodollar refers to the profits made by oil exporting countries when the price rose during the 1970s, and their preference for holding these profits in U.S. dollar-denominated assets, either in the U.S. or in Europe as Eurodollars.
Developing country	Developing country refers to a country whose per capita income is low by world standards. Same as LDC. As usually used, it does not necessarily connote that the country's income is rising.
Credit risk	The risk of loss due to a counterparty defaulting on a contract, or more generally the risk of loss due to some "credit event" is called credit risk.
Deficit	The deficit is the amount by which expenditure exceed revenue.
Recession	A significant decline in economic activity. In the U.S., recession is approximately defined as two successive quarters of falling GDP, as judged by NBER.
Commodity	Could refer to any good, but in trade a commodity is usually a raw material or primary product that enters into international trade, such as metals or basic agricultural products.
Export	In economics, an export is any good or commodity, shipped or otherwise transported out of a country, province, town to another part of the world in a legitimate fashion, typically for use in trade or sale.
Creditor	A person to whom a debt or legal obligation is owed, and who has the right to enforce payment of that debt or obligation is referred to as creditor.
Developed country	A developed country is one that enjoys a relatively high standard of living derived through an industrialized, diversified economy. Countries with a very high Human Development Index are generally considered developed countries.
Debtor nation	Debtor nation refers to a country whose assets owned abroad are worth less than the assets

303

	within the country that are owned by foreigners. Contrasts with creditor nation.
Lender	Suppliers and financial institutions that lend money to companies is referred to as a lender.
Firm	An organization that employs resources to produce a good or service for profit and owns and operates one or more plants is referred to as a firm.
Commercial bank	A firm that engages in the business of banking is a commercial bank.
Operation	A standardized method or technique that is performed repetitively, often on different materials resulting in different finished goods is called an operation.
Service	Service refers to a "non tangible product" that is not embodied in a physical good and that typically effects some change in another product, person, or institution. Contrasts with good.
Mutual fund	A mutual fund is a form of collective investment that pools money from many investors and invests the money in stocks, bonds, short-term money market instruments, and/or other securities. In a mutual fund, the fund manager trades the fund's underlying securities, realizing capital gains or loss, and collects the dividend or interest income.
Compliance	A type of influence process where a receiver accepts the position advocated by a source to obtain favorable outcomes or to avoid punishment is the compliance.
Stock	In financial terminology, stock is the capital raized by a corporation, through the issuance and sale of shares.
Property	Assets defined in the broadest legal sense. Property includes the unrealized receivables of a cash basis taxpayer, but not services rendered.
Interest payment	The payment to holders of bonds payable, calculated by multiplying the stated rate on the face of the bond by the par, or face, value of the bond. If bonds are issued at a discount or premium, the interest payment does not equal the interest expense.
Variable	A variable is something measured by a number; it is used to analyze what happens to other things when the size of that number changes.
Principal	In agency law, one under whose direction an agent acts and for whose benefit that agent acts is a principal.
Debt rescheduling	Debt rescheduling refers to an agreement between banks and borrowers through which a new schedule of repayments of the debt is negotiated; often some of the debt is written off and the repayment period is extended.
Default	In finance, default occurs when a debtor has not met its legal obligations according to the debt contract, e.g. it has not made a scheduled payment, or violated a covenant (condition) of the debt contract.
Negotiation	Negotiation is the process whereby interested parties resolve disputes, agree upon courses of action, bargain for individual or collective advantage, and/or attempt to craft outcomes which serve their mutual interests.
Committee	A long-lasting, sometimes permanent team in the organization structure created to deal with tasks that recur regularly is the committee.
Equity	Equity is the name given to the set of legal principles, in countries following the English common law tradition, which supplement strict rules of law where their application would operate harshly, so as to achieve what is sometimes referred to as "natural justice."
Debt/equity swap	Debt/equity swap refers to an exchange of debt for equity, in which a lender is given a share of ownership to replace a loan. Used as a method of resolving debt crises.

Exchange	The trade of things of value between buyer and seller so that each is better off after the trade is called the exchange.
Swap	In finance a swap is a derivative, where two counterparties exchange one stream of cash flows against another stream. These streams are called the legs of the swap. The cash flows are calculated over a notional principal amount. Swaps are often used to hedge certain risks, for instance interest rate risk. Another use is speculation.
Buyer	A buyer refers to a role in the buying center with formal authority and responsibility to select the supplier and negotiate the terms of the contract.
Manufacturing	Production of goods primarily by the application of labor and capital to raw materials and other intermediate inputs, in contrast to agriculture, mining, forestry, fishing, and services a manufacturing.
Market price	Market price is an economic concept with commonplace familiarity; it is the price that a good or service is offered at, or will fetch, in the marketplace; it is of interest mainly in the study of microeconomics.
Broker	In commerce, a broker is a party that mediates between a buyer and a seller. A broker who also acts as a seller or as a buyer becomes a principal party to the deal.
Nissan	Nissan is Japan's second largest car company after Toyota. Nissan is among the top three Asian rivals of the "big three" in the US.
Face value	The nominal or par value of an instrument as expressed on its face is referred to as the face value.
Conditionality	A conditionality in international development is a condition attached to a loan or to debt relief, typically by the International Monetary Fund or World Bank. They may involve relatively uncontroversial requirements to enhance aid effectiveness, such as anti-corruption measures, but they may involve highly controversial ones, such as austerity or the privatization of key public services, which may provoke strong political opposition in the recipient country. These are often grouped under the label structural adjustment.
Economic policy	Economic policy refers to the actions that governments take in the economic field. It covers the systems for setting interest rates and government deficit as well as the labor market, national ownership, and many other areas of government.
Policy	Similar to a script in that a policy can be a less than completely rational decision-making method. Involves the use of a pre-existing set of decision steps for any problem that presents itself.
Economic problem	Economic problem refers to how to determine the use of scarce resources among competing uses. Because resources are scarce, the economy must choose what products to produce; how these products are to be produced: and for whom.
Collateral	Property that is pledged to the lender to guarantee payment in the event that the borrower is unable to make debt payments is called collateral.
Contract	A contract is a "promise" or an "agreement" that is enforced or recognized by the law. In the civil law, a contract is considered to be part of the general law of obligations.
Contribution	In business organization law, the cash or property contributed to a business by its owners is referred to as contribution.
Reserve currency	A reserve currency is a currency which is held in significant quantities by many governments and institutions as part of their foreign exchange reserves.
Economic growth	Economic growth refers to the increase over time in the capacity of an economy to produce goods and services and to improve the well-being of its citizens.

Government spending	Government spending refers to spending by all levels of government on goods and services.
Economy	The income, expenditures, and resources that affect the cost of running a business and household are called an economy.
Private sector	The households and business firms of the economy are referred to as private sector.
Long run	In economic models, the long run time frame assumes no fixed factors of production. Firms can enter or leave the marketplace, and the cost (and availability) of land, labor, raw materials, and capital goods can be assumed to vary.
Subsidy	Subsidy refers to government financial assistance to a domestic producer.
Corruption	The unauthorized use of public office for private gain. The most common forms of corruption are bribery, extortion, and the misuse of inside information.
World Bank	The World Bank is a group of five international organizations responsible for providing finance and advice to countries for the purposes of economic development and poverty reduction, and for encouraging and safeguarding international investment.
Exchange rate	Exchange rate refers to the price at which one country's currency trades for another, typically on the exchange market.
Publicity	Publicity refers to any information about an individual, product, or organization that's distributed to the public through the media and that's not paid for or controlled by the seller.
Forming	The first stage of team development, where the team is formed and the objectives for the team are set is referred to as forming.
Conversion	Conversion refers to any distinct act of dominion wrongfully exerted over another's personal property in denial of or inconsistent with his rights therein. That tort committed by a person who deals with chattels not belonging to him in a manner that is inconsistent with the ownership of the lawful owner.
Holding	The holding is a court's determination of a matter of law based on the issue presented in the particular case. In other words: under this law, with these facts, this result.
Financial assets	Financial assets refer to monetary claims or obligations by one party against another party. Examples are bonds, mortgages, bank loans, and equities.
Estate	An estate is the totality of the legal rights, interests, entitlements and obligations attaching to property. In the context of wills and probate, it refers to the totality of the property which the deceased owned or in which some interest was held.
Subsidiary	A company that is controlled by another company or corporation is a subsidiary.
Parent company	Parent company refers to the entity that has a controlling influence over another company. It may have its own operations, or it may have been set up solely for the purpose of owning the Subject Company.
Short run	Short run refers to a period of time that permits an increase or decrease in current production volume with existing capacity, but one that is too short to permit enlargement of that capacity itself (eg, the building of new plants, training of additional workers, etc.).
Private property	The right of private persons and firms to obtain, own, control, employ, dispose of, and bequeath land, capital, and other property is referred to as private property.
Property rights	Bundle of legal rights over the use to which a resource is put and over the use made of any income that may be derived from that resource are referred to as property rights.

Host country	The country in which the parent-country organization seeks to locate or has already located a facility is a host country.
International Business	International business refers to any firm that engages in international trade or investment.
Country risk	Country risk relates to the likelihood that changes in the business environment will occur that reduce the profitability of doing business in a country. These changes can adversely affect operating profits as well as the value of assets.
Frequency	Frequency refers to the speed of the up and down movements of a fluctuating economic variable; that is, the number of times per unit of time that the variable completes a cycle of up and down movement.
International reserves	International reserves refers to the assets denominated in foreign currency, plus gold, held by a central bank, sometimes for the purpose of intervening in the exchange market to influence or peg the exchange rate.
Liquidity	Liquidity refers to the capacity to turn assets into cash, or the amount of assets in a portfolio that have that capacity.
Foreign exchange	In finance, foreign exchange means currencies, such as U.S. Dollars and Euros. These are traded on foreign exchange markets.
Evaluation	The consumer's appraisal of the product or brand on important attributes is called evaluation.
Foundation	A Foundation is a type of philanthropic organization set up by either individuals or institutions as a legal entity (either as a corporation or trust) with the purpose of distributing grants to support causes in line with the goals of the foundation.
Creditworthiness	Creditworthiness indicates whether a borrower has in the past made loan payments when due.
Secondary market	Secondary market refers to the market for securities that have already been issued. It is a market in which investors trade back and forth with each other.
Covered interest rate	The covered interest rate, in a currency other than your own, is the nominal interest rate plus the forward premium on the currency.
Interest Rate Parity	The Interest Rate Parity is the basic identity that relates interest rates and exchange rates. The identity is theoretical, and usually follows from assumptions imposed in economics models.
Drawback	Drawback refers to rebate of import duties when the imported good is re-exported or used as input to the production of an exported good.
Per capita	Per capita refers to per person. Usually used to indicate the average per person of any given statistic, commonly income.
Economic perspective	A viewpoint that envisions individuals and institutions making rational decisions by comparing the marginal benefits and marginal costs associated with their actions is an economic perspective.

Economy	The income, expenditures, and resources that affect the cost of running a business and household are called an economy.
Unemployment rate	The unemployment rate is the number of unemployed workers divided by the total civilian labor force, which includes both the unemployed and those with jobs (all those willing and able to work for pay).
Internal balance	A target level for domestic aggregate economic activity, such as a level of GDP that minimizes unemployment without being inflationary is called internal balance.
Domestic	From or in one's own country. A domestic producer is one that produces inside the home country. A domestic price is the price inside the home country. Opposite of 'foreign' or 'world.'.
Balance	In banking and accountancy, the outstanding balance is the amount of money owned, (or due), that remains in a deposit account (or a loan account) at a given date, after all past remittances, payments and withdrawal have been accounted for. It can be positive (then, in the balance sheet of a firm, it is an asset) or negative (a liability).
Trade balance	Balance of trade in terms of exports versus imports is called trade balance.
Economics	The social science dealing with the use of scarce resources to obtain the maximum satisfaction of society's virtually unlimited economic wants is an economics.
Economic growth	Economic growth refers to the increase over time in the capacity of an economy to produce goods and services and to improve the well-being of its citizens.
Inflation	An increase in the overall price level of an economy, usually as measured by the CPI or by the implicit price deflator is called inflation.
Capital account	The capital account is one of two primary components of the balance of payments. It tracks the movement of funds for investments and loans into and out of a country.
External balance	External balance refers to balance of payments equilibrium. A performance goal in which the country's economy has an overall balance of payments that is sustainable over time.
Consideration	Consideration in contract law, a basic requirement for an enforceable agreement under traditional contract principles, defined in this text as legal value, bargained for and given in exchange for an act or promise. In corporation law, cash or property contributed to a corporation in exchange for shares, or a promise to contribute such cash or property.
Capital	Capital generally refers to financial wealth, especially that used to start or maintain a business. In classical economics, capital is one of four factors of production, the others being land and labor and entrepreneurship.
Complexity	The technical sophistication of the product and hence the amount of understanding required to use it is referred to as complexity. It is the opposite of simplicity.
Yield	The interest rate that equates a future value or an annuity to a given present value is a yield.
Policy	Similar to a script in that a policy can be a less than completely rational decision-making method. Involves the use of a pre-existing set of decision steps for any problem that presents itself.
Government spending	Government spending refers to spending by all levels of government on goods and services.
Monetary policy	The use of the money supply and/or the interest rate to influence the level of economic activity and other policy objectives including the balance of payments or the exchange rate is called monetary policy.

Go to **Cram101.com** for the Practice Tests for this Chapter.

Fiscal policy	Fiscal policy refers to any macroeconomic policy involving the levels of government purchases, transfers, or taxes, usually implicitly focused on domestic goods, residents, or firms.
Money supply	There are several formal definitions, but all include the quantity of currency in circulation plus the amount of demand deposits. The money supply, together with the amount of real economic activity in a country, is an important determinant of price.
Supply	Supply is the aggregate amount of any material good that can be called into being at a certain price point; it comprises one half of the equation of supply and demand. In classical economic theory, a curve representing supply is one of the factors that produce price.
Macroeconomic equilibrium	Macroeconomic equilibrium refers to the GDP level at which intended aggregate demand equals intended aggregate supply.
Quantity demanded	The amount of a good or service that buyers desire to purchase at a particular price during some period is a quantity demanded.
Balance of payments	Balance of payments refers to a list, or accounting, of all of a country's international transactions for a given time period, usually one year.
Current account	Current account refers to a country's international transactions arising from current flows, as opposed to changes in stocks which are part of the capital account. Includes trade in goods and services plus inflows and outflows of transfers. A current account is a deposit account in the UK and countries with a UK banking heritage.
Deficit	The deficit is the amount by which expenditure exceed revenue.
Current Account deficit	Current account deficit occurs when a country imports more goods and services than it exports.
Capital account surplus	Capital account surplus refers to the amount by which the purchase of domestic financial assets by foreigners exceeds the purchase of foreign financial assets by domestic consumers.
LM curve	The relationship that describes the combinations of interest rates and aggregate output for which the quantity of money demanded equals the quantity of money supplied is referred to as the LM curve.
Macroeconomics	Macroeconomics refers to the part of economics concerned with the economy as a whole; with such major aggregates as the household, business, and government sectors; and with measures of the total economy.
Investment	Investment refers to spending for the production and accumulation of capital and additions to inventories. In a financial sense, buying an asset with the expectation of making a return.
Interest rate	The rate of return on bonds, loans, or deposits. When one speaks of 'the' interest rate, it is usually in a model where there is only one.
Money market	The money market, in macroeconomics and international finance, refers to the equilibration of demand for a country's domestic money to its money supply; market for short-term financial instruments.
Interest	In finance and economics, interest is the price paid by a borrower for the use of a lender's money. In other words, interest is the amount of paid to "rent" money for a period of time.
Market	A market is, as defined in economics, a social arrangement that allows buyers and sellers to discover information and carry out a voluntary exchange of goods or services.
Is curve	The relationship that describes the combinations of aggregate output and interest rates for which the total quantity of goods produced equals the total quantity demanded is called the IS curve.

Service	Service refers to a "non tangible product" that is not embodied in a physical good and that typically effects some change in another product, person, or institution. Contrasts with good.
Leakage	Leakage refers to a withdrawal of potential spending from the income-expenditures stream via saving, tax payments, or imports; a withdrawal that reduces the lending potential of the banking system.
Export	In economics, an export is any good or commodity, shipped or otherwise transported out of a country, province, town to another part of the world in a legitimate fashion, typically for use in trade or sale.
Firm	An organization that employs resources to produce a good or service for profit and owns and operates one or more plants is referred to as a firm.
Fund	Independent accounting entity with a self-balancing set of accounts segregated for the purposes of carrying on specific activities is referred to as a fund.
Points	Loan origination fees that may be deductible as interest by a buyer of property. A seller of property who pays points reduces the selling price by the amount of the points paid for the buyer.
Domestic price	The price of a good or service within a country, determined by domestic demand and supply is referred to as domestic price.
Price level	The overall level of prices in a country, as usually measured empirically by a price index, but often captured in theoretical models by a single variable is a price level.
Holding	The holding is a court's determination of a matter of law based on the issue presented in the particular case. In other words: under this law, with these facts, this result.
Exchange rate	Exchange rate refers to the price at which one country's currency trades for another, typically on the exchange market.
Exchange	The trade of things of value between buyer and seller so that each is better off after the trade is called the exchange.
Inverse relationship	The relationship between two variables that change in opposite directions, for example, product price and quantity demanded is an inverse relationship.
Opportunity cost	The cost of something in terms of opportunity foregone. The opportunity cost to a country of producing a unit more of a good, such as for export or to replace an import, is the quantity of some other good that could have been produced instead.
Interest income	Interest income refers to payments of income to those who supply the economy with capital.
Asset	An item of property, such as land, capital, money, a share in ownership, or a claim on others for future payment, such as a bond or a bank deposit is an asset.
Current account surplus	A current account surplus is when a country exports more goods and services than it imports.
Capital account deficit	Capital account deficit refers to the amount by which the purchase of foreign financial assets by consumers exceeds the purchase of domestic financial assets by foreigners .
Financial assets	Financial assets refer to monetary claims or obligations by one party against another party. Examples are bonds, mortgages, bank loans, and equities.
Buyer	A buyer refers to a role in the buying center with formal authority and responsibility to select the supplier and negotiate the terms of the contract.
Official	A record of the change in a country's official reserves is an official settlements account.

settlements account	Also referred to as reserve transaction account.
Fixed exchange rate	A fixed exchange rate, sometimes is a type of exchange rate regime wherein a currency's value is matched to the value of another single currency or to a basket of other currencies, or to another measure of value, such as gold.
Central Bank	Central bank refers to the institution in a country that is normally responsible for managing the supply of the country's money and the value of its currency on the foreign exchange market.
Short run	Short run refers to a period of time that permits an increase or decrease in current production volume with existing capacity, but one that is too short to permit enlargement of that capacity itself (eg, the building of new plants, training of additional workers, etc.).
Perfect substitute	A good that is regarded by its demanders as identical to another good, so that the elasticity of substitution between them is infinite is referred to as perfect substitute.
Capital mobility	The ability of capital to move internationally. The degree of capital mobility depends on government policies restricting or taxing capital inflows and/or outflows, plus the risk that investors in one country associate with assets in another.
Perfect capital mobility	The absence of any barriers to international capital movements is referred to as perfect capital mobility. Under this scenario a practically unlimited amount of lending shifts between countries in response to the slightest change in one country's interest rate.
Capital Outflow	Capital outflow is an economic term describing capital flowing out of (or leaving) a particular economy. Outflowing capital can be caused by any number of economic or political reasons but can often originate from instability in either sphere.
Capital inflow	Capital inflow refers to a net flow of capital, real and/or financial, into a country, in the form of increased purchases of domestic assets by foreigners and/or reduced holdings of foreign assets by domestic residents.
Foreign exchange	In finance, foreign exchange means currencies, such as U.S. Dollars and Euros. These are traded on foreign exchange markets.
Intervention	Intervention refers to an activity in which a government buys or sells its currency in the foreign exchange market in order to affect its currency's exchange rate.
Authority	Authority in agency law, refers to an agent's ability to affect his principal's legal relations with third parties. Also used to refer to an actor's legal power or ability to do something. In addition, sometimes used to refer to a statute, case, or other legal source that justifies a particular result.
Depreciation	Depreciation is an accounting and finance term for the method of attributing the cost of an asset across the useful life of the asset. Depreciation is a reduction in the value of a currency in floating exchange rate.
Net exports	Net exports refers to exports minus imports; same as the balance of trade. They are the sum of the money gained by a given economy by selling exports, minus the cost of buying imports. They form part of the balance of payments, which also includes other transactions such as the international investment position.
Total spending	Total spending refers to the total amount that buyers of goods and services spend or plan to spend.
Appreciation	Appreciation refers to a rise in the value of a country's currency on the exchange market, relative either to a particular other currency or to a weighted average of other currencies. The currency is said to appreciate. Opposite of 'depreciation.' Appreciation can also refer

	to the increase in value of any asset.
Floating exchange rate	A system under which the exchange rate for converting one currency into another is continuously adjusted depending on the laws of supply and demand is referred to as a floating exchange rate.
Expansionary fiscal policy	An increase in government purchases of goods and services, a decrease in net taxes, or some combination of the two for the purpose of increasing aggregate demand and expanding real output is an expansionary fiscal policy.
Flexible exchange rate	Exchange rates with a fixed parity against one or more currencies with frequent revaluation's is referred to as a flexible exchange rate.
Crowding out	In economics, crowding out theoretically occurs when the government expands its borrowing more to finance increased expenditure or tax cuts in excess of revenue crowding out private sector investment by way of higher interest rates.
Open economy	Open economy refers to an economy that permits transactions with the outside world, at least including trade of some goods. Contrasts with closed economy.
Fixed price	Fixed price is a phrase used to mean that no bargaining is allowed over the price of a good or, less commonly, a service.
Household	An economic unit that provides the economy with resources and uses the income received to purchase goods and services that satisfy economic wants is called household.
Stabilization policy	Stabilization policy refers to the use of monetary and fiscal policies to reduce business fluctuations in aggregate employment and prices.
Journal	Book of original entry, in which transactions are recorded in a general ledger system, is referred to as a journal.
International macroeconomics	Same as international finance, but with more emphasis on the international determination of macroeconomic variables such as national income and the price level are called international macroeconomics.
Federal Reserve	The Federal Reserve System was created via the Federal Reserve Act of December 23rd, 1913. All national banks were required to join the system and other banks could join. The Reserve Banks opened for business on November 16th, 1914. Federal Reserve Notes were created as part of the legislation, to provide an elastic supply of currency.
Political economy	Early name for the discipline of economics. A field within economics encompassing several alternatives to neoclassical economics, including Marxist economics. Also called radical political economy.
Interdependence	The extent to which departments depend on each other for resources or materials to accomplish their tasks is referred to as interdependence.
Welfare	Welfare refers to the economic well being of an individual, group, or economy. For individuals, it is conceptualized by a utility function. For groups, including countries and the world, it is a tricky philosophical concept, since individuals fare differently.
Variable	A variable is something measured by a number; it is used to analyze what happens to other things when the size of that number changes.
Long run	In economic models, the long run time frame assumes no fixed factors of production. Firms can enter or leave the marketplace, and the cost (and availability) of land, labor, raw materials, and capital goods can be assumed to vary.
Purchasing power	The amount of goods that money will buy, usually measured by the CPI is referred to as purchasing power.

Go to **Cram101.com** for the Practice Tests for this Chapter.

Supply shock	Supply shock refers to a shift in aggregate supply caused by some external factor that causes costs of production to change.
Consumption	In Keynesian economics consumption refers to personal consumption expenditure, i.e., the purchase of currently produced goods and services out of income, out of savings (net worth), or from borrowed funds. It refers to that part of disposable income that does not go to saving.
Purchasing	Purchasing refers to the function in a firm that searches for quality material resources, finds the best suppliers, and negotiates the best price for goods and services.
Purchasing power parity	purchasing power parity is a theory based on the law of one price which says that the long-run equilibrium exchange rate of two currencies is the rate that equalizes the currencies' purchasing power.
Law of one price	The principle that identical goods should sell for the same price throughout the world if trade were free and frictionless is referred to as the law of one price.
Developed country	A developed country is one that enjoys a relatively high standard of living derived through an industrialized, diversified economy. Countries with a very high Human Development Index are generally considered developed countries.
Expansionary monetary policy	Increases aggregate demand by increasing the money supply are referred to as expansionary monetary policy.
Euro	The common currency of a subset of the countries of the EU, adopted January 1, 1999 is called euro.
Convergence	The blending of various facets of marketing functions and communication technology to create more efficient and expanded synergies is a convergence.
International policy coordination	International policy coordination refers to agreements among countries to enact policies cooperatively.
Argument	The discussion by counsel for the respective parties of their contentions on the law and the facts of the case being tried in order to aid the jury in arriving at a correct and just conclusion is called argument.
International trade	The export of goods and services from a country and the import of goods and services into a country is referred to as the international trade.
Economic policy	Economic policy refers to the actions that governments take in the economic field. It covers the systems for setting interest rates and government deficit as well as the labor market, national ownership, and many other areas of government.
Context	The effect of the background under which a message often takes on more and richer meaning is a context. Context is especially important in cross-cultural interactions because some cultures are said to be high context or low context.
Technology	The body of knowledge and techniques that can be used to combine economic resources to produce goods and services is called technology.
Tariff	A tax imposed by a nation on an imported good is called a tariff.
Quota	A government-imposed restriction on quantity, or sometimes on total value, used to restrict the import of something to a specific quantity is called a quota.
Depreciate	A nation's currency is said to depreciate when exchange rates change so that a unit of its currency can buy fewer units of foreign currency.
Economic forces	Forces that affect the availability, production, and distribution of a society's resources

Go to **Cram101.com** for the Practice Tests for this Chapter.

among competing users are referred to as economic forces.

Administration	Administration refers to the management and direction of the affairs of governments and institutions; a collective term for all policymaking officials of a government; the execution and implementation of public policy.
Nominal exchange rate	Nominal exchange rate refers to the actual exchange rate at which currencies are exchanged on an exchange market. Contrasts with real exchange rate.
Devaluation	Lowering the value of a nation's currency relative to other currencies is called devaluation.
Expense	In accounting, an expense represents an event in which an asset is used up or a liability is incurred. In terms of the accounting equation, expenses reduce owners' equity.
Large country	Large country refers to a country that is large enough for its international transactions to affect economic variables abroad, usually for its trade to matter for world prices.
Incentive	An incentive is any factor (financial or non-financial) that provides a motive for a particular course of action, or counts as a reason for preferring one choice to the alternatives.
Locomotive effect	The effect that economic expansion in one large country can have on other parts of the world economy, causing them to expand as well, as the large country demands more of their exports is called locomotive effect.
National income	National income refers to the income generated by a country's production, and therefore the total income of its factors of production.
Marginal propensity to save	The increase in saving per unit increase in income is referred to as marginal propensity to save.
Marginal propensity to import	Marginal propensity to import refers to the increase in expenditure on imports per unit increase in income.
Multiplier effect	The effect on equilibrium GDP of a change in aggregate expenditures or aggregate demand is called the multiplier effect.
Industry	A group of firms that produce identical or similar products is an industry. It is also used specifically to refer to an area of economic production focused on manufacturing which involves large amounts of capital investment before any profit can be realized, also called "heavy industry".
Capital flow	International capital movement is referred to as capital flow.
Exchange rate regime	Exchange rate regime refers to the rules under which a country's exchange rate is determined, especially the way the monetary or other government authorities do or do not intervene in the exchange market.